Teacher Learning

Editor	Contributors
Gwyneth Dow	Rory Barnes
	Gwyneth Dow
	Rod Foster
	Noel P. Gough
	Bill Hannan
	Doug White

Routledge & Kegan Paul. ISBN 0-7100-9020-X. For copyright reasons, this book must not be sold, issued on loan or otherwise disposed of, except in its original paper cover. Printed in Great Britain (TY).

Teacher learning

Routledge Education Books

Advisory Editor: John Eggleston
Professor of Education
University of Keele

T.M

Teacher learning)

Edited by
Gwyneth Dow

with contributions from
Rory Barnes, Rod Foster, Noel P. Gough,
Bill Hannan and Doug White

Routledge & Kegan Paul

London, Boston, Melbourne and Henley

First published in 1982
by Routledge & Kegan Paul Ltd
39 Store Street, London WC1E 7DD,
9 Park Street, Boston, Mass. 02108, USA,
296 Beaconsfield Parade, Middle Park,
Melbourne, 3206, Australia and
Broadway House, Newtown Road,
Henley-on-Thames, Oxon, RG9 1EN
Set in IBM Press Roman by
Donald Typesetting, Bristol
and printed in Great Britain by
St Edmundsbury Press, Bury St Edmunds, Suffolk

Library of Congress Cataloging in Publication Data

Teacher Learning

(Routledge education books)
Includes index.
1. Teachers–Training of–Australia–
Victoria. 2. Teacher-student relationships.
I. Dow, Gwyneth M. II. Barnes, Rory.
III. Series.
LB1727.A7T38   371.1'02   81-23382

ISBN 0-7100-9020-X   AACR2

Contents

Notes on contributors

Rory Barnes — creative writer and free-lance lecturer. Formerly a member of the Curriculum Advisory Board, who worked on curriculum planning in many schools.

Rod Foster — Lecturer in Curriculum and Philosophy of Education, University of Melbourne. He maintains close contacts with schools.

Noel P. Gough — Senior Lecturer, Rusden College of Advanced Education, Clayton, Victoria, and part-time Lecturer in Curriculum, University of Melbourne.

Bill Hannan — author, especially of school books for English and of articles on education. Editor of teachers' journals. Former teacher of English and languages and prominent in curriculum reform in Victoria.

Doug White — Senior Lecturer, La Trobe University. Active as a writer on and a leader of school reform. Formerly a member of the Curriculum Advisory Board.

Acknowledgments

Editing and writing for a book that contains separate contributors' chapters is more difficult than writing the whole oneself, and I can say this with uncommon conviction because I worked with an uncommonly co-operative and constructively critical group of contributors to whom my first acknowledgment is due. They were all concerned with the book as a whole and so were willing to read and comment on each other's work, as well as to meet for lengthy discussions to thrash out the most difficult educational dilemmas it raised. It is very much *our* book, which fostered new friendships and strengthened old ones.

During the writing of the book all but one of the writers lived for a time overseas; each of us often worked under great pressure; and all had periods either of acute intellectual paralysis or of overflowing wastepaper baskets — or of both. But there were never irresponsible or uncommunicative hold-ups, which makes me a very lucky editor. A part of that same luck came from the sort of support the general editor, Professor John Eggleston, gave. He was quick to spot what might be most original and valuable in both our ideas and the way we presented them. This forced us into a much more difficult undertaking than we had initially envisaged; but he was forthright in a way that we respected, and he offered many constructive suggestions about the finer points of our work, without ever trying to influence our interpretations.

There are too many friends and colleagues to be named individually for their help, but a few must be singled out. At the University of Melbourne, Gloria Johnson and Gita Grimaud never once groaned at having to type yet another revision of work resulting from none of *their* mistakes, and they made the work easier by their generous help; Gwen McDowall made a great contribution to our research, the organization of work, and her textual criticisms were always valuable; and Olive Battersby was unfailing in giving us help from the Library. Our research students at Rusden State College as well as at Melbourne

University, often studied drafts of chapters as part of their seminar work, and their responses were both challenging and helpful to us. Jan Andrews, a graduate student and part-time lecturer at Melbourne as well as school teacher, kept records of her pupils in class and made some penetrating pedagogical points from them which are incorporated in the book, as are the ideas of Gillian Gough and Lorna Hannan. Bill Hannan drew extensively, too, on his four daughters' own education as he and they saw it. I called on my husband, Hume, at every sticky point during the writing and editing, for he has the misfortune to be closest to hand and to possess the critic's unerring eye for faults. I also thank my friend, Barbara Falk, for reading my chapter and making helpful suggestions, and Cameron Jackson for painstakingly giving me detailed comments that helped me to clarify and drastically revise an early draft.

The authors and publishers are grateful to Penguin Books Ltd for permission to reproduce an extract from Jeremy Seabrook: *The Unprivileged* (copyright © Jeremy Seabrook, 1967), and to the Geography Teachers' Association of Victoria for permission to reproduce p. 28 of *SGEP-PAK: a Teacher's Resource File for the Development of Geography Courses and Materials*, Melbourne, 1977.

Introduction

Several connected themes run through this book. Its central concern is with learning — pupils' learning and teachers' learning — in schools. And it argues, sometimes explicitly and sometimes by implication, that there are no quick routes to proper learning because learning is the acquisition of self-knowledge and an understanding of oneself as part of a particular culture. This ambitious view entails a recognition that learning is achieved by reflective action; that it is stunted by a sense of uselessness and powerlessness as well as by an undue love of power; and that the theories that best inform it defy the exactness of explanatory scientific theories.

Thus, the various contributors draw on philosophy, politics, sociology, psychology and history for enlightenment. We are not of one mind in all things; indeed, our ideological positions probably vary considerably; but I have worked with each contributor both in teaching and curriculum planning, and we usually work well together because we share a number of broad beliefs as well as experiences. We have all been engaged in reforming curriculum and teacher education, and we have all been critical of the sloppiness that accompanied some of the reforms of the late sixties, early seventies. We believed that these weaknesses resulted from faulty thinking — poor social analysis, romantic psychological theories, slip-shod pedagogy.

But the reversal in the seventies came not only from climatic economic changes; it came also from a frenzied attempt to halt the good things that were being tried. Those good things that we want to salvage, and about which we agree, are the subject of this book. They include the revitalizing of curriculum to the extent that it now shows greater consciousness of pupils' concerns. At the same time, teachers are increasingly aware that their pupils' experiences, their families' values and customs, do matter and are to be respected as well as questioned. Simple as this might seem, underlying it is a democratic

1

resurgence which affirms that, if pupils are to gain in self-respect and self-knowledge, they must learn in an environment that allows them to influence the direction of their own schooling. According to this view, teachers and pupils are partners — not antagonists — and the teacher's authority derives from her greater maturity, from the greater understanding and wisdom that her success in learning has brought her and from which pupils can learn. There is no place for permissiveness in such a view; but because it challenges the whole authority structure that has grown and thrived in the school system, it is regarded as heretically radical in many quarters.

The emphasis in such a view on the importance of experience and reflection rules out the possibility that culture and knowledge can be treated as static entities to be handed down *de haut en bas*. It also rules out learning theories that are manipulative in the way that stimulus-response theories are. They may have their place in instilling some of the 'basics'; but they have a subordinate role in our scheme of things.

Three of the contributors to this book taught with me in an experimental teacher-training course in which we attempted to close the gap between theory and practice, between the talk in the seminar room and what happens when young adults find themselves in front of thirty fourteen-year-olds whom they are meant to 'instruct' from ten till eleven on Monday morning. We attempted to base the content of sessions at the university on our students' actual experiences and problems in the schools in which they spent two days a week teaching. We tried to make university studies such that our students' classroom and staffroom behaviour would be influenced by their increasing understanding of the roles schools were playing in the lives of pupils and of the political processes in society at large that affected school practices. I have told the story of that course in *Learning to Teach: Teaching to Learn* (London, Routledge & Kegan Paul, 1979) although much of the 'telling' in that book is actually done by our students themselves who were encouraged to keep diaries which they generously made available for publication. This book stands for the same principles as those in the previous book; but in this book we address ourselves to the learning of a hypothetical young teacher through her early experiences as a teacher.

This imaginary teacher, Maria, has to learn not only to tolerate ambiguity (to quote a popular phrase of Professor Denis Lawton); she has also to learn to live with some errors, just as her pupils have to learn to recognize failure in themselves, for, as we several times point out, there can be no success without failure. Our adoption of this view comes from our own experience in planning and implementing curriculum reforms. Every one of the contributors has been involved in educational innovation in the secondary school system and teacher education. Many of us were active members of an influential advisory committee, the Curriculum Advisory Board (CAB), which was set up in 1966 by the State Department of Education to advise on curriculum innovation in Victoria, Australia. It was made up of representatives from independent and state schools, from unions, parents' organizations and faculties of education in response to the abolition of the external examinations taken at fourth form (year ten).

In helping schools in Victoria to take responsibility for their own curriculum planning, we were in tune with modern development elsewhere. Education in the six Australian States had long been regarded as rigidly centralized. England, though boasting that every school through its principal was the owner of its own curriculum, in effect placed a severe limitation on curriculum planning in academic schools through external examinations and university requirements. And secondary modern schools, in the search for status, came increasingly to enter their pupils for a variety of external examinations. In North America there were both exciting and deplorable examples of curriculum innovation, but restrictions from state bureaucracies and more local authorities were widespread and became infamous in the USA during the repressive mood of McCarthyism after the Second World War.

It would be false to suggest that the freedom suddenly offered to secondary teachers in Victoria was unique, but it was certainly unique in Australia and was far from common all told. And this book must be read in that context.

The CAB never recommended, let alone imposed, specific reforms. As a Board which contained more than a normal number of educational experts, we discovered a series of questions rather than a set of answers. We agonized; we consulted subject experts and learning theorists; we read; we discussed; we worked with many schools. At the end of our first year we were humbler than at the beginning of it. We were pretty confident about a whole lot of things that were wrong: we were far less confident about what was right.

The responsibility that had been put upon us as a sort of 'think tank' led us to frustrating indecision along with a far greater clarification of the problems than we had had hitherto. How, then, could we expect teachers to move any faster than we did? They had to go through the same processes for themselves before they could even see the problems in all their complexity. This meant, we believed, that they had to be entrusted with responsibilities similar to those carried by the CAB. All schools were therefore invited to reconsider their curriculum and to submit their proposed reforms. We, meanwhile, enunciated a number of broad principles that we believed might profitably guide the schools, and a series of state-wide conferences was organized.

My concern here is not with the detailed narrative, but with the

3

modus operandi, which was sound though adventurous, even risky. We gave up the search for one all-embracing, consistent theory on the grounds that, whether or not one was ever likely to be found, it certainly did not exist at the time, and probably we were looking for the wrong kind of theory anyway. This book, then, is an attempt to pass on what we have learned from ten years or more of having tested our ideas in the classroom and in an innovatory course in teacher education. During that time there have been advances in educational theorizing, which, in the light of greatly broadened and enriched experiences, have helped us to reformulate many old ideas, to verbalize some that were previously only well-informed hunches, and to clarify what sort of theorizing is appropriate to educational problems.

Quite early in our deliberations in Victoria we found an ingenious solution to the problem of priorities by dividing our task into three: learning, conditions of learning, and supportive services. Thus we came to see school policies such as school organization, procedures for grouping pupils, and provisions for transfer from primary to secondary school as conditions which either promoted or impeded pupils' learning; while relations with parents, with the local area, with social agencies, with churches, with employers and the like were seen as the development of supporting structures and practices sharing a common interest in pupils' learning. We were then able to focus sharply on learning as the specific role of the school.

What gave our committee shared ground was agreement on the malpractices that resulted from the heritage of external examinations. When we came to look at new organizing principles, nuns, Marxists, members of the Headmasters' Conference, academics — this heterogeneous group of members that shared little but experience of education in many different kinds of schools — seemed to find a form of words that they agreed expressed what was wrong and we were then able to move from that to what might replace it. We had battled futilely for months in trying to start with a statement of aims and objectives. Some of us, like our fictitious Maria, were convinced that this would not work, and in fact it nearly destroyed our organization. Nuns, Marxists, members of the HMC, academics fought furiously and doggedly over aims that ranged from what they meant by citizenship to the place of physical fitness (and that one nearly scuttled us) in a school curriculum. Then we turned to examining those school practices that created our major problems and we began to see differing ways in which these could be replaced. There were a few who kept trying to drag us back to the old debate over aims, and insisting that we couldn't say anything respectable or consistent until we put it in a framework of aims and objectives. We had to move sideways by adopting activities that were clearly effective to avoid the verbal collision over aims and behavioural

4

objectives that threatened to destroy the CAB.

Certainly we believed that, after generations of highly centralized control that characterized our system and that was commoner (through external examinations) in less centralized systems than they recognized, teachers (like our committee in Victoria) had to work through their problems for themselves in order to revise curriculum in their schools on the basis of shared experience. Our committee resisted the popular demand to provide pedagogically exciting resources not only as a crutch for weak teachers, but more importantly to show teachers in general how to improve their ways. We recognized that when we had bumper crops of packaged materials teachers were brought into the production process and were relied on to try out the materials all along the line, but there were no means by which they could extend their experiences and insight to the intended consumers — the bulk of the teachers. Hence, in England and the USA, there developed widespread concern that the money invested in producing resources was missing the mark because of the problem of dissemination. Sweden, too, had luxurious resource centres lying almost idle despite the elaborate services and quick communications offered to all neighbouring schools. In Victoria, by contrast, our ideas caught fire and spread so rapidly that we could give guidelines and samples but we could in no way keep pace with the demand for a supporting structure that was needed. Ours was a riskier way because it caught on, giving us too little time for the reflective evaluation that we wanted to accompany the rapid changes. It took us some time even to find the right words for what we were doing, but 'school-based' innovation was what was achieved. Pilot schools were established before packaged courses or resource centres.

The principle of school-based decision-making has remained as explicit policy in Victoria. It is interesting that for years the external sixth-form examination, Higher School Certificate (HSC), has been attacked and sometimes blackballed by teachers, and one of the main criticisms has been its effect on the school's autonomy. It is in that context that a new body — the Victorian Institute of Secondary Education, recently set up to review curriculum and revise HSC — must be seen. It offers sixth forms a considerable degree of self-determination by inviting them to submit their own syllabuses for a large proportion of the sixth-form work that will be accredited. There are no external examinations before HSC.

It should perhaps be explained that Victoria, which we are momentarily considering, having just over 3,000,000 inhabitants in the 1960s, is more comparable with a large English Local Education Authority that contains several populous cities than with England as a whole. Yet its area of 88,000 square miles is as big as Great Britain and a little larger than Minnesota or Utah. We began our work before any real attempts had been made to decentralize the administration of the Education Department into regions or to establish effective parental consultation in the schools. Whether or not a strong communications network would have helped or hindered us must remain a matter for speculation; but the remarkable thing is that a professional network sprang up that was part of our attempt to encourage schools to go through the thinking for themselves as we had been made to do. R.A. Reed, the then Director of Secondary Education, about the same time that he invited each school (in pressing tones) to prepare to submit plans for curriculum revision, set up two trial schools — one old and one new — to try out new ideas and to be pace-makers. Four of the contributors to this book worked in those schools. Within their first two years the schools had thousands of teachers visiting them. 'We work by infection, not direction', we confidently affirmed. Or, to use another metaphor, the rapidity of change was declared to be the veritable opening of Pandora's box — whether this implied that blessings were being prodigally lost in the process or that the system was being purged of ancient ills depended on one's point of view.

It would have been much easier for us, and sociologically sounder to boot, if we had been able to locate Maria in a specific school in an area that could be precisely described and analysed. But in trying to make her situation more widely relevant we found ourselves seeing her variously in Leicester, in Peckham, in Quebec, in Footscray, in the Bronx, in Brunswick, in Dublin. It created many passing difficulties which led to changes in the detailed illustrations we could use, especially in such questions as pupils' ethnic languages. But the more we were tripped up by specific details that had to be international the more depressingly evident it became to find how often the problems were universal.

We know that Maria's problems and dilemmas are real — they are faced by teachers like her, every day — but we are under few illusions that we have provided any sure-fire solutions that can be put quickly and effortlessly into practice with guaranteed success. We have all spent too much time inside schools for that. But since we are all academics and/or writers, and since we are expected to reflect on what we know and experience in a way that teachers such as Maria are denied by the sheer pressures of their jobs, we have written this book. And while we have few illusions about solutions, we know the value of informed exploration in discovering guides to the action that all of us — teachers, academics and writers alike — should take.

It is no accident that, after introducing Maria and her problems in chapter 1, Rory Barnes and I move straight into the classroom and staffroom to look at curriculum planning in action. In 'Looking at topic-centred teaching', we briefly trace the attack on the traditional subject-centred curriculum which fractures the knowledge that schools attempt to impart, thus dividing teachers' time between a number of different classes each week, requiring teachers to know upward of a hundred children and isolating teachers in their work.

Maria's school was fairly typical in that, in attempting to reform the curriculum, the staff planned a programme of integrated studies with direct relevance to the pupils' problems and in which pastoral care would be built in by the way the programme was to be carried out. This indicated a recognition that the care of individual children should be seen as related to the teacher's concern for the child's work in school and not as an afterthought in which counselling and therapy would be 'administered' in attempts to patch up a poor organization that made no allowance for it as an organic part of sound teaching. Maria's team also had sound sociological and political reasons for drawing their content from what they saw as the mainsprings of the pupils' lives. They saw self-knowledge as coming from what they called 'consciousness-raising' (though they dislike the term), which entails looking hard and critically at the society of which they are a part as well as developing a critical awareness and tolerance of the sub-cultures that compose it.

These were all concerns that clearly overcome the remoteness that many of Maria's pupils complained about in their studies, and the issues that are to be raised cannot be understood adequately by the insights offered by any one subject. But new difficulties have to be averted. In chapter 2 we give examples of badly planned topic studies drawn from what we have seen in schools, and compared with different approaches that avoid superficiality and incoherence; thus, we have moved sideways to by-pass (though not ignore) arid academic debate about 'disciplines'.

While teachers of old and tested subjects acquire ready-made coherence handed down by generations of scholars, teachers of newly integrated studies have to find new structures of their own. It is at least to be said in favour of integration that this cannot be done absent-mindedly, as so much of routine teaching appears to be. There are, however, further difficulties that have to be overcome. Teachers can be uneasy at having to handle material that normally belongs in someone else's province, and they foresee the probability that their own specialism might be watered down and distorted. Such difficulties inherent in team-teaching are raised in 'Introducing Maria', examined in chapter 2, and developed further in chapter 3, 'Curriculum development: a practical view', by Noel Gough. Gough demonstrates that what he calls the classical model of curriculum development — a means-end model in which behavioural objectives are specified in advance — has little use in practice, whatever elegance, rationality or logical simplicity it might appear to have in theory. Gough, in short, addresses himself to the question already raised — what sort of theorizing is appropriate in education? This question comes up again and again, most notably in Rod Foster's chapter and in my 'Yin and Yang'. Gough is concerned largely with developing curriculum through active deliberation of a small school-based team of teachers who may be viewed as conducting on-site research. He justifies this as conforming to the canons of practical or action research.

Built into Gough's proposals is a component of participatory evaluation. We say little in the book about evaluation, although it is clear that we have little faith in competence- or performance-based (that is, Behaviourist) evaluation. Gough's chapter quite explicitly points the way towards building in evaluative procedures during curriculum planning in ways that avoid the restrictiveness of the ends–means model.

Bill Hannan's chapter, 'The multicultural school', deals with questions that concern Maria in selecting content for her new course. Although Hannan confines himself largely to the ethnocentric selection of content and methods of treating content, he draws attention to how, underlying much teaching, the assumptions are undemocratic and culturally biased. He deals with Maria's concern for 'relevance' — a conception that allows the pupil to seek his own identity and to believe in himself as a critical agent of change in a society that might have convinced him of his own powerlessness. Because teachers so often unthinkingly adopt the standards of the dominant culture of which they have become a part, they reinforce pupils' sense of inferiority or set them at odds with their parents. Hannan seeks an attitude of critical tolerance that avoids both cultural relativism and dogmatism. While he sees that many of Maria's pupils' difficulties are not of the school's making and cannot be resolved by schools, he also encourages her to see in what ways schools can be in the vanguard of reform.

Perhaps Hannan's most original contribution lies in his ideas for language work in multicultural schools, which imply a belief that language is central to a child's culture. A particular culture or sub-culture cannot be given full expression in a different language. Hannan's language proposals attempt to take into account pupils who bring with them a sophisticated mastery of a foreign tongue — the language they were born to — and a ready adoption of the standard norms of their new host language, as well as the pupils who are inarticulate speakers of an unwritten foreign dialect. Although Hannan's chapter shows his practicality as an enthusiastic linguist and an experienced language teacher, he makes telling criticisms of how teachers are so often under the sway of the dominant culture in their approach to children's language. Thus his educational proposals also have political implications.

In a sense, Doug White takes up where Hannan leaves off, but he does this from a reversed viewing point. Hannan sees the political policy of 'multiculturalism' as having such direct educational implications that schools could properly give political leadership, whereas White, in 'A core curriculum − a political answer to a social problem', sees what purports to be educational policy (the widespread demand for a core curriculum) as being political in motive.

When he points to the disguised political intent, he is not treating it simplistically according to some cryptic conspiratorial theorizing: he is, rather, concerned with the truly frightening world-wide trends that centralize decision-making at an ever-increasing distance from those who must carry out the decisions. In grappling with Maria's difficulties, White sees alienation as one of the major causes. He points to the dissonance between the school's acceptance of responsibility for all pupils while it, itself, is subject to increasing manipulation and loss of power. Teachers, in defending themselves against the 'experts' who tell them what they must teach, tend to try to strengthen their professionalism by becoming exclusive and inegalitarian. Thus they find themselves intensifying the very division of labour (particularly into thinkers and doers) that they deplore when they think of its effects on their own pupils' self-esteem.

The core curriculum, then, in White's view, is significant not because of the effect it will have on the content of education, and not because teachers would necessarily object to it on educational grounds, but because of how it might be determined and by whom. If unwatched, it could disfranchise teachers and local communities even further in the power politics of educational control. White seeks a means by which teachers can be authoritative without being authoritarian, and he finds it in the 'intellectual culture', exemplified by international science at its best. A community of researchers can become, *de facto*, the arbiters of tentatively held truths and debunkers of received wisdom, working together co-operatively but autonomously. Teachers as scholars also represent this tradition − a point raised in other chapters, too, particularly 2 and 3.

In general the book shows schools to be in a state of constant tension between their progressive role of cultural regeneration and the inevitability of their also being the victim of cultural lag. This tension is examined most explicitly by Hannan and White. We have chosen, after much thought, not to take up explicitly the debate about equality and social class, with its related question of whether schools can make a difference to society or can merely reproduce it. So much has been written at such length on the theoretical and semantic implications of the debate that we decided to concentrate on its importance in action. We see in Maria's dilemmas that her options are at one and the same time both open and closed. It is with that focus that our ideas on equality are presented and we have, we hope, avoided the more obscurantist thinking in sociological literature. We have looked at very familiar ideological conflicts that arise from the sort of inner suburban, industrial, ethnically mixed community in which we placed the fictional school where Maria teaches. We have dealt with the practical decisions she has to make as a member of staff and as a member of her professional associations and union.

In chapters 6 and 7 the book is concerned with that part of Maria's work in which she has the most unquestionable autonomy – her teaching style. We return to issues already raised, but our emphasis is on pedagogy – a word that we believe should enjoy a revived status.

Foster and I, in our various ways, try to indicate how Gradgrind's didactic inflexibility, Skinner's conditioning policies, and Rousseau's or Neill's trust in untrammelled innate goodness, just to mention a few pedagogical fashions, may be corrected. It would be too grandiose to say that we formulate a learning theory; but we are concerned with approaches which we believe show new promise.

Paradoxically, although these two chapters focus at least in part on how to teach, Foster and I have found it hardest to give specific help to Maria. This, on further reflection, should not be too surprising because learning itself is full of paradoxes, contradictions, conflicts, struggles and satisfactions, none of which is susceptible to tight scientific analysis or generalizations – for reasons also outlined by Gough. That is why what we have to say to Maria at least starts by forearming her against specious theories or half-baked but homely generalizations once imprinted on her memory as a pupil, in her teacher-training year, or later heard in the staffroom or the union meeting – though homespun wisdom is possibly less misleading than the pretentiously mystifying 'in' talk of educational scientism.

Teaching, like history or art, is always a particular response to an enormously variable number of possible conditions. What Foster says about this is in some ways an extension of Gough's argument about the unsuitability of abstract scientific theory applied to human beings and their practical pursuits. Thus chapter 6 recommends looking afresh at behaviour instead of drawing false conclusions from controlled laboratory experiments on rats and pigeons. It is significant that we first turned to the work of a highly successful teacher of youngsters with impoverished language skills and tried to relate her methods to our own thinking about the importance of the learning environment – the social organization of the classroom and the school – in learning.

A philosopher by trade, Foster is wary of big philosophical ideas about human nature and rationality; but his interest in Ethology leads him to value exploratory behaviour and problem-solving in the

10

development of insight and intellect. Large, impersonal, bureaucratic schools, he suggests, provide a most unfavourable environment.

Like Hannan, in my chapter 'Yin and Yang', I am concerned with communication, and I develop the book's recurrent theme about the unsuitability of both repressive and romantic extremes in education. In a somewhat different context I, too, examine the importance in intellectual development of intuition and insight — mental skills that are so often overlooked in the western world's preoccupation with analytic rationality. And I emphasize a theme that runs through the whole book — the simplistic nature of 'either/or' thinking. Where both right and left have gone wrong is in adopting dualistic thought that is static, doctrinaire and productive of stock behaviour as well as inert ideas.

Foster and I both point to ways in which Maria might help her least successful pupils to improve their achievement. We are concerned with effective classroom management that is neither repressive nor laissez-faire; and I try to give some guidelines that might help teachers in the making of difficult and subtle decisions about when to encourage exploratory speculation and when to drill, when to ignore mistakes and when to correct them — in short, decisions about intervening and letting go.

At the end of the chapter 'Yin and Yang', I commend the sort of curriculum planning and pedagogical practice illustrated in what Barnes and I described as Plan E in chapter 2, which deliberately guides children towards the formulation of concepts of ever-increasing power and applicability until they can swing between synthesizing and analysing, between intuiting and verbalizing, between generalizing and particularizing. I accept as the pinnacle of educated thinking Vygotsky's notion of 'the consciousness of being conscious'. This notion epitomizes the importance of reflection.

In the final chapter 'And then?', I return to a major thesis in the book — the interplay between individual learning and cultural/social influences.

I come back briefly to White, who in chapter 5 has shown the tendency for new technology in modern societies to increase the distance between the makers of our world and the common man. The increasing concentration of power with the growth of transnationals widens the structural split between thought (or planning) and possible action that diminishes man. When the individual is isolated and sees herself as powerless to influence social reconstruction or political policy, and when this sense of fatalism is intensified by the increasing remoteness of the makers of the most influential mass communications, we can be seen to have created alienation, new inequalities, cynicism and inertia — all of which are the deadliest enemies of education.

Gwyneth Dow

Chapter 1

Introducing Maria

Gwyneth Dow and Rory Barnes

This book is concerned with schooling: what it is thought to do, what it in fact does, what it possibly might do. Its focus is the classroom, but it looks behind popular talk and accepted practice to examine the maze of problems and tensions that constitute the contemporary teacher's lot. There is no one starting point, the maze has many entrances, and any point marked 'Finish' invariably discloses new paths that demand exploration.

Throughout the book, education is seen to be endlessly changing in response to the constant reconstruction of theory in the light of practice, and the reverse. Theory and practice so often go their separate ways that it is tempting to write a book with a title like 'What Lecturers Say and Teachers Do', but instead this book tries to point to ideas that can be shown to stand the test of practice, and to practices that have inspired the reformulation of theory.

During the early stages of writing this book, Barnes looked for a way into the ever-moving scene by creating a young teacher who was personally experiencing the kinds of problems that bothered us. Since then, she has grown in importance to embody the central concerns of the book.

Let us then start by considering this young teacher. Call her Maria. Let us say that Maria has been teaching for a year in a coeducational secondary school in a large industrial city. Many of the children she teaches are from non-English-speaking backgrounds. As a student teacher Maria learnt a considerable amount about herself and the society she lives in, knowledge that has been consolidated by her teaching experience. She is constantly aware of the way in which the children of affluent parents, with their access to well-equipped schools, libraries and a literate English-speaking environment, fulfil their parents', their teachers' and their own ambitions by gaining places in institutions of tertiary learning which alone can lead to the professions. Maria is even more aware of the way in which the children of working-class parents do not reap such benefits. At times the unfairness depresses her, at times it makes her angry, at other times she ignores it. But the awareness colours her political outlook and informs her ideas about what the school in which she teaches is doing for its particular children. She is also aware of what teaching has done to her own sense of herself. Despite the frustrations of the job, and the occasional bouts of cynicism that she shares with many of her staffroom colleagues, much of her satisfaction in life comes from being a good teacher, concerned within her classroom, possessed of a useful body of knowledge and the skills to communicate it. While she scorns much of 'professionalism', she spends more energy and longer hours than are strictly necessary both in her teaching and in her pastoral work with her pupils.

Let us say that Maria's school is in an area that has caused the Education Department grave concern. It could be in an industrial suburb of any modern city, but, for our purposes, it happens to be in one where the school leaving age is sixteen. Stories of crime and violence committed by some of its pupils have reached the headlines, but many signs of demoralization remain concealed from the public. The school has an annual intake of 150 first-form pupils, but these numbers dwindle to twenty-five at sixth form, and local employers are wary of employing ex-pupils.

A new deputy principal had been appointed to try to regenerate the school. The staff had agreed that fourth form (year ten), being the final year for many of the school's pupils, was most urgently in need of overhauling if the school were to overcome the indifference and disruptiveness of those who were there under sufferance and if a bigger proportion were to be persuaded to proceed to higher classes. Even so, David, the head of the geography department, and Betty, the home economics teacher, were the only experienced teachers to volunteer to plan a pilot scheme, and Paul, a recent English graduate, enthusiastically offered to give what help he could.

It was at this stage that the deputy principal appointed Maria because she had graduated in sociology, which the team felt was a necessary component in their planning. Though hesitant about taking anyone else who was so inexperienced, the deputy principal felt that this was offset by her enthusiasm. He was also impressed by her awareness of her inexperience, which had led her to discuss his proposals tentatively rather than with the too ready self-assurance of the most suitable mature applicants.

Paul soon became one of Maria's closest friends as she quickly realized that, though slightly nervous and reserved, he was deeply committed to the success of the task. The other two members of the committee remained more enigmatic; but the planning had proceeded fairly smoothly.

It was decided very quickly that block-timetabling of an integrated studies course would enable each teacher to work for ten periods a week with one class – a considerable improvement, it was felt, on the situation where one specialist might 'teach' 200 pupils per week. Somewhat less confidently the committee realized that they must pool resources, must be prepared to teach beyond their own speciality and must devise a course that Maria, at least, had no hesitation in calling 'consciousness-raising'. The theme first chosen was social and occupational structure and it was decided to concentrate on a special study of the local area. It was later broadened to 'Equality' to give scope for the integration of a greater number of disciplines and to make it more controversial. In her first year at the school, Maria was the form teacher of a year nine class, and so she was able to confer with her pupils, getting ideas from them and testing her own ideas with them from the very beginning of the team's planning.

Working together, Maria and the geographer had been designing the local study which was to be carried out by the pupils as independent work in first and second term with joint reporting in third term. Maria secretly thought of David as the epitome of the dedicated, not-overly-bright, career teacher: good with the kids in a rough you-can't-fool-me manner, interested in new developments but not eager to move very far from areas or methods with which he felt comfortable. Paul had undertaken to prepare a series of classroom projects based on drama, literature, film, records and tapes all with some bearing on the local social questions; but, much to Maria's astonishment, he suddenly started to insist quite dogmatically that four periods a week be set aside for English as such, taught by an English specialist. Since he could not be persuaded otherwise and since the planning committee were all agreed that the ten periods of integrated work should not be reduced to six, a compromise was reached in which the deputy principal allotted twelve periods to them, two of which were for unadulterated English. At which point a strong counter-attack on the whole project was mounted by other members of the school staff who until then had been sitting back with barely concealed silent hostility, and who now started a territorial battle for their own subjects. The committee had been embattled enough as it was when it was suddenly divided internally by David's announcing that he was all in favour of interdisciplinary teaching provided that there was a prior statement of aims and specification of learning outcomes expressed quite precisely, so that subsequent success or failure could be measured, and judged objectively. Maria and the other two members of the committee suspected that in this sudden concern with scientific respectability David was running for cover when under pressure from his colleagues in the rest of the school; but they had little effect on him. He forcefully rested his case on the psychometric arguments that he had learnt some time ago during his teacher-training course.

'Don't get me wrong,' David said late one night at Paul's place, 'I want our project to go ahead, it's just that we must be careful not to . . .'

'Throw the bloody baby out with the bathwater' - Maria finished his sentence.

'Quite so,' he replied, and Maria wondered if he even suspected that she was sending him up.

Betty's response to all this was more alarming. She quite abruptly declared that all the detailed plans were fine as guidelines but of course she would do her own thing (apart from the local study) because a programme must be open-ended so that it could respond to the children's spontaneity. Admittedly resources had to be pooled, but settling for a firm structure in advance, while paying lip-service to giving children freedom, was mock-democracy.

David replied with some tired phrases Maria had heard before about freedom not licence. Paul said nothing. Betty restated her position more dogmatically. Maria wandered out to Paul's kitchen to make coffee. She leant against the sink. Jesus, who'd be a bloody teacher? There are times, she thought, when the flood of kids down a corridor, that mixture of grey flannel and dirty white cotton of the uniform, was depressing beyond words. Half the kids treated the rule about school uniform with contempt and few of the teachers tried to enforce it, but to get involved in fighting that hypocrisy would force her into a triviality that it was more dignified to ignore. The smell of that stuff they used to clean the floors and of the felt-tipped pens for use on the whiteboards (a right little educational innovation that one, such an improvement on blackboards and chalk), the dead foot-shuffling hours of Assembly, the repeated intrusion of the loud-speaker system into any serious classroom work — what an environment in which to attempt anything at all. And now the urge to walk back into Paul's scruffy little living-room and bang her colleagues' heads together . . . If a hand-picked team of dedicated teachers can't agree on anything, what chance have the kids? And yet, how should a curriculum planning team proceed? How do you allow for kids to exercise their own initiative? What are the risks in designing a topic-centred course? What sort of a mess will non-sociologist colleagues make when they come to teach sociological concepts like 'social stratification' or 'sector inequality'? How well will she, herself, cope with the attempt to improve children's writing capacity by the sort of concentration on writing that Paul wants?

Maria took the coffee into the living-room. Not during that meeting, but three meetings later, a compromise of sorts was arrived at. Maria saw that the tensions had been by-passed rather than resolved. David and Paul, it had been agreed, were to spell out their detailed programmes within the framework of their own individual statements of aims and pre-specified objectives. When it had come to the point, they could not agree even on the statement of broad aims, and so it was decided that the programme was flexible enough to allow them to teach it to fit their own convictions while allowing Betty and Maria to dissent from their approach altogether. They were all to keep detailed work records, but Maria and Betty were to require their pupils to keep diaries and to write monthly appraisals of their own progress.

The deputy principal intended to evaluate the whole project and to report to the Education Department by the end of the first year. Maria knew that he would find it easier to evaluate much of David's and Paul's work than hers, but such an evaluation could more readily miss what was at the heart of the project unless she and Betty could produce some kind of evidence more basic than that in the 'pre-tests' and 'post-tests' that Paul wanted of the children's language competence and David wanted of their understanding of specific geographical concepts covered in the course. Maria and Betty were prepared to have their pupils take the same tests, though sceptical about their worth. Maria had it in her favour that the deputy principal understood and sympathized with her stand, and that Paul was aware that standardized English and content tests of various kinds revealed nothing about a child's love of literature and very little about his imagination or fluency in using language, his curiosity or his independence as a student. Nevertheless Paul and David were both retaining a marking system and formal school reports. Maria had abandoned marks the previous year, and re-placed the stereotyped report with detailed statements. Each pupil wrote a report each term on her progress and difficulties. This was discussed with Maria before she composed her report for the parents, who were then encouraged to confer with her. This was one means she adopted to challenge her ablest pupils, while, without a doubt, her weakest pupils profited from no longer suffering the ignominy of public failure. She saw it as fundamentally important that pupils should help each other, sharing their knowledge and skills in a common pursuit that yet left room for the development of individual interests and abilities.

Each member of the team was to take a quarter of the year group. In an attempt to relate the school more closely to the adult world, a programme of part-time work experience was offered for those pupils who undertook to remain at school until the end of the academic year. Maria and David had included sections in the local study project that pupils in that outside work would take, thus enabling them to draw on their actual experiences. There was a general maths programme for the year as a whole, but options in pure or applied maths could be taken additionally. The maths staff had agreed that David and Maria would offer the 'applied' unit which they could relate to the integrated studies and the pupils' work experience. The scientists remained aloof, but it was hoped that they might be persuaded to take over some parts of the integrated studies later in the year in return for Betty's taking over their junior forms for a home economics unit. Mondays were kept for work experiences or other options (it was planned eventually to offer sandwich courses in year eleven), and Friday afternoons were reserved for crafts, arts and sports.

Thus, David, whom the team acknowledged as the co-ordinator of the integrated studies project, could timetable it for all classes for all four periods of Tuesday mornings and the three periods of Wednesday and Thursday afternoons. This meant that all pupils could come together for films, outside speakers, excursions, lectures or even work periods on assignment sheets. During such large group sessions some teachers could gain spare periods. It was possible for teaching groups to range from very small to very large, although the basic unit, the tutorial group, was to be approximately thirty pupils. And simultaneous time-tabling would allow the teachers to switch classes, thus making their speciality more widely available. An old building, once used for infants and first-graders and retaining the patronizing title 'Pigmy Hall' in common discourse, suited the project very well. It consisted of a central area with several smaller classrooms off it. The central area became the resources centre, and could take the total number of 120-odd year ten pupils.

To make the best use of these conditions, it was necessary to plan ahead so that each class could usefully come together for the purposes outlined. To make this possible, the team divided the term into segments, each teacher undertaking to cover an agreed topic for which resources could be collected and more difficult fixtures, such as hiring expensive films, could be arranged for set times. Beyond these broad commitments, there was room for great diversity in the teaching. The deputy principal's determination not to impose radical ideas on reluctant staff, but to allow, indeed encourage, teachers like Maria to innovate and be tested in action without having others' views imposed on them, made it relatively easy for a team to agree to differ though still to work as a team. On the other hand, it was essential that parents and pupils also be given the right to choose, and every effort had been made to consult them so that they could make informed decisions about which group to join. Maria, for example, in explaining her plans, noted that she expected to see the parents of her class, 10M, at least once a term. The fact that the pupils were not grouped randomly, and that the programmes would vary greatly in each group, increased immeasurably the deputy principal's problems in making a comparative

17

evaluation of the innovation – indeed in making any safe generalization at all.

By the same token, a more rigid approach would probably have meant abandoning innovation altogether or alienating both staff and parents. Despite his considerable success in winning the support of those parents whose children were to undertake the new course, and despite the backing the parents of 10M gave to Maria's plans, she realized that the real tests were yet to come. In particular, many parents (especially of some of the migrant children) were only partly reassured that their children would not be handicapped in later external examinations. And the team knew that they would have to navigate stormy waters when their course led to comparative cultural studies which they had decided must be undertaken.

Maria was already in trouble on that score: her contact with the children of immigrants had given her a strong sense of the discrimination that handicaps many children from non-English-speaking backgrounds. She was concerned that many of her pupils appeared to deny their migrant backgrounds under pressure of the mainstream of English-speaking culture. Maria believed that the school's curriculum should, in some way, foster a love and knowledge of their cultural heritage and languages. As a corollary of her concern about the discrimination suffered by ethnic minority groups, Maria held strong feminist views on the discrimination suffered by the majority group of girls.

Let us illustrate her difficulties by citing a specific student, call her Fatima, fifteen, living within a mile of the school with her Islamic Turkish family. When Fatima said to Maria one day, 'My mother is a peasant,' she was not joking. Maria is convinced that Fatima could pass any official exam or hurdle necessary to gain a place in a university or other tertiary institution. Fatima's father is distraught by what he sees as his daughter's increasingly decadent and foreign ways, and he identifies the school to which he is compelled to send her by the laws of this affluent, but hostile, land as one of the chief forces in his daughter's alienation (indeed as the only real force): for, once Fatima returns from school, she remains strictly within the parental home except for such sanctioned outings as visits to the mosque or relatives, all of which are chaperoned by one of her brothers or another member of the family.

Fatima's father is thinking of sending her back to Turkey where a marriage has been arranged with a suitable boy from the village. Fatima and her new husband may well return at a future date, but by then she will be a good Turkish wife. Fatima is upset by these plans, and turns to Maria as the only adult she can talk to. Maria, the feminist, arrived at her own liberated state after a long and continuing struggle against conditioned roles, chauvinist assumptions, overt and covert prejudice. Although her father had left Italy when young and had married an

English-speaking woman, Maria felt pleasure and pride in her Italian heritage that she clung to even during her most ferocious conflicts with her father and grandmother over their sexism. Yet she had never faced anything like an arranged marriage at fifteen.

What price, now, her concern for migrant cultures. All the Arab cooking classes, the glory of Greek civilization, the ethnic folk-dancing and the Italian language lessons on Saturday mornings suddenly don't amount to very much. Only recently Maria had come to regret her earlier childish and stubborn refusal to learn Italian, against her father's repeated attempts to interest her and talk to her in Italian. Like so many of her school friends, she studied just enough French to pass at school and then she dropped it gleefully at sixth form. Regretting now that she had chosen to be 'language deficient', Maria wonders at times if she has allowed herself to be culturally brainwashed in other ways too. Perhaps so, she reflects; but to take the immediate question, if the liberation of women entails the destruction of many of the modes and institutions of her father's and even her mother's culture she is prepared to take her stand at the barricades any day.

But what of the cultures of many of her students born elsewhere? Is she committed to the destruction of large slabs of various Mediterranean cultures? Is she perhaps a greater threat to Fatima's father's cultural heritage than are all the xenophobes who frankly proclaim that the sooner the wogs learn English and start supporting the local football team the better? Is there an escape into cultural relativism? Can Maria insist that the restraints placed on Turkish children by their parents can be understood only in an all-embracing understanding and acceptance of Turkish culture and society as a whole? Possibly, as far as Fatima's mother is concerned, but what about Fatima herself? She has the haziest memories of Turkey, she doesn't want to be married to a boy she's never seen, and she has turned to Maria for guidance and help. But is it Maria's job to offer guidance (even if she can think of anything to say)? Maria is, after all, a teacher, not a social worker. As a trainee teacher, Maria read widely in the literature of 'progressive education'. If asked, she would place her position somewhere between the education-as-therapy and the hard skills-for-the revolution schools of thought. But what about Fatima? To whom does Maria owe allegiance? Should she try to be true to her own vision of women's place in the world, or to that of Fatima's ethnic background? She cannot be both, and to be one is to be directly in conflict with the other.

Leaving aside Fatima's immediate problems brings up the question of which skills need to be taught. Even if Fatima's parents do not see their daughter's future as depending upon success in exams, many parents of other children in her classes see the whole point of school as just that — the road to success measured in terms of the status and money that follow from good exam results. And many of the parents see this as being more important for their sons than for their daughters. The aspirations of many of her boy pupils are also higher than those of her girls. Should her teaching then be directed to allowing her pupils to compete most effectively in the exam rat-race? Maria, politically committed to a more egalitarian society, knows perfectly well that, even were she to succeed in teaching her pupils to the level where they all pass with the highest honours, she wouldn't have magically increased the number of places available in tertiary institutions: for every success above the average, somewhere else some other teacher is seeing one of his pupils fail to pass the dividing line. And what if all her pupils did make it to the affluent middle classes? It's an odd form of revolutionary activity that posits the teacher's role as that of lifting a select group from the subservient to the dominant position while leaving the structure of society as a whole untouched. And yet, of course, Maria's sympathies are with her own particular pupils rather than with anyone else's. If her sixth-formers do well in the selective examination system they will be elated, they will have what they wanted, and Maria, also will be pleased that she has been in part the cause of their success. Similarly, if they fail, their dashed hopes will in part be her own. From the point of view of a committee such as the one concerned with the planning of the work on the social and occupational structure of the local area, it would be ideal if all that the pupils and the parents were interested in was a curriculum devoted to understanding the world with a view to changing it. But if many of the pupils (and parents) are primarily concerned with achieving the greatest economic potential from their education (and who is a middle-class teacher, reasonably well paid and secure, to tell them that they shouldn't be?), how much should Maria and her colleagues bow to demands which conflict with their own views about what is worth teaching?

Now, moreover, the Education Department is conferring with schools under its jurisdiction about introducing a common core curriculum in all schools in the area and keeping a tally on pupils' performance in the basic subjects. The deputy principal is resisting this, and he and Maria have become very active in fighting within the union and local professional associations to prevent the adoption of the policy Maria feels that she is always embattled. She and her friends will fight against stereotyping and standardizing from above, but can they also be committed to the view that the pupils and their parents cannot impose curricular demands? Maria feels stretched to the limits.

So that is a picture of one particular teacher. We've invented her much as a novelist invents a character in a work of fiction. William Faulkner said he wrote his novels by mentally following his people around and recording what they said and did. And in our writing of this introduction Maria has taken on a form, a personality of her own. We must confess we are fond of her, although at times she seems a bit too intense, too lacking in the ability to stand back from the action in order to view herself and her work in perspective. She has a sense of humour, but does she ever really laugh? Perhaps if she learned to relax a little . . . Ah well, we could write more, of course, show her in the pub after school, describe her childhood, give her a happy or a tragic love affair, but this is a sober book about education, not a novel, and so it's probably best to leave her be and see what this book has to say that could be of use to her as a teacher.

It has been tempting at times to let Maria become a literary creation on the one hand, or a puppet on the other. She was invented by Barnes in an attempt to particularize some of our arguments when they become (like so much educational theory) too abstract. As the book went through various drafts, Maria came to personify such consensus as the contributors share. Where we might disagree in detailed ideological discussion, we have seldom disagreed about what to do in schools. Thus, under Professor John Eggleston's prompting, we came increasingly to use Maria as our focus and as our reminder that the worth of our ideas must be tested in action.

Maria, as we have depicted her, is in a healthy state of disequilibrium that must not be confused with crippling indecisiveness. On the other hand, if the road she is to take ever becomes absolutely clear and predictable, we can assume that she has settled for stereotyped teaching and, very possibly, her certainty may become dangerously close to bigotry.

If there is a main theme in this book it is that Maria must learn that good teaching consists in for ever making the best possible choices by weighing up things as they arise — by developing habits of knowledgeable reflection, speculation and rationality, and not by mindlessly settling for a store of received truths.

Chapter 2

Looking at topic-centred teaching

Rory Barnes and Gwyneth Dow

The movement to reform traditional teaching

In the late sixties and early seventies much of the impetus behind the
introduction of new teaching methods came from dissatisfaction with
the ways in which knowledge and skills were being treated in schools.
In traditional schools it was common to divide curriculum into discrete
subjects whose content pupils were encouraged to master in order to
vie effectively in a series of examinations. If any thought was given to
the consequent fragmentation it seemed to be assumed that pupils
would integrate their learning experiences in a way that their staff
were apparently unable to do. In reaction to these criticisms, it was
argued that pupils should be introduced to knowledge in such a way
that they could recognize its power to give meaning to their world.
Its value should be shared: thus, acquiring knowledge should be socially
enriching, not divisive.

Amongst reformers who had studied the history of the progressivism of the thirties there was a strong feeling that changes in the social
context of learning must be achieved without debasing the intellectual
content of what was taught. One example that suggested itself was the
community of research scientists who, it was felt, existed within an
intellectual culture as made up of people who[1]

> act autonomously, yet co-operatively, for its existence depends
> upon the free circulation and the common use of information,
> ideas, images and theories. Although it is participatory and
> co-operative, it does not demand that its members surrender their
> individuality. The intellectual culture is universal in the sense that it
> transcends national and historical barriers and it is anti-
> authoritarian in that the criterion for assessing an idea is not its
> appeal to official authority but to experience. Like all cultures, it

is shared and transmitted and the characteristic form of
communication is the book and the journal.

Whatever reservations we may have about the realities of academia,
the model itself, with its insistence that the content of education is
negotiable, represents a non-authoritarian ideal of considerable appeal.
It was held that anyone conducting an investigation within the spirit
of this intellectual culture must be free to cross and recross the boundaries of the traditional disciplines; that to confine a student to any
formal 'subject' was to place an externally determined restraint on the
pursuit of knowledge, a condition at variance with the anti-authoritarian
nature of the culture itself. And, of course, hand in glove with this
belief went the encouragement of pupils' initiative. The participation of
a pupil in influencing the directions of his own learning was vital to a
participation in the wider culture. The result of these beliefs was the
introduction in many schools of a topic-centred rather than a subject-
discipline approach to teaching.

It would be misleading to pretend that such a theoretical formulation
preceded the general studies, integrated studies, or inter-disciplinary
enquiries movement in any one country let alone in the many that
witnessed it at the time we are considering. It is significant that the
term 'social studies' was seldom used, and we may fairly assume that it
was studiously avoided because of its association with the progressive
movement in the USA that had so recently been widely discredited in
the post-Sputnik frenzied search for an educational scapegoat.[2] Somewhere in the movement to open up the curriculum, wherever it
occurred, were people to remind the young of valid criticisms of
progressivism in the USA.

The contributors to this book, most of whom were leaders in curriculum reform in Victoria, focus firmly on the centrality of learning as
the specific role of the school. We two worked with Bill Hannan and
Doug White in establishing two pilot schools to try out new approaches.
Both schools planned a core of interdisciplinary studies and, for want
of a better term (and certainly carefully avoiding a label that would be
reminiscent of the early progressivism), chose the term, 'general studies'.
The reasons for this attempt to cross subject boundaries were largely to
do with content and sound pedagogy. Like Maria and her team those
two schools were determined to replace a fragmented curriculum with
one that had coherence and spin-off. They expected to replace the
automatic mastery of inert ideas, displayed at examinations and for-
gotten for ever after, with the pursuit of generative ones that would
draw first of all on the unique and shared experiences of the pupils
themselves.

It was in the course of introducing topic-centred studies that organizational concerns took on unexpected importance. First, as a prerequisite to planning the work, a team of teachers had to talk to each other and work with each other in a frank interchange. In Maria's school this was a radical departure from tradition. It was partly contrived by her deputy principal and partly the result of the formation of a group of volunteers who, so far as they knew, had little more in common than a willingness to give the new ideas a go. In the pilot schools established in Victoria only volunteer staff who were keen to implement new principles participated in the innovations. It is significant that Maria's deputy principal, too, never tried to persuade doubtful staff to join the experiment.

The second departure from tradition, we found, was that school organization had to be drastically adjusted to make way for curricular innovation – the gigantic jigsaw that results in the immutable school timetable is inimical to innovation. The teams running the innovation began to organize their own timetables. Thus, a desperate response to what seemed an intractable problem led to a decentralizing of school administration, the eventual recognition by the principal of one of the pilot schools that his own duties had become considerably less onerous as a result of the innovations and, as he put it wryly, he could now find time to teach – a pursuit that he had always enjoyed and done well, but that he had thought ruefully he would never enjoy again. Some of the staff showed unsuspected organizational skills and it was generally recognized, as school staff put it, that the school timetable turned out to be the tail that had always wagged the dog. A flexible approach to timetabling enabled the innovative teams to try out various kinds of grouping in an attempt to discover in action what we sought for in vain from theorists. We have no doubt that Maria's team will become preoccupied for a time with trying out various grouping strategies.

Adjusting schools to topic-centred teaching

When innovation spread to other schools, we discovered that school organization had to be changed before any major changes of curriculum itself could occur. With hindsight we can see that for it to have been otherwise would be like designing an open-plan school and then trying to teach by old classroom talk and chalk methods (which, of course, happened in numberless cases and was interpreted to be a basic flaw in open classrooms generally).

And then a further phenomenon manifested itself as reforms were put into practice. Just as giving freedom to teachers had opened Pandora's box, so too taking the lid off for pupils forced teachers to focus their attention on urgently important day-to-day matters like counselling and the setting up of supportive group structures. We are not saying that pupils ran riot (although in some cases they did), but rather that once they were treated as individuals and the teachers had a relatively small number to get to know, the silent minority (or was it a majority in some schools?) suddenly became conspicuous. Countless children who had sat quietly and apparently co-operative but dumb, and others who had been subdued by impersonal disciplinary measures were (often for the first time) seen to be beset by crippling personal problems. Right, learning was the first concern of the school, but how could Sam learn anything while his mother kept him at home every time she had a headache? How could Sam grow up under such a tyranny of affection? How could Penny care about her course on 'Women in History' when she was out on the streets every night with the connivance of her father, a drunken widower who was also an unpaying customer? How did Jim survive at all when his teacher discovered on visiting his home that his small sister was strapped to the bed all day until he came back from school to look after her while waiting for her parents to return from work? And Jim had had the same treatment until he was big enough to look after himself. Hyperbole? Each example is true, and all too many more, equally gruesome, could be cited whether the school was like Maria's or at the other end of the spectrum – a wealthy independent school. We foresee that Maria, worried as she is by the problem that Fatima is creating for her – a problem that for the moment is making Fatima slip back alarmingly in her studies – could be submerged by her pupils' problems.

Maria does not want to turn her teaching into therapy. She would have chosen social work if so; but the problems before her are urgent, and some, we know, will be heart-rending. Because she is not callous, she has to keep her cool and remind herself that she is there primarily to teach; she cannot take on all society's problems. The best that she can do is to run her classroom in such a way that children can help each other, and to have a strong working contact with local professional and lay groups that will help. But there are too few of them, and making the right contacts takes time as well as ingenuity. She has to tell herself constantly that she is in danger of letting her thinking about the content of her teaching and the planning of her lessons go on taking second place. Also, Paul is there constantly reminding Maria, as he reminds himself, that it is all too easy to get a taste for pupils' dependence, thereby giving problems an importance that at best aggravates them, and at worst helps to create them.

In her training year, Maria had ample opportunity to see and work with innovative schools. She recognizes that some teachers seem to thrive on their pupils' vulnerability and even, she suspects, originally undertook to innovate for this reason, however dimly perceived at the time. Of course, like Maria, we recognize that the reasons for introducing topic-centred teaching are not identical in every school, and in many cases the reasons for *retaining* the new teaching methods are often quite different from those which originally justified their introduction. Many of the reasons given by teachers for topic-centred studies are concerned with pastoral care or with the improved relations between teacher and pupils that we have shown to be likely in classrooms in which much of the activity involves pupils working individually or in groups rather than participating in a teacher-orchestrated lesson. These sorts of changes, of course, can be effected while keeping the learning within one of the traditional disciplines. However, partly for reasons already mentioned above, and partly because at the time of the introduction of topic-centred studies the teaching profession in Victoria and many other places was in a mood of militant professionalism, all changes away from an authoritarian mode of teaching appeared to come as a package deal. Enquiry learning, open-endedness, self-direction, spontaneity and a number of other slogans were almost always associated with an abandonment of traditional school 'subjects' for 'topics'.

Some characteristic approaches to topic-centred teaching

In this chapter we wish to say little about the debate between the proponents of subject-teaching and those of topic-centred teaching. We shall, rather, consider the claim that the methods used in topic-centred teaching provide a way of engaging knowledge that is not only different from that in the traditional disciplines, but can be more coherent and rational. When the first overwhelming problems settle down, our experience suggests that teachers' interest in content and pedagogy revives, and that they then seek some guidance, perhaps it would not be too grand to say some 'conceptual tools', for choosing one approach to knowledge rather than another.

If one of the distinguishing features of topic-centred courses is that they all involve at least the possibility of working with more than one discipline on a topic, we probably have as good a starting point as any other for comparing various approaches to topics. We can make this comparison independently of how important the designers of the different courses consider 'subject-integration' to be. In any inter-disciplinary team, we can expect the kinds of tensions Maria's group faced. If subjects are 'integrated', or if no attempt is made to confine the area of study within the traditionally construed boundaries of knowledge, how is this integration achieved, what is allowed, what not allowed, what is encouraged and what discouraged? As an aid to looking at this problem let us construct five types of planning which show how an investigation into an area of knowledge might be organized. These will be simplifications. When looking at actual examples of classroom practice, we need not expect to find them realized in these pure forms.

Plan A: nominal correlation or the general knowledge quiz

Let us take some examples from programmes we have seen in schools. We might start with form four (year ten) integrated studies taught by a team comprising a historian, a geographer and two English teachers, taking two classes of thirty pupils for eleven periods a week. The topic is 'Asia and her Pacific Neighbours'. In first term the historian takes IVc for India's history, and the geographer takes the geography of India. They each have three periods a week. One of the English specialists has three periods on Indian literature. Two periods every Friday afternoon are given to creative writing supervised for both classes by the English staff with some help in small group work from the other two. To economize in resources a similar approach is taken with IVp, except their country is China. In second term they switch over. In third term each child in the classes 'does' Indonesia and chooses two countries from New Guinea, Japan, Malaysia, Vietnam.

The starting point in planning this 'innovation' was content. It was agreed by the staff that all Australians should know about their Asian neighbours. The science and maths staff had refused to enter into the interdisciplinary project, and so the small group who wanted to try it decided to work with year ten because in this year the pupils could start foreign language work in either Chinese or Indonesian – a good reason. But when the staff started to plan a thematically integrated course, there were sharp differences over territorial rights, and so in desperation they decided to keep the subject boundaries but to bind them with a common topic for study. The teachers did co-operate somewhat at first, but the extent of the overlap diminished under the pressure of time. When it came to planning the final term's work, they were so pressed that each member took the major responsibility for one country (the one he knew best), worked out a series of written assignments, and gave each of the other specialists the opportunity to add some sections of their own, and that was that.

Here we have an example of integrated studies in name only. The only difference between it and subject teaching is that there is less variety, and the assignment sheet in third term becomes the surrogate teacher that is even more boring than the most boring member of the team whose frailties are at least interesting. Each term there is a demonstration of great relief when each form organizes an Indonesian Day or a China Day, and parents, students and staff enjoy foreign cooking, dancing, singing and whatever other cultural expressions can be found. As Bill Hannan will show, this is a poor imitation of multicultural education. It is enjoyable entertainment but it is skin-deep multiculturalism.

If we may now convert this to a grossly exaggerated diagram, we can represent what has happened as something like Plan A. If a whole curriculum is content-dominated, it can end up with an infinitely proliferated number of circles each of which indicates some area of information.

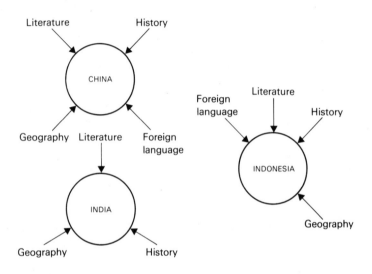

Plan A   Nominal correlation: general knowledge quiz approach to 'Asia and her Pacific Neighbours'

Plan B: cross-disciplinary approach to a concept

Plan B is only a slight variant of A in that its central idea, 'Movement', is so broad an umbrella that all the elements can exist independently without there necessarily being any criss-crossing network. We saw a slight modification of Plan B in a general studies course in year seven of a convent. The central circle was 'Creation', which was filled with the Bible (from Genesis through the Virgin birth to the Resurrection). The arrows then pointed inwards from the following circles: religious

28

music, motherhood and the family, the propagation of plants, scientific discoveries. No member of staff need have felt left out. There was a circle for each.

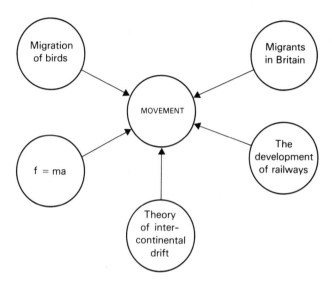

Plan B   Cross-disciplinary approach to a concept, 'Movement', studied through biology, sociology, history, physics and geo- morphology (f − force; ma − mass acceleration)

Plan C: the cross-disciplinary ramble

Plan C develops a little like a stream-of-consciousness narrative − one thing leads to another, though some of the links are tenuous and the material is stretched to join them. There is in this plan some awareness of logical links as we move from formless content to some explanatory, organizing ideas. This, of course, was the idea behind 'Creation', but it kept its individual staff in their individual circles, whereas Plan C could be taught by a team in various ways. It could have started with Ancient Egypt and the sun taught by a historian and geographer, and the two parallel studies could then have criss-crossed, while the historian might have led on to other ancient civilizations and the geographer might have led on to irrigation and the harnessing of water power. Because the connecting links are more generative in this plan, the two (or more) teachers could teach in tandem throughout, switching over as the development of the themes leaned more directly in the geographer's or the historian's direction, or they could have kept their own group so that they might build in pastoral care, but have switched over temporarily, by special arrangement, if either got into difficulties. The plan tends, however, to be linear rather than interactive, and there is a tendency for each new link to lead further away from the starting point, thus encouraging superficial teaching.

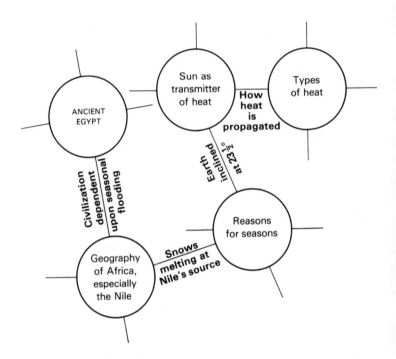

Plan C   A cross-disciplinary ramble around a topic. 'Ancient Egypt' studied through history, geography, physics

The danger of superficiality in trying to fit everything into a theme or a topic is illustrated by Plan C. Only a generation or so ago it was thought by some historians that the discipline of history was too difficult for youngsters and for the weaker members of the weaker sex at a rather later age. And so it was argued with the specious appeal of half-truths that, since adolescent girls were obsessed with their appearance, history might be taught, for example, by taking the theme,

'The History of Clothing', which would have the added advantage of cutting down on reading and concentrating on pictures. Thus, it was bravely supposed, every period studied could branch out into imaginative sociological explorations, biographies and other related studies. And so, by looking at pictures of, say, convicts, agricultural and town labourers, Queen Alexandra and King Edward VII, we would get a feel for the period. Let us not disparage the use of good visual aids in history. Far from it. But this particular approach is far too frivolous to have any gripping meaning for modern adolescents. Try interpreting our own times by examining our own fashions. Far from being simple, it is extremely complex, requiring a wealth of background knowledge from which to make tentative informed guesses. This sort of slanting of history towards simplistic sociology was indeed, to use Maria's sarcastic term, throwing out the baby (history) with the bathwater (irrelevant history).

Or again, let us look at a similar fashion of the time — the extraction of masses of bits from short stories, novels, plays and even poetry to illustrate, let us say in Maria's project, oppressive poverty. No wonder that Paul entered the venture enthusiastically and then discovered that he was starting to look at what he was reading, for pleasure or for work, solely in terms of what the kids could get out of it for the project. Thus the integrity of each writer's work was being subsumed in some quite other purpose. No wonder he started protesting that he was being required to bend his subject shamefully and he must have time to study things for their own sake. And the same complaint could be made by any subject specialist.

Without being too dogmatic, we conclude that 'subject-integration' is not automatically good in itself. Certainly there is nothing to suggest that just because work on a topic has included material and methods from six different disciplines it is somehow better than one that has managed to include only two. Bill Hannan's comment is completely germane here.[3]

> It cannot be said too often that General Studies do not aim to integrate subjects. A topic involves only the work which the subject matter warrants. If a topic does require some maths or some history well and good. If it does not there is (or should be) no attempt to force it.

There are many ways in which integration can occur without bending subjects. One way is by having a specialist teacher who is so widely based that she can move out from a piece of literature or an historical topic or a laboratory experiment (depending on her specialism) in a number of directions that the study inherently points to. We would agree with the Crowther Report[4] that a good subject specialist invariably goes beyond subject-centredness into all kinds of associated studies. But the *reductio ad absurdum* of this is that one really good teacher of one subject is all that is needed to give a child a liberal or general education.

There is the further point that a good teacher can do wonders with a badly conceived plan and a bad teacher can wreck a splendid one. One cannot judge what happens in a school solely from its written documents. That being said, however, much thought needs to be given to starting with a promising plan, which itself is an indication that the teachers concerned have done some searching thinking. The designers of Plans A and B show little awareness of the need for coherence, and they also betray, as Bill Hannan implies in his warning, ignorance of the nature of knowledge — a point we shall return to later.

For the moment let us concentrate on the fact that Plans A and B are information-bound. We are not setting up Aunt Sallies here: our Plans were constructed from what we have seen in schools. Plan C shows some signs of seeking associative and causal links in the material that could require pupils to exercise their imagination and reasoning and not merely their memories. It could tempt them to try to find out more about some of the matters raised. But it could also ramble all over the place because there are not organizing ideas that bind the various topics.

All three Plans appear on paper to be value-free, and so, even if connections could be found between the presently discrete elements, they suggest an aridly cerebral approach. There are key concepts or organizing ideas at the heart of the disciplines (or, if you prefer, the main branches of learning), and there are values that concern them. Scholarly teachers will bias their selection of content so that it leads pupils towards the sort of fertile understanding that they themselves have and that they recognize among scholars they respect — or towards what Doug White and Eva Wynn have called 'the intellectual culture'. Dow will take up these points in greater detail in a later chapter, but the question at issue at the moment is: Is one sort of curriculum plan better than another? We have already shown some sort of progression in the planning. Let us take Bill Hannan's observations a little further.

Plan D: a network branching from a single study

Let us now choose a subject-centred study that works outwards and raises a number of interdisciplinary topics for investigation. The work to be done would be helped less by asking the question, 'What has my special area of expertise to offer on this study', than by asking, 'What is central about this study? What further investigation is needed to

32

Are there similarities with brainwashing?

How are sex-roles induced?

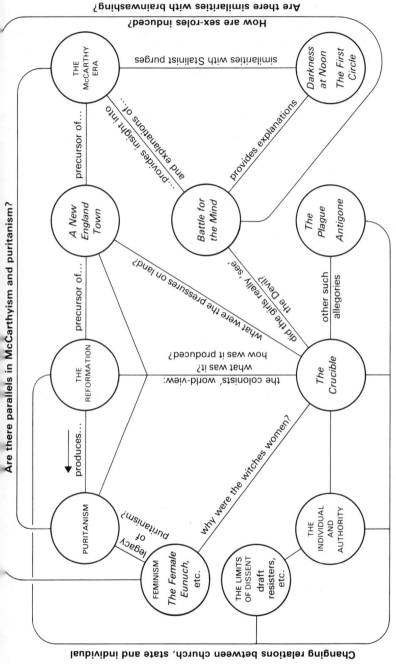

Are there parallels in McCarthyism and puritanism?

Changing relations between church, state and individual

Plan D A branching network growing from one study in one subject, English (Arthur Miller's play, The Crucible)

understand it? How do we go about investigating it?' If, for example, a class were looking at Arthur Miller's play, *The Crucible*, a number of questions and possible areas of investigation present themselves. How did the early American colonists see themselves in relation to God, to the state, to each other? How and why does Miller link the McCarthy era with earlier puritanism? How have other writers used this technique of historical allegory? Why were witches always women? And so on. All these possible lines of investigation are suggested by the play and to follow them up would help to illuminate, explain and deepen a student's understanding of the play. Each suggested question is linked to the central issue and thus to each other question.

As well as the links that tie the secondary areas of investigation to the central one of Miller's play, it is possible to show links between these secondary areas and the tertiary and further areas of investigation that present themselves. In this way an interlocking network can be constructed. This possible map can be shown as in Plan D.

Thus one teacher using one play well can open up many kinds of understanding. It might be noted in passing that if Paul had been giving this unit he could well have called on other members of the team, particularly Maria, to develop some of the lines of enquiry with his pupils. It might also be noted that no interdisciplinary unit should preclude the possibility that each member of the team be given scope to develop his speciality in depth with a group of pupils. Paul's doubts in chapter 1 deserve to be taken very seriously.

Team-teaching

What can we say so far about topic-centred studies? Plan B, which in some senses is most topic-centred in that it takes a broad theme and allows a team of teachers to branch out from it yet keeping relevant to the theme, is far more fragmented than Plan D, which is subject-centred (literature), has one play as the topic, can well be taught, and can be well taught by one teacher. Why many courses tend towards Plan B rather than Plan D may be found not in the nature of the knowledge being pursued, but in the demands of team-teaching.

Team-teaching is often, but not always, associated with a topic-centred approach. Plans A and B illustrate how content can be divided in an attempt to respect the individuality of each teacher in a so-called team. Even the most gifted team would be unlikely to make Plan A any more attractive than straight-out subject-teaching. Plan B could be taught by one teacher or a team, but either way it would inevitably be fragmented. Plan C could have some coherence if the team's work was organized with that in mind. If so the eventual programme taught would be an improvement on the Plan, for it would show links that are absent in the initial planning. Plan D is one teacher's *modus operandi*, but she could well call on others' expertise for quite extensive segments without loss of shape in the programme.

Setting up a team like Maria's has obvious advantages if the major problems of team-teaching can be resolved. The very exercise makes it necessary to give new emphasis to curriculum planning in sharing wisdom and experience. In thinking seriously about any difficult question one moves across subject boundaries without any consciousness that at this moment it is helpful to think like a historian, but the next step requires psychological insight. Any good teacher will try to take pupils along the lines of thought she finds most germane. But in thinking about a serious question no two people take exactly the same route. This diversity of approach is both the strength and weakness of team-teaching. To retain coherence while several people bring to bear their separate and several perspectives, those members of the team have to be unusually well tuned in to each other. Thus a small team is likely to work better than a large one. Further safeguards can be provided. The work can be so divided that one person's conception of the pattern prevails in each section and is respected by the 'visitors' who come to help. This is what we saw in Plan D.

There is no one best way of taking account of the problems of team-teaching; but we can distinguish two basically different methods of organizing a team of teachers. In the first case the team may draw up a common topic-centred course, each teacher contributing to the planning of the syllabus in whatever way he or she can. The course is then taught by each teacher to his or her own class. Alternatively, each teacher may offer different components of the course to the pupils who move between the team members in order to benefit from the different approaches being pursued. There are obviously pitfalls in both methods. In the first (which is probably more common in the junior forms) there is always the possibility that teachers will find themselves supervising work that was devised by someone else in an area they know little about or are unenthusiastic about teaching; pupils risk having a great deal of time with an unexciting teacher; or their one teacher can become too clucky about his pupils, and make them too dependent; and pupils miss being taught by teachers with diverse, even conflicting, ideas, which is a safeguard against indoctrination. In the second it is possible that the individual teachers will only imperfectly know what the others are doing and that chances for constructing real links between sections of the course will be lost. In both cases it is possible to see how ease of curriculum planning can be achieved by trying to broaden the base of the investigation to accommodate every member of the team, but also how this broadening may in fact become fragmentation. There are, of course, all kinds of variations possible between the two extremes.

Maria's team, for example, could organize their course (pp. 14ff.) in many ways. They could, if they wished, call in a maths teacher to demonstrate to all the pupils what equality means in mathematical terms. If he were of philosophical bent, he could show that equality is a construct, which he could exemplify in many ways. He might examine parallel lines in geometry; he might examine our perception of them (for example, what happens to railway lines as our distance from them increases); and he might, perhaps with David's help, look at them geographically on curved surfaces, through latitude and longitude. Inviting speculation of such a kind need not be too difficult for pupils in year ten. Most of Maria's pupils knew in advance a great deal about the project, having been consulted all along during the planning; but they now needed to be given a more detailed introduction to the proposed lines of enquiry. The team might discuss at some length the various ways in which 'equality' could be examined, thus pointing out the shape that the whole unit of work might take. They might each give samples. Paul might look at some poems or parables (say Brecht's 'Questions from a Worker who Reads', or Luke 14, 10-14; 16, 19-25; 18, 22-25); David might introduce the pupils to the notion of inequalities in the world's resources and what this means to different nations; Betty might relate David's material to the different diets that different peoples have, and even to the different budgetary allowances to be found in the school's neighbourhood; and Maria might look at studies of identical twins.

One could think of any number of ways into the topic. The selection of material would be based on the team's sensing what would both engage the pupils' interest initially and be rich in meanings; on what they felt competent to teach; and on the very practical matter of the availability of sound teaching materials for later study. The key issue here is that the team should so understand each other's thinking that coherence would be gained first by the way they would explicitly point to the links they would be making, and later by repeated cross-references to what the others were doing. The pupils might then choose from a number of options arising directly from the content introduced. The introductions would ensure that pupils did not have to make choices in a state of stone-cold sober ignorance. They could then break into smallish groups which would allow various forms of supervision, though each child and each group would be attached specifically to the teacher who designed his unit, and other teachers would be available as consultants. They could create larger groups for specific purposes from time to time, and they would meet the whole year group for sessions at the end in which there would be a pooling of all the different kinds of work. The pupils at that time would use as many different media as possible in presenting their findings, and the teachers would see that they would come back to a consideration of the different kinds of equality, some in conflict with others, and none of them being absolutely attainable in reality except as a mathematical construct.

There are all kinds of other ways in which the team's work could be divided and organized. Using something like Plan D as a starting point, Paul might keep his own class and focus on literature throughout the unit. He might choose one novel like *Hard Times*, compare a number of poems, short stories, newspaper articles, folk and pop songs and even some serious essays. David might examine some issue arising from his work on unequal energy resources, such as oil. He could start with the shortages the children might face in their lifetime; he might then look at the new wealth of the Middle East and its relations with the USSR; and from that he might turn to a study of alternative forms of power. Betty might have her class read the School of Barbiana's *Letter to a Teacher* (Penguin Education, 1970) with a view to setting up a similar research project into educational inequalities and trying out the method the Barbiana pupils adopted to ensure that their reporting was fluent and clear. Their work might explore such questions as the different kinds of schooling for the rich and the rest, why in England the eleven-plus largely gave way to comprehensive schools, and the student composition in various kinds of higher education. Maria might pursue the question of the effect on identical twins of radically different kinds of upbringing and environments and then lead on to the question of whether Aboriginal tribes or Eskimos developed hierarchies or were basically egalitarian. David and Betty might decide to change groups after two weeks, and Paul and Maria after three. Like the first group they would all come together after a set period for a sharing and summing up.

Plan E shows some of the possibilities of interaction and coherence in such planning. It is the kind of plan that would allow many other topics to be introduced in response to teachers' expertise and pupils' interests, without loss of relevance. It also provides for treatment of concepts at many levels of difficulty, but always straining towards an interplay of greater generalization and richer particularization.

Coherence in curriculum plans

What can we learn by a comparison of the different plans and approaches? It is clear from our examples that some sorts of investigations of topics produce a far more complex internal structure than others. While complexity in itself is neither good nor bad, we would

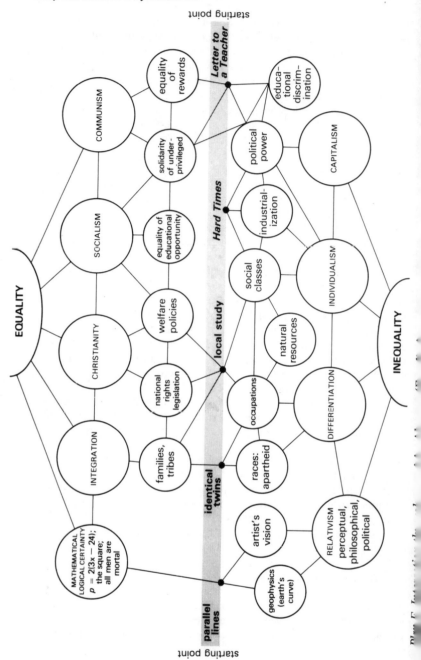

starting point

Letter to a Teacher

COMMUNISM

equality of rewards

educational discrimination

solidarity of under-privileged

political power

CAPITALISM

SOCIALISM

Hard Times

equality of educational opportunity

industrialization

EQUALITY

welfare policies

social classes

INDIVIDUALISM

CHRISTIANITY

local study

national rights legislation

natural resources

INEQUALITY

INTEGRATION

families, tribes

occupations

DIFFERENTIATION

identical twins

races: apartheid

MATHEMATICAL (LOGICAL CERTAINTY) $p = 2(3x - 24)$; the square; all men are mortal

artist's vision

RELATIVISM perceptual, philosophical, political

parallel lines

geophysics (earth's curve)

starting point

38

like to suggest that the greater the number of valid links that can be drawn within the area covered by an investigation, the greater will be the pupil's understanding and control of the knowledge he gains by pursuing the investigation. If, for example, work from both history and literature is included in the same study, as it is in *The Crucible*, it could be expected that reading the historical material would illuminate, explain, fill in and, most importantly, raise questions about the literary material and vice versa. In order that this should occur, it seems imperative that both the historical and literary material be concerned with the same quite specific questions or areas. If there is only a vague relationship between the two approaches, or if the material is stretched to appear to make some connection, the amount of illumination that one will provide on the other will be minimal. Thus in Plan B there are no direct links shown between the area marked 'Migration of birds' and the one marked 'The development of railways'. Although the two areas can be subsumed under the broad heading, 'Movement', that about exhausts the capacity of one area to illuminate the other. The pupil can learn as much as he likes about the migratory patterns of Arctic terns and still be none the wiser about the part played by the railways in making a country economically self-sufficient. The two areas of enquiry really have nothing to do with each other, though, if an approach like Plan D were used, a book like Geoffrey Blainey's *Tyranny of Distance* may make very effective links.

We should recall that the first approach we suggested for Maria's group was for one teacher to examine the concept 'equality' in mathematics, and then other teachers would all take a turn at exploring what 'equality' might mean in, say, geography, literature, sociology and home economics — in whatever speciality they happened to command. The second suggested possibility was that each teacher would begin with examining the concept through his speciality, and that pupils might later change to another member of the team for a different perspective. In Plan D, which we commended, a really good teacher is a *sine qua non*, whereas an equally good teacher in Maria's team can influence the whole team, and each can learn from the other's particular skills. One important way in which the structure inherent in a topic is conveyed to pupils is through the teacher. The teacher makes available to the pupils the meanings and values that she has acquired from her own learning. It is difficult for one person to convey another's richness of meanings, which is why teachers find it hard to use pre-packaged materials. In close relationships, however, teachers will be aware of each other's strengths, and the cohesion in team-teaching will reflect that relationship. Thus the bigger the team the harder it is to avoid fragmentation. Team-teaching is educative for *teachers* if done well.

It is not too optimistic to hope that team-teaching, in drawing attention to the significantly different ways in which the participant teachers construct meanings and seek solutions, will heighten their awareness of the different backgrounds of experiences and understanding to be expected in a group of pupils. There is nothing in Plans A, B, C or D that suggests that they would stimulate that sort of enlightenment, as do some of the proposals for Maria's team. They also make possible flexible grouping of pupils so that teachers could engineer the structures in such a way that diffident and slow learners might be placed in supportive groups where child teaches child when studying, and pupils' work is made accessible to the whole group.

Written assignments as training in question-answering

We noted in Plan A that most of the work in third term was based on a large number of written assignments. Maria's team plans assignments in the local study, and no doubt others will be used. We want good assignments to be used, but not even good ones should be used too extensively, for if they are they become the surrogate teacher; they can be subtly manipulative and yet impersonal, and too much of them is boring, boring, boring.

In particular we should be wary of the assignment that is nothing more than a fact-finding, comprehension exercise, however many titillating things it invites the pupil to do, such as illustrate, draw maps, fill in blanks. Again, we should avoid assignments that allow solely for individual work. Our observations of a number of schools in which assignment sheets are regularly used is that pupils see them as programmes to be worked through, usually starting at the top of page 1 and continuing until the bottom of the last page. Pupils see the work as a series of questions, each of which has a correct answer. The main point of doing any reference work is assumed to be fact-finding. The exclusively sequential nature of the assignments and the spaces for answers on the duplicated sheets themselves help the development of these attitudes. Let us take one example.

Topic 4 The Disadvantaged: St Urban's Comprehensive School, Year Ten, General Studies

Read the following passages with care. If there is anything you do not understand, ask a teacher. Words you do not know you should look up in your dictionary and note, with meanings, in your folder.

The first two extracts come from a book written by an Englishman about his own family who, with the growth of industry, had moved from the country to 'Green St', Northampton. Before reading the passages, look up Northampton on the map and find out as much as you can about it and write it in your folder before answering the questions.

The third passage was written by a fifteen-year-old black girl from Harlem. Explain in one sentence what and where Harlem is.

1 Speech in 'Green St'

. . . Nobody developed an independent, personal way of speaking. They shared a tongue assimilated uncritically from the past. Everything spoke of their origin; the idioms borrowed from obsolete crafts and occupations of the countryside ('tup-reddle' for lipstick; 'She looks like a sow with sidepockets', said of a woman unnecessarily adorned); expressions connected with the weather and the passage of the seasons ('You come like snow in harvest' would be the greeting to an unexpected and unwelcome visitor); vegetable or animal life ('It's a poor hen as can't scrat for one chick', said of a woman with only one child who complains that she is unable to manage it; 'It's a sign of a hard winter when the hay starts to run after the horse', referring to a girl who reverses the conventional process of courtship by openly and shamelessly setting her cap at the man) . . .

Like popular speech in any tongue their idiom had at its core many images and similes taken from the human body and its functions, and often of great crudity and immediacy. 'She looks at him as if the sun shone out of his arse' was a pejorative and disapproving reference to anyone so immoderately preoccupied with a lover that she had no time for anyone else.

. . . Whenever anyone suggested that he felt sorry for Vera or Dopey Freda, they would shake their head sagely and declare, 'Aah. Pity without relief is like mustard without beef.' . . .

Allusive sayings abounded in all their speech. Of a woman who disapproved of other people's sexual success, they would say, 'It's easy enough to hold the latch down when nobody's trying to get in.' . . . They spoke with great economy of language. Nothing was ever said for the sake of speaking, nothing added to impress or to excite admiration. They never trusted articulate people, and always held 'the gift of the gab' in great contempt. Long silences supervened in all their conversations . . . They had many evasive answers for those who asked indiscreet questions. They were guarded in all replies, unwilling to disclose to anyone . . . more than a minimum about themselves and their own lives. If anyone asked them how much something had cost the stern and uncommunicative reply would be 'Money and fair words'. Curiosity about the purpose

of an errand would be met with the invariable unsmiling rebuff
'To see a man about a dog' . . . When S. left his wife and the children
asked where he was, the only information their mother offered
was 'Two fields the other side China'. They were reluctant to give
praise. If a daughter asked how she looked before going out, the
highest compliment she could expect would be, 'You'll pass in a
crowd with a good push.'

2 Work in 'Green St'
There was neither dignity nor self-fulfilment in their labour, in
spite of the frequent sermons and exhortations to which they were
exposed and which exalted the sanctity of toil and the salubrity of
industry. They were directed into occupations that corresponded
neither to their abilities nor to their preferences . . .

As the machinery became complex more factories became
established . . . All the children of Ellen Youl began work in one of
those early factories, and of this novelty and privilege they still
bear the marks today − backs so bent that as they shuffle along the
road . . . all they can see is the pavement beneath them, the . . .
head-turban covering Aunt Lou's baldness, which resulted from
some unguarded machinery in the factory where she worked at the
age of twenty.

The employment of children as human scarecrows, the necessity
of serving imperious and ungrateful gentlefolk as maids and
gardeners did not bring them any . . . satisfaction . . . I cannot
imagine anyone wanting to perpetuate proletarian culture . . . we
had been as effectively deprived of freedom as if we had been
physically confined. (from Jeremy Seabrook, *The Unprivileged*,
London, Longmans Green, 1967, pp. 111-15, 118, 120-1)

3 Youth in the Ghetto
We look into the schools in Harlem and we find that our young
people can't read and they can't write. They don't know who they
are or where they come from and they have teachers who don't
care, who will never teach them this. They don't have enough
teachers . . . The black man has the most deplorable housing in New
York, in the United States. He has landlords who do nothing but
constantly rob him deaf, dumb and blind . . . [He] looks at television
and he sees those news reporters saying the city is making a move
to inspect housing conditions . . . and then the days roll by and the
rat-bites still show up on the children, and parents find that they
still have to sleep in shifts to keep the rats away from the baby at
night, and the children are still catching pneumonia in the winter
because of the cold, and are still not being able to go to school,

which are inferior anyway . . . The system that we live in becomes a vicious cycle and there is never a way out . . . So, when this anger builds up in black people, not knowing how to let it out and how to retaliate against the power structures, the black man finds a way out; but the way out is often in a bottle of wine or in a needle containing heroin or in a reefer, or in the power of his fists when he slaps his wife down. The woman finds a way out in the power of her hand when she slaps a child down, and so the cycle goes on. (Quoted in Peter Marris and Martin Rein, *Dilemmas of Social Reform*, Penguin Books, 1974, pp. 78-9 — first published London, Routledge & Kegan Paul, 1967)

Answer the following questions

1 What was the date of first publication of the two books?
2 Write out the sentences or phrases that are comments on (a) the characteristics of speech in Green St and (b) literacy in Harlem.
3 (a) In discussion with others in your group try to work out what the underlined sayings or words might mean. You should also use your dictionaries.
   (b) Try to find as many common sayings that we use as you can and list them with meanings.
4 What present hardships are described by the two writers?
5 What do you think Seabrook might mean when he writes that his people 'had been as effectively deprived of freedom as if we had been physically confined'? Write down a sentence from the Harlem girl's account that says much the same sort of thing.
6 Choose one of the packages of material brought into class for this assignment and use it to write at least a page on one of the following (you may illustrate it if you wish):
   (a) Some achievements by American blacks
   (b) Local industries in this school's neighbourhood
   (c) The work of the St Urban council in housing and education
   (d) Where the people of St Urban work
   (e) Paul Robeson
7 Find a group of four with whom you will make a tape-recording of readings from Negro poems. Read as well as you possible can. *OR* Write an account of any book you have read by James Baldwin. *OR* Write a letter to a friend telling him about the occupation you most want to follow.

These sorts of courses, however good the materials or enjoyable some of the tasks may be, help the pupils to become question-answerers, but not question-askers. In some schools a large collection of these assignments has been built up over the years. It is possible for pupils who have finished one assignment to proceed directly to the next. Having pupils working at differing speeds in the same classroom at any one time results in up to ten or so different assignments being worked on. This effectively prevents the teacher from engaging the whole class in discussion of some aspect of the work, since only a few pupils may be familiar with the relevant section.

While almost all teachers who use assignment sheets in this fashion admit these disadvantages, many hold that the advantages of allowing the pupils to 'work at their own pace', and of having a store of well-constructed units of work always on hand, outweigh them. Because the assignments can be reproduced for as many pupils as necessary over as many years, a good deal of time and effort can go into making them of high quality. In terms of the Plans outlined above, it is possible to find a great deal of interconnection between the different sections of the work. In terms of the number of subject-areas that can be integrated into work on the central topic, the range is often very extensive. But even if we discern a tight formal structure within the assignment sheets themselves, the real question is still: To what extent do the pupils gain a feeling for the structure as they proceed with the work? As previously mentioned, the prevailing attitude among the pupils seems to be that the goal of assignment work is quick, unquestioning, sequential form-completion. In most classes where assignments of this type are used, it is possible to find a small group of 'assignment-racers' vying with each other to see who can complete the assignments in the shortest time. With this attitude to the work, taking time to explore in depth a particular, interesting part of the topic can only be seen as counter-productive, since it slows down the giddy pace.

Interviews with pupils about their work reveal that even though they may be happy with the continual use of prepared assignments of this nature, and may be deriving a considerable sense of achievement from their ordered completion, there is little feeling for the structure of the work as a whole and very little feeling that learning about a topic should be a process in which the pupil actively questions the subject-matter and tries to devise his own ways of coming to grips with it. The effective use of assignment sheets, then, seems to rest very much on the amount of ordinary classroom teaching and discussion that the teacher can intermingle with the work outlined on the duplicated sheets. It goes without saying, of course, that an assignment that invites enquiry is better than one that does not.

44

Guidelines for topic-centred units

It is worth noting that Maria's topic-centred unit has more far-reaching interconnections than Plan D which relates only to literature, history and sociology. If one reason for interdisciplinary topic-centred teaching is to show pupils the interdependence of many branches of knowledge in terms of the information, skills, insights and values embedded in them it is probably wise to choose a vexed question of topical interest (say, planning for the energy crisis), a complex concept (say, frames of reference) or an unrealizable ideal (say, democratic equality). By taking a central issue or area of investigation and asking oneself, what do we need to know about this topic? and how are we to find out? it should be possible to build up a coherent plan of attack. The degree of subject integration is something one can go on discovering after the investigation has been completed. It is not something that can be totally programmed into it beforehand. Topics like 'Movement', 'Clothing', 'Transport' or 'Poverty' may be taught dynamically, but there is nothing in the descriptive term given to the topic that suggests such an approach.

Maria's topic, 'Equality', is both a vexed question and one that arises from an unrealizable ideal. Lawrence Stenhouse, in preparing his famous school materials on sex, war, family relations and the like for the Humanities Curriculum Project in the UK, deliberately chose controversial (vexed) issues. The pressing human problems that pupils face do break across subject boundaries; but we have to be very careful in raising such sensitive questions. Maria's team, for example, would need to take care to avoid dealing with poverty in the locality in a way that might draw attention to any one pupil.

The old social studies idea of moving in concentric circles, say, out from the school, and then the family, and then the locality, and then the nation and finally to the world is in danger of being merely informational in intent. It is also based on the assumption that the things closest to us are both simplest and of most interest, whereas in reality 'distance (often) lends enchantment' and our problems may also be more easily understandable if we distance them than if we tackle the immediate thing, which in the process of simplification easily becomes simplistic. It was this sort of superficial distortion that led to academic criticism of progressives' concentration on what is contemporary.

The written assignment that we concocted on 'The Disadvantaged' illustrates not only the dangers inherent in reliance on written projects but also how to dwell on the trivial. There seems no point in the suggested illustrations in question 6. The unit emphasizes acquiring and comprehending information. The links between questions 6 and 7 and the passages are tenuous. Very many illuminating enquiries could have

45

been introduced and followed but were not.

By contrast, in the local study that David and Maria plan on 'Equality', they send the children on all kinds of fact-finding missions on their own. They ask them not only to collect and analyse statistics on employment and unemployment but also to seek information from their parents and grandparents on changes in their locality if they are old residents, or on immigration if they are migrants. Every opportunity is given for pupils to follow their own hunches.

Encouragement of question-asking

The invitation to what we might call question-asking, exploratory enquiry methods and associative thinking cannot be pursued equally well in all disciplines. Pupils in science may follow ingeniously designed enquiries, but rarely are the questions put to them genuinely open-ended — they are rather of the 'find the answers that the teacher wants you to know' kind. In any topic, pupils must first become acquainted with what is already known. In science this means learning what has been discovered and also the methods used in scientific enterprises.

This is a formidable task even if the teachers select, as they must, only samples. The teachers themselves cannot master more than a fragment of scientific knowledge, and they must in turn choose for their courses topics that have great social importance and that provide methodological training that is highly generalizable (and thus has transfer value). But there are also genuinely open-ended questions in science resulting from imperfect knowledge (for example, Why is the mutton-bird population declining?), as well as questions of a controversial moral nature about the value of scientific research (for example, Is the decline in the mutton-bird population a matter for human concern, and should it be investigated?) to which there is no simple answer. And if the answer to the last question is 'Yes', the further action required (How are we to stop the decline?) might present further questions about whether we should proceed. Questions concerning the moral responsibility of the scientist need not necessarily have a prominent role in the actual acquisition of scientific knowledge, since they are about the *application* of findings rather than about the nature of the search and of the findings themselves.

This point is well made in *The Web of Life* when it distinguishes between understanding science, which is 'to recognize the spirit of scientific investigation and appreciate the methods that the scientists use' and applying the findings:[5]

the application of the findings of science towards human welfare is not necessarily a part of the scientific process. Many scientists make no conscious effort to apply what they have found in the interests of human welfare, though, collectively, the whole process of science has materially altered the circumstances of human life.

As a corollary to this, it is important to recognize that science may have limited or no value in some fields of human activity — a point also made in *The Web of Life*:[6]

A full appreciation of the nature of science also brings with it the realization that there are some parts of everyday living to which science alone has little to contribute — which go, in fact, well beyond the realms of science.

Hence to try to force a scientific component into an inappropriate topic (say, neighbourliness) would be absurd, while it is less obviously absurd but just as inappropriate to try to squeeze human affairs into a highly theoretical scientific model — a point that is central to our examination of educational theory in this book. Science courses that lead pupils to ask questions and that familiarize them with the different *kinds* of questions that can be asked are unlikely to be tedious.

One of the values in interdisciplinary studies is that they can and should be used to help pupils grasp what are appropriate and inappropriate modes of enquiry. Or to take another example, Plan D is a generative way of studying a play that opens up many lines of thought and points to many problems that are integral to or derived from the main theme. The same sort of plan would be inappropriate for a topic requiring the use of geometry to solve an engineering problem. This is a problem-solving topic that may be approached in various ways in the search for the right conclusion or conclusions. The learning experiences in appreciating a poem and conducting a scientific experiment are qualitatively different, and different again from writing a poem and writing up an experiment for the uninitiated or for the expert. The poet tries to give us his *particular* vision and he may find his meaning expressed best in figurative or metaphorical images; the scientist's report to laymen might be best expressed through many illustrations of a *general* point; whereas the scientific researcher writing for his peers may make his point with what scientists call 'elegant' economy in the most *abstract* all-embracing generalization.

Almost any material can be presented to pupils in a way that will prompt them to ask questions of it, thus learning to initiate their own work and develop their own interests. Good pedagogy will always try to foster curiosity and initiative in the acquisition of knowledge. There is also great scope for individuality and versatility in the way people express their meanings. Of course pupils cannot write a highly theoretical paper on some original scientific investigation of their own, but they can learn to assess the kind of exposition that best expresses the different kinds of meanings provided by different kinds of knowledge, and they can be introduced to the far more subtle aptitude of establishing rapport with a particular audience by means of discussions and writing.

Balance in the curriculum

Not all knowledge and all kinds of understanding are accessible to immature students. We have dealt at greater length here with the sciences than with other branches of knowledge partly because the effects of scientific imperialism are still with us, and attempts to give all kinds of inappropriate activities the status of science are still quite common. Also, however, 'hard' subjects like maths, foreign languages and sciences do not perhaps so readily give some taste of their deepest meanings in simple ways as literature and humane studies can. This has led some writers and teachers to mystify humane and social subjects by using unnecessarily obscure language and concepts.

Bill Hannan will be raising the question of foreign language programmes in his chapter. We want to conclude by suggesting that parts of science can be selected because they are still problematic, and other parts can be humanized. It is important for pupils to recognize when a scientific enquiry is genuinely open-ended and when it is not; when tightly controlled experimentation with results that can be verified by replication is necessary and when it is not — a point that will be developed in chapter 6, whose theme is the unsuitability of that method in the study of human behaviour.

Some physical phenomena necessitate more speculation than others. Hence, *The Web of Life* invites pupils to speculate on and test out various hypotheses on the origin of life because we are here dealing with scientific questions that we cannot answer with certainty. We might draw a comparison with speculation in history — we cannot know explanations, or even some facts, with certainty because we were not there to do the scientific tests (in history, we cannot have all the evidence), and events cannot be repeated to give us a verification. Similarly, *The Web of Life* takes examples of how scientific explanations have been reached (of the causes of malaria, for example) thus showing a progression of knowledge from one tentative hypothesis to another which resembles somewhat one way in which the historian works.

All kinds of enquiry fall between the most objective and the most subjective kinds of knowing. We cannot *know* a person's motives though we might make pretty accurate generalizations about how they will make him behave. Nor can we *know* the nature of the universe in the way we *know* the second law of thermodynamics, or better still mathematical axioms. Some divisions of science, like geology and astronomy, we can feel less confident about than others, and this remains true even though we know enough to launch artificial satellites with minimal risk of error. Even the more speculative branches of science, however, do not invite speculation in the way that a poem, or a painting or a symphony does. Nor can the sciences make us *feel* vicariously how it is to be someone else. The pursuit of science might be deeply satisfying and far more personal and imaginative than is often supposed — a point developed by Dow in a later chapter. The findings of science might be awesome, exciting or horrifying; but these emotional qualities are different from the feelings and insights engendered by the arts and humanities.

In designing curriculum units, our degree of specificity or alternatively flexibility must be judged in terms of its appropriateness to the material being explored. And to gain a general education pupils need to experience tightly structured logic as well as suggestive, evocative speculation.

A tightly designed unit of programmed learning or even a computerized hook-up can be useful for developing routine skills such as those practised in language or number drill, but more generative plans must allow for, indeed try to incite, incidental explorations. The child whose curiosity and interest are fully engaged will suggest his own parallels, illustrations (perhaps even analogies), and further questions; and pupils may see significance in the material before them that escaped the designers and the teachers on the spot. In this sense, a good unit of work is open-ended, ever ready to allow pupils to steer it in a quite unforeseen direction. If that new direction forces the teacher to join pupils as a fellow learner, instead of as an expert, all to the good. If, on the other hand, every triviality is allowed to run its course, the unit becomes a mish-mash.

Finally, if learning calls into play the exercise of low-level and high-level intellectual skills, if it is concerned with gut responses as well as sensitivity and moral values, and if some content is more important than others, teachers must not only be selecting what they will teach and how they will teach it; they must also ensure that some sort of learning map is kept of each child's curriculum. Scientific, historical and literary imagination are not identical; nor are the standards of proof employed by the physical scientist feasible for the magistrate, the jury and the parole officer (the topic 'Proof' would be an excellent one for interdisciplinary study). The social responsibility that the scientific researcher has for the unknown consequences of his experimentation and consequent discoveries is not identical with the judgments the doctor makes in trying out a course of treatment, the sociologist makes in setting up a commune, or the teacher makes in trying out grouping policies with her pupils. We cannot teach our pupils every skill, the source of every prejudice or the whole gamut of every political and economic problem, but we can give them skills with the greatest power of transferability, we can tackle the most conspicuous prejudices; and we can be sure that they have sampled first-hand or, if necessary, vicariously, examples of the gravest political and economic problems. That is what a general education is about.

It would be doctrinaire to insist that the best way is always through interdisciplinary teaching. Tensions in Maria's group arose because Paul, David and even Maria herself feared that their pupils would lose something important if they could not focus on literature, geography and sociology sufficiently to gain more than superficial glimmerings. We have respected and tried to meet those objections by the approaches we suggest. Neither do we want to rule out 'straight' subject-teaching; but we do feel that, since the major dilemmas we face can rarely be solved by the insight of one 'straight' subject, pupils should gain experience of calling on a number of 'disciplines' through problem- or topic-centred studies.

Notes

1 D.C. White and Eva Wynn, 'An approach to general studies', *Secondary Teacher* (Melbourne), July 1970, p. 3 (a document written for the Curriculum Advisory Board, Victoria).
2 Lawrence A. Cremin, in *The Transformation of the School: Progressivism in American Education, 1876–1957*, New York, Knopf, 1961, p. 328, places the finale of American 'progressivism' at 1957.
3 *Secondary Teacher* (Melbourne), July 1970.
4 *15 to 18*: Report of the Central Advisory Council for Education (England), London, HMSO, 1959.
5 *Biological Science: the Web of Life*, Student's Manual, Canberra, Australian Academy of Science, 1973, part 1, p. 1.
6 Ibid.

Chapter 3

Curriculum development: a practical view

Noel P. Gough

Maria and curriculum theory

Many of the dilemmas which beset Maria concern curriculum decision-making — about what and how to teach, about who teaches what, about how such decisions are made and who makes them. Maria has had only limited experience in making curriculum decisions, and, like many teachers, her knowledge of curriculum development is largely restricted to what she learned during her pre-service teacher training.

No matter how enlightened Maria's teacher-training programme might have been, it is unlikely that she would have had more than a brief introduction to the practical problems of curriculum development. Teacher training usually sharpens critical skills: Maria can see what is wrong with the curriculum she and her colleagues are planning, but is less certain about how to go about improving it. Studies in philosophy of education might have helped her to recognize an unstated assumption, but she still may not know what to do about it. Similarly, studies in educational psychology might have enabled her to recognize that some classroom activities demand cognitive skills not yet developed in her pupils, but she would probably have learned little about appropriate substitutes. As a sociology graduate, Maria almost certainly gained a great deal from studies in the sociology of education — as is clear in chapter 1, she can spot a 'hidden curriculum' with the greatest of ease. But it is equally clear that she is much less certain as to what she should do with a hidden curriculum when she finds one. Finally, it is likely that anything Maria learned in her teacher training that could be identified as 'curriculum theory' now seems hopelessly irrelevant in day-to-day school life. To her credit, she seems to be resisting the temptation to clutch at half-baked memories of such theory as a means of defending herself in debate (although the same cannot be said of David's avowed desire for the group to plan the integrated studies programme in the light of objectives stated in behavioural terms).

This chapter is concerned with curriculum 'theory' to the extent that it discusses *ideas* about curriculum and curriculum development. Much of the chapter will be devoted to positive recommendations — after all, Maria needs to be acquainted with ideas that she can put into practice. But there are also some less useful ideas which, unfortunately have embedded themselves rather firmly in conventional curriculum thinking. It is therefore in Maria's interests to start with some cautionary notes.

Educational objectives and curriculum planning

If one were to rank the various beliefs or assumptions in the field of curriculum that are thought most secure, the belief in the need for clarity and specificity in stating educational objectives would surely rank among the highest.[1]

More than a decade has passed since Elliot W. Eisner made that comment, but it is doubtful whether time has diminished its accuracy very greatly. Despite growing criticism of objectives as the main focus in curriculum planning, it is possible to find even new texts which consider the statement of clear and specific objectives to be an essential early step in constructing a curriculum.[2]

Planning on the basis of objectives assumes that it is most useful to think of curriculum in terms of *means* and *ends* (sometimes this is represented as *process* and *product*). Thus objectives (ends/products) are stated, and learning experiences (means/processes) are devised to achieve them. In much writing about curriculum, the term 'objectives' has a narrow, specialized meaning, and cannot be used interchangeably with other statements of intention (such as 'aims' or 'goals'). An objective usually describes a desired *behavioural outcome* of learning, e.g. 'at the end of the lesson the pupil will be able to spell correctly 80 per cent of the words in the unit word list.' Such *behavioural objectives* are the preferred method of describing educational intentions in the means–ends model of curriculum.

Lawrence Stenhouse has suggested that the central problem of curriculum study is the gap between curriculum as intention and curriculum as reality.[3] This gap between aspirations and practice is clearly a very real and frustrating one for Maria, and it will not help her to pretend that the gap is smaller than it is. But it is all too easy to do this, either by ignoring some intentions or ignoring some of the realities. Thus, the means–ends model achieves its apparent simplicity partly by ignoring those intentions which cannot easily be translated into behavioural outcomes. Maria and her colleagues have intentions which will affect the curriculum experienced by their pupils but which can be expressed as objectives only by the most tortuous rationalizations. These intentions include: preferred ways of interacting with pupils; desires not to alienate parents and other staff; the wish to be seen as a 'good teacher' by others, and so on. Such intentions are too important to be merely tacit influences on the curriculum, but they are rarely accommodated into the means–ends model.

In practice, when teachers work at curriculum development, any objectives they formulate seem to be a diversion from their work rather than an integral part of it. The situation described in chapter 1 is typical: David's demand for the integrated studies course to be planned and evaluated by reference to explicit objectives is made only after a great deal of groundwork in preparing classroom activities has already been completed. Although Maria sees this as a politically expedient exercise in attempting to subdue criticism from the rest of the staff, she can also see that the resulting conflicts threaten to render the planning group powerless. Maria seems justified in questioning the value of an approach which causes such disruption within her group but which will probably provide no more than a lifeless blueprint, ignored in practice. (Betty, for one, is unlikely to treat stated objectives as real directives for her teaching.)

The degree to which objectives *are* useful criteria for curriculum decisions depends to some extent on the subject-matter. In certain subject areas (e.g., mathematics, languages, and some aspects of the arts and sciences) it is often possible and appropriate to specify with great precision the particular behaviour the student is to perform after instruction. In other subject areas (e.g., the creative arts, and the experimental/enquiry aspects of the sciences) such specification is not possible or, when possible, may not be desirable. If novel or creative responses are desired, the particular behaviours to be developed cannot easily be identified; it can be argued that an educational objective could specify novelty, originality or creativeness as a desired outcome, but the referents for such terms cannot be specified in advance; one can only judge after the fact whether the product or behaviour is novel.[4]

It is common to see this problem with objectives as applying mainly to the creative arts, but it should also be noted that novel responses are often desired (if not often enough encouraged) in the sciences. If a pupil is undertaking a true investigation or an experiment (as distinct from following prescribed techniques in order to demonstrate a predicted occurrence, or illustrate a phenomenon), it is neither possible nor desirable to specify in advance the particular behaviour the student is to perform after undertaking that enquiry. If one could, there would be no real enquiry taking place.

For example, several years ago I was teaching science to year ten pupils in a school very like Maria's. To accommodate the varied interests of the pupils, I frequently gave the class an extended period of time (usually three or four weeks) to pursue an enquiry of their own choice, either individually or in small groups. The nominal ground rules for the enquiry were based on the standard schoolbook version of 'the scientific method' which, in practice, meant only that I encouraged pupils to articulate problems for investigation which were researchable with the available time and resources. These enquiries involved a great deal of teacher–pupil and pupil–pupil dialogue, and almost always progressed in unexpected ways. One case started when three boys said that they wanted 'to do something about astronomy'. I discussed with them the difficulty of finding something 'do-able' with our limited resources, and suggested that they try to come up with a more definite proposal. During the class-time that immediately followed, the boys examined the school's astronomical telescope and its accompanying instruction manual. They obtained a rough working knowledge of how to operate it and what its capabilities were. They also consulted some library references and local star maps and, from the daily newspapers, found out which planets were currently visible in the early part of the evening. But, by the next time the boys saw me, the focus of their attentions had shifted somewhat. They were still keen to use the school's tele-scope to observe the planets (particularly the moons of Jupiter and Saturn) and, indeed, they demonstrated their proficiency with the telescope by locating the planets several nights later. However, they now perceived a technical problem of greater importance: the in-accessibility of the school's telescope and the difficulty of setting it up afresh every time it was used. What the school needed, they con-sidered, was an observatory!

We agreed that their enquiries should now be directed to designing a practical school observatory. Over the next two weeks, with no additional help from me, the three pupils designed a small, manually operated, rotating weather-proof observatory (the basic framework was a rotary clothes hoist) suitable for mounting on the flat roof of one of the school buildings. All measurements and materials were specified and costed; on their own initiative, the boys convinced the school principal of the observatory's practicability and obtained his promise that the school would meet the cost of the materials if they decided to build it. (As it happened, it was never built at the school, although one of the boys did construct a similar observatory at home.)

Clearly, it would have served no useful purpose to attempt to specify in advance any detailed objectives of this segment of my science curriculum (especially bearing in mind that I had forty-three pupils, and I have described only what happened with three of them). Indeed, adherence to stated objectives would have precluded the valuable result that did occur. It might have been possible to *justify* the pupils' activities in terms of ends which were, in fact, achieved, but this can only be done after the event and does not really assist curriculum *planning*.

Similarly, David's demand for behavioural objectives is made in order to justify learning experiences rather than to plan them. Objectives may, then, be more useful as aids to communication among teachers and administrators than as tools for curriculum development. Certainly, David would be correct in assuming that teachers should be able to answer in a satisfactory way enquiries about the purposes of their teaching programmes. But Maria could also argue that many of her intentions might be more effectively communicated to colleagues by observation of her actions in the classroom.

In my experience, queries about the aims and objectives of classroom activities usually arise in connection with stated or implied negative criticisms. If, after observing a classroom in action, one has to ask the teacher what she was trying to achieve through the activities she initiated, one is in effect saying, 'I could not infer your intentions from your actions', which is either a confession of ignorance of classroom processes on the part of the observer, or a veiled criticism of the teacher's performance. On the other hand, positive reactions to classroom activities are not usually accompanied by queries about aims and objectives. It would be decidedly odd to say to a teacher: 'I really liked what you just did; now, why were you doing it?' Agreement about what constitutes effective teaching does not usually seem to depend on agreement about (or a statement of) pre-specified aims and objectives.

Nevertheless, we cannot disregard objectives as elements in curriculum design just because many teachers cope quite well without specifying them. The means–ends model is intended to be prescriptive rather than descriptive, and those who recommend it presumably believe that practice guided by the model is better than ordinary practice. A means–ends model of curriculum is also a *theory* of curriculum. By this I do not mean that the model is fanciful: I am treating theories as 'beliefs about what relations hold between existing entities, that is, beliefs about what is true.'[5] Supporters of a means–ends approach believe that the elements they have identified (objectives and learning experiences) exist in rationally constructed curricula, and that the true relationship that ought to hold between these elements is as described by the model, i.e., learning experiences should be selected in order to achieve clearly stated outcomes.

It is true that objectives are invariably found – in one form or another – in planned curricula. But the point I am making is that teachers rarely use these 'objectives' as specific criteria for selecting content and learning experiences. For example, a unit developed as part of the Secondary Geographical Education Project (SGEP) in Victoria begins:[6]

> *Title*: Why are timber mills located where they are [in the particular local area studied which, in this example, is Gippsland]?
>
> *Rationale*: To introduce pupils to a variety of organizing concepts through a study of the timber milling industry. In this case we are using an industry which most students are familiar with, and which should have a high motivational value. The unit could best be started with a field trip to a saw mill, or with slides of the activities carried out at a saw mill. Thus the unit (using field trip and/or slides) is based on 'real world' examples which the student has before him. It begins with a particular mill and expands to the milling industry in the whole of Gippsland.
>
> *Objectives*: This unit should increase the student's ability to:
> (a) plot simple phenomena on maps — the location of sawmills in his home region; simple goods flows;
> (b) collect and use fieldwork data;
> (c) describe simple map distributions — e.g., the distribution of local saw mills;
> (d) provide explanations for these distributions;
> (e) understand some changes that have taken place in the distribution of saw mills;
> (f) understand the effect of changing transport technology on mill location.

It is clear in this example that the objectives have not preceded the selection of content and activities but vice versa. The 'objectives' are predicted outcomes of predetermined content and activities. On the other hand, the 'title' does take the form of a fairly broad aim which is vaguely justified in the 'rationale'. Elsewhere in the SGEP materials[7] it is stated that the Project was concerned with developing procedures for the selection and organization of content primarily in terms of the structure of the discipline, the process of intellectual development, and the nature of learning experiences. Despite this, when developing SGEP units, it is suggested that teachers write objectives in behavioural terms. That is, the content of the unit is not to be selected in terms of intended learner outcomes, *yet it is meant to be written up that way*. Thus, the Project pays lip-service to means-ends curriculum theory, but largely ignores it in the more practical phases of unit planning. In fact, the SGEP unit development sequence suggests that teachers decide on *key questions* and their sequence in the unit prior to considering 'general objectives'. However, it is also suggested that consideration of objectives could be left until after decisions about pupil activities, teaching strategies, resources and materials have been made.[8]

Thus, very little of what is planned follows from a *prior* statement of objectives, although this is not clear from the suggested format for progressively writing up the unit plan:[9] it is suggested that this format

Unit title:				
Key questions	Objectives	Activities	Resources	Possible evaluation procedures
1				
2				
3				
4 etc.				

may be useful because activities, resources, etc., can be related closely to the key questions. Some people may find it useful to *include reference to only the key questions and activities in the very earliest stages*, gradually adding to the details as development progresses'[10] (my emphasis). A more realistic representation of the SGEP unit development sequence would be given if the columns were headed (from left to right): Key Questions, Activities, Resources, Outcomes, Possible Evaluation Procedures. However, the extent to which the objectives dogma has moulded teachers' thinking is reflected in the observation of one of the SGEP leaders: 'In unit planning workshops, teachers often appeared to feel guilty if they designed a unit without writing down some objectives, even if this meant making them up afterwards.'[11]

The SGEP unit development sequence appears to work well in practice, in so far as groups of teachers are able to use the suggested sequence to produce unit plans which they feel confident about translating into action. The success of the SGEP sequence, in my view, does not depend on teachers' being clear about their objectives, although it does appear to depend on their being clear about their *intentions*. In this case, the most productive clarification of intentions seems to be agreement on the *key questions* to be addressed during the unit. Reaching such agreement does not necessarily require teachers to separate 'objectives' from 'content' or 'methods' at this crucial stage of unit planning, because certain commitments about outcomes, content and methods are implicit in the questions agreed to. That is, teachers might agree that a key question in the unit on Gippsland timber mills is 'What is the relationship between mill location and changing transport technology?' Agreement that this is a key question carries with it agreement about conceptual outcomes (at the end of the unit, pupils will be able to give an explanatory answer to the key question), content (pupils are to be exposed to concepts, generalizations and facts concerning location and transport) and methods (pupils are intended to explore key questions partly through their own enquiries).

The SGEP approach to planning may be useful in Maria's situation. Because its most important element is reaching agreement about key questions, such a focus for planning would allow Maria's team to avoid the pitfalls inherent in separating ends from means (or product from process) too early in the planning stages. Later, it may be politically expedient to separate ends and means when they are called upon to defend their programme but, by that time, such separation will not interfere with their planning and it will be obvious to them that they are providing a rationalization rather than developing a rationale.

It should now be apparent why Maria and her colleagues cannot rely on clearly specified objectives to guide their curriculum planning. It is true that a means–ends model is *logical*, but it would be a mistake to suggest that logic − and linear logic at that − is the only path to rationality. Rational curriculum planning consists of more than selecting objectives, developing learning experiences through which to achieve them, and evaluating the extent to which the objectives have been achieved. If there were no more to objectives than clearly stating one's intentions, then there would be little to quarrel about. But behavioural objectives − though they express only a fraction of our educational intentions − are often presumed to be the criteria by which all other elements of the curriculum are to be selected and justified; materials, methods, activities of pupil and teacher, evaluation procedures, and so on. Finally, as Eisner has pointed out, if objectives were really useful tools for curriculum planning then teachers would use them; and if they do not use them, then perhaps it is not because there is something wrong with the teachers but because there might be something wrong with the theory.[12]

Eisner's observation, like Maria's predicament, reminds me that during my first year of lecturing in a teachers' college I was part of a staff team that tried (with considerable lack of success, I am now pleased to say) to convince student teachers that behavioural objectives were an essential part of rational curriculum planning. One of the tasks we required of students was that they analyse the curriculum development process in their practice teaching school, and that they present a schematic model of that process. Many students rationalized what they observed in terms of a means–end model but others, less well indoctrinated (or, perhaps, more honest), came to rather different conclusions, as the student's model illustrates. This model is a rather cynical comment

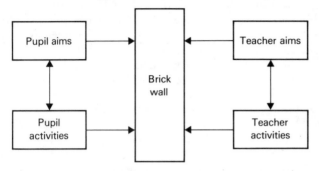

on the gap, referred to earlier, between curriculum as intention and curriculum as reality. It may also be seen as a comment on the gap between curriculum theory and practice which has long frustrated teachers and administrators who have attempted to use the simplistic means-ends models prescribed by some curriculum scholars. School personnel often suggest that the gap exists because curriculum theorists are out of touch with the realities of schools and classrooms, and this is no doubt true to some extent: the ivory tower has all too frequently been as impenetrable as the brick wall.

Stenhouse's process model of curriculum

The approach to curriculum development used by the SGEP participants illustrates that it is possible to choose content and learning experiences rationally without prior reference to objectives. SGEP exemplifies the 'process model' of curriculum, as outlined by Lawrence Stenhouse.[13] It assumes that a form of knowledge has a structure which includes procedures, concepts and criteria, and that content can be selected to exemplify the most important of these structural elements. If these were stated as objectives they would be distorted, since the key procedures, concepts and criteria in a discipline are more importantly the focus of speculation, rather than the object of mastery: they are important for the very reason that they are problematic.

Thus, an important preliminary stage of SGEP was concerned with identifying the organizing concepts of the discipline – such as location, distance, distribution, spatial association, spatial interaction, movement, diffusion, region and scale – in order to help teachers achieve a balance of content and to help pupils to understand generalizations that hold great illuminating power. These concepts were selected to help teachers specify content and activities rather than outcomes. Concepts like *location* and *distance* are grasped while being *used*, rather than being mastered once and for all.

Stenhouse's model can most readily be applied to the traditional disciplines of knowledge, and it may have less applicability in topic-centred teaching where the traditional disciplines do not necessarily provide the major focus of attention. A further limitation of the process model is that, while it does not stress objectives as such, it uses similar elements to a means–ends model (such as process and product) to characterize curriculum development. These elements are usually not readily separable in practice (see also pp. 153-4), and in the remainder of this chapter I intend to explore two approaches which are considerably different from the classical model. They are approaches which have led to a fundamental reorientation of curriculum thinking during the last decade and, I predict, will considerably influence curriculum theory and practice in future years.

On the one hand, Joseph Schwab has presented a view of curriculum which he calls 'the practical', in the course of which he argues that curriculum workers should rely less on theory and adopt more practical methods and principles.[14] Schwab's proposal has received widespread endorsement in North American curriculum literature. On the other hand, Stenhouse has proposed a research model for curriculum development, focusing on classrooms and the work of teachers,[15] a view which similarly pervades much curriculum writing in the United Kingdom. The two approaches have some important similarities, and what follows will be an attempt to clarify some of their key elements, with particular emphasis on those features of the proposals which have direct application to curriculum development in schools.

'The practical' as a focus for curriculum development

Earlier in this chapter it was suggested that if teachers did not *use* objectives (as distinct from paying lip-service to them), it was not through any deficiency in the teachers but in the theory which produced the means–ends model. Maria's reactions to David's theories about planning indicate that she was convinced of the point I am making but that she was somewhat at a loss in articulating her view. Schwab's conceptualization of curriculum as 'practical' would help her to see that the weakness of a means–ends (or process–product) model lies not in *the* particular theory but in the nature of theory itself. Schwab believes that the failures of curriculum theory are due to an essential difference between theory and practice: in practice, we are concerned with making *defensible decisions* about what to teach and how to teach it, whereas curriculum theory is concerned with drawing *warranted conclusions* which contribute to our general knowledge and understanding of curriculum. Schwab's central thesis is that theories of curriculum and of teaching and learning cannot, *alone*, tell us what and how to teach, because these questions arise in actual situations loaded with particulars of time, place, person and circumstance.[16] This is not to say that relevant educational theories should be ignored but, rather, that we cannot base a realistic curriculum on a single theory of teaching, learning, motivation, cognitive development, structure of knowledge, or what have you. Further, many of the theories commonly applied to curriculum are in themselves partial, and lack theoretical connection with one another, so that no *one* theoretical basis for action can be sufficient. Practical problems therefore require an *eclectic* approach.

For example, it is common for curriculum projects dealing with the early years of secondary school to use Piaget's theory of cognitive development as a guide in selecting content and learning experiences which will match the pupil's stage of intellectual development. Piaget's theory enables us to conclude that, in general, children in year seven will be unlikely to cope with activities requiring a preponderance of abstract thought, but it tells us little about what a specific child in a specific school will be able to cope with. That is, Piaget's theory *alone* does not allow us to make a defensible decision about the introduction of a unit involving abstract thought to particular year seven pupils; consideration of the particular situation, and its special characteristics, is required.

A research model for curriculum development

Although Stenhouse does not refer directly to Schwab's arguments, he also pleads for the adoption of more practical classroom-oriented approaches to curriculum development.

Stenhouse considers that all well-founded curriculum research and development is based on the study of classrooms and thus rests on the work of teachers.[17] Like Schwab, Stenhouse believes that no two schools or classrooms are so alike in their circumstances that external prescriptions can replace the judgment of the people in them. Since each classroom is importantly different from every other, the research model which Stenhouse advocates emphasizes teachers' own perceptions of their work, so that they are able to accumulate data about the curriculum with which they are involved and apply this information when making practical decisions. The findings of such research must be presented in such a way that a teacher is encouraged not to *accept*

61

them but to *test* them in his own situation.[18] Teachers already do this to some extent; certainly they all reflect on their teaching in some way. Sometimes the reflection is a deliberate strategy, a soul-searching analysis of their own performance as well as that of their pupils. Sometimes the reflection is more casual, limited only to a brief consideration of how well a particular lesson went. This kind of reflection is valuable and necessary but it has some weaknesses: it usually is unplanned and based on rather erratic observations; it normally remains undocumented; the teacher's recollections may be vague, and certainly much detail is lost; the teacher's attention is usually held by a multiplicity of events, making it difficult to focus on more specific events; and the teacher's personal attitudes towards the pupils, or subject matter, may colour his perception of what is happening.

Research-based teaching builds on this informal reflection on classroom activities. It aims at increasing teachers' understanding of a unique school situation and, as a result, their ability to make decisions in that situation with more confidence. The success of situational research in schools and classrooms is dependent to a large degree on teachers' attitudes. The teacher-as-researcher is involved in studying not just the pupil and the environment but also himself and his own behaviour. Research-based teaching involves self-knowledge, self-development, and potentially threatening self-assessment. Research also implies working with others, a situation which may be perceived as supportive, but may also appear threatening to some teachers. Situational research may be formal or informal, and although the degree of formality is likely to depend on many factors, there are sound reasons for formalizing the research in part. The understandings gained, problems faced and the questions generated should not be lost.

Some of the difficulties faced by Maria and her colleagues might have been circumvented if, from the outset, they had treated the course they were planning as a hypothesis (or several hypotheses) to be tested. The programme is intended to be experimental but what, precisely, is the nature of this 'experiment'? For example, it is claimed that the experimental programme is to 'have meaning for the pupils', but how is this to be verified? What might the tangible *effects* of the course be? If, at an early stage, the planners had given some attention to how they intended to test their hypotheses, some of the problems now facing the group might be seen in a new light (if they had emerged at all). For example, Paul's proposal to set aside four out of the ten periods of 'integrated' study for specialist English study might be perceived by the group as more (or less) defensible if presented as a research proposal. On the other hand, Paul might never have insisted on this line of action if the original idea (that English be integrated within the total programme) had been presented in research terms. The need to collect evidence relating to the research hypotheses maintains the prominence of the issues which are important to Paul so that they are not overlooked by other members of the team. Treating the integration of English as a research problem rather than as a design *fait accompli* should ensure that Paul's doubts about the idea continue to be taken seriously. Apart from anything else, testing ideas in action *as a group*, rather than as individuals, is more likely to generate evidence which will be accepted by others both within and without the group, and therefore be accepted as a basis for further curriculum action (that is, the testing of further hypotheses about the effects of the curriculum as developed). The research model of school-based curriculum development also militates against the possibility that teachers will forget either their powers or their responsibilities: they are, as it were, managers of the only valid laboratory for research in curriculum and teaching.

Planning with a research focus: a suggested sequence

Maria and David, it will be remembered, worked fairly well together when designing the local study for — like most teachers in my experience — they are readily able to find common ground by concentrating on plans for classroom action. Teachers frequently identify activities that seem useful, appropriate or rich in educational possibilities, and from a consideration of what *can* be done in class they identify the possible *effects* of using these activities. These hypothetical relationships between *activities* and *effects* (*some* of which will be behavioural outcomes in the pupils) can provide a framework for curriculum planning. *Testing* these hypothetical relationships through relatively informal situational research can then become a means of monitoring and further developing the curriculum.

This relationship between activities and effects is at the heart of the suggested unit development sequence which follows. It is the product of several years of experience in using the sequence with classroom teachers and is, therefore, a 'minimum effort/maximum effect' strategy. It has already been suggested that a central problem of curriculum study is the gap between curriculum as intention and curriculum as reality; for busy classroom teachers, an effective strategy is one which brings intentions and realities closer together with the expenditure of minimal additional effort.

The approach suggested here attempts to keep the relationship between aspirations and practice in the forefront of teachers' minds during planning. It encourages teachers to work in a flexible yet systematic way towards the goals they have identified as being important (both for themselves and for their pupils), and also takes account of desirable adjustments or deviations that arise during teaching. At the risk of labouring the point, it must be emphasized that 'goals' are not to be equated with 'objectives'. Rather, the reference to goals is merely stating the obvious: that teachers behave purposively when planning units of study. But curriculum units are rarely designed with a *single* purpose in mind. When planning a unit of study, teachers usually intend to do some or all of the following: teach some factual information; develop skills in thinking, social competences and, perhaps, manipulation of objects; explore values and feelings; excite and maintain pupil interest; maintain class control; use styles of teacher/learner interaction with which they are comfortable. Teachers also want the work they put into doing these things to be personally and professionally rewarding. Clearly, it is difficult to concentrate on all these things at once, but many conventional approaches to unit planning ignore some of these important and legitimate teacher intentions from the outset.

Although there is a *suggested* sequence in what follows, it must not be thought that any part of a curriculum can be produced by following a few simple, logical steps. Certainly, there is no attempt to suggest that any of the following steps are anything but complex. Each involves deliberation, i.e., negotiation, debate, discussion of reasons for and against, consideration of alternatives, and careful consideration of the anticipated consequences of decisions. The sequence which follows does not minimize the complexities of curriculum deliberations but, rather, presents them as a series of manageable tasks. Like any recipe, the sequence can be varied according to taste.

Step 1: Group formation

When teachers like Maria and her colleagues begin to plan units to study, they will already have made (or had made for them) some decisions that will impose constraints on the remaining steps. They will already have identified the subject-matter in broad terms, and they will know some of their resource limitations (time, finance, materials, their own background knowledge and interests, and so on). In other words, their planning will take place in a context comprising numerous assumptions about what can and cannot be done. Many of these assumptions will remain unconscious unless the group of teachers can talk about them with one another. Although the steps which follow can all be performed by an individual teacher, experience shows that a group (even if it is of only two teachers) is more efficient and productive. Maria's group of four teachers is a good size for the kind of unit planning they are engaged in. Some further aspects of group composition will be discussed in a later section of this chapter.

Step 2: Clarify major teaching purpose

Maria and her colleagues have already decided on many of their major teaching purposes in the integrated studies course, but not all of them may be in the most useful form for unit planning. For example, in planning a unit within the broad theme of 'Equality', they may already have decided that one of their aims is 'to encourage pupils to be more aware of equalities and inequalities of job opportunities in the local area'. However, the aim may be more useful in unit development if it is phrased in terms of developing a generalization which pupils can apply in thinking about certain kinds of problems, e.g., 'job opportunities in a given local area are related to its history and its development of a particular social structure.'

If they have not already done so, Maria's team should now decide on the broad area(s) of content appropriate to the major teaching purpose of the unit. The content should also meet other criteria, such as being interesting to pupils (and teachers). The generalization above could be taught using a variety of content from several of the social sciences. If the broad content area has already been decided at this stage, the generalization should reflect it. The generalization as stated so far reflects Maria's background in sociology. David might have approached a similar major teaching purpose through a more 'geographical' generalization, e.g., 'employment opportunities are related to the location of industries and transport services'.

Step 3: Devise key question(s)

Maria and her colleagues can further usefully refine their major teaching purpose by deciding on a *key question* (or, depending on the length of the unit, a series of key questions) that could be answered by applying the generalization. This key question (or topic question) provides a focus for both pupils and teacher, giving a sense of 'going somewhere' in the unit. For example, Maria might see the key question arising from her generalization as being: 'Who gets the available jobs in our area?' David might take a more geographical line of enquiry in exploring the topic: 'How are jobs (spatially) distributed in our area?'

Step 4: Checklist of supplementary outcomes

Maria and her colleagues might now find it useful to prepare a list of the broad types of learning outcomes that they will be encouraging pupils to achieve. They will almost certainly be concerned with pupils remembering some factual information, exploring various attitudes and values, developing social, intellectual and manipulative skills, and so on. It may be useful to list these in groups of similar outcomes. For example, the topic as so far developed could include the following:

Knowing and thinking:	Remembering factual information
	Understanding information
	Formulating generalizations
	Identifying problems
	Problem solving
	Justifying actions
Attitudes:	Exploring feelings
	Clarifying values
Skills:	Collecting information
	Report writing
	Working collaboratively

Different topics will require a different checklist of supplementary outcomes, although the broad groupings will probably remain similar. For example, some units may need to include 'manipulation of apparatus' and 'measurement' under Skills, or 'developing empathy' under Attitudes, or 'independent enquiry' under Knowing and thinking. Furthermore, the broad groupings should not be rigid for they are merely to help the team bring order to what they are doing: it does not particularly matter if, say, Maria thinks of 'working collaboratively' in attitudinal terms and David regards it as a skill, provided that the two *are* agreed that (i) both attitudes and skills are to be developed in the unit and (ii) group co-operation is to be encouraged.

It is important that the checklist includes a fairly comprehensive range of the broad categories of possible *effects* of learning experiences on pupils. For example, a teacher's explicit purpose in teaching a unit on social and occupational structure may be to provide pupils with information, but the *effects* of this information, and of the learning experiences used to transmit the information, may be largely attitudinal. Teachers may not want to identify these effects any more precisely than, say, 'consciousness-raising', but it is important that attitudinal effects are recognized as a *possible* outcome. Above all, the checklist must make sense to the teachers involved, and need not necessarily resemble a learning 'hierarchy' or 'taxonomies of educational objectives'.

Step 5: Develop a planning worksheet

Several kinds of planning worksheet may be appropriate. If the topic is focused on a single key question, to which several supplementary outcomes are related, the sample worksheet illustrated is recommended.[19]

SAMPLE PLANNING WORKSHEET

Major purpose:
Topic question:

	SUPPLEMENTARY OUTCOMES										
	Remembering and thinking					Attitudes			Skills		
	Remembering factual information	Developing concepts	Inferring and generalizing	Applying generalizations	Enquiring and problem-solving	Exploring feelings/values/attitudes	Developing empathy	Working co-operatively	Collecting data	Report-writing	Manipulating objects
INTRODUCTORY ACTIVITIES (interest, diagnosis) WORKING SESSIONS											
CONCLUDING ACTIVITIES (closure, application, evaluation)											

Step 6: Activities brainstorm

Maria and her colleagues should list as many ideas as possible about *activities* that the pupils might be involved in during the unit. It is worth including even the wildest ideas at this stage, for they may lead to others that are more plausible. Included in this list should be any resources that might be needed for each activity.

Step 7: A good beginning

An introductory activity can then be selected from the list. It must create interest in the topic question and give the teacher a good idea of pupils' previous knowledge and interest. Ideally, it will make a contribution to the major teaching purpose and to a range of supplementary outcomes. Usually activities which are open-ended and which involve all pupils actively will be most useful at this stage.

For example, in a unit on equality which focuses on the social and occupational structure of the school's neighbourhood, pupils might begin by surveying the kinds of employment available in a cross-section of the area. In a school very like Maria's, I observed an activity which involved pupils in walking the length of their community's main street, noting on a map all of the locations where people were employed. Back in the classroom, they listed categories of jobs in each location. Pupils were surprised at the size of the lists they generated, and several stereotypes were exposed. For example, many pupils had thought of schools as offering employment opportunities only to teachers, but this activity led them to realize that their own school also employed three secretaries, four cleaners, two laboratory assistants, three teacher-aides, a nurse, three gardeners and a canteen manageress.

Step 8: A satisfying end

A concluding activity (or activities) should also be selected. This should draw together the activities pupils have been involved in and focus on the topic question to give both teacher and pupils a sense of closure. If the major teaching purpose is developing a generalization the concluding activity should provide opportunities for it to be applied in a new situation. This will give the teacher a chance to see whether pupils will transfer and apply the generalization when appropriate. The concluding activity should also provide opportunities for formal and informal evaluation of the unit and of pupils' learning. Sometimes a similar activity can be used for both introduction and conclusion, and the difference in performance can partly serve as a guide to what has been learned. Selecting this activity will need considerable thought, for the conclusion should mark a stage passed or a job done for both quick and slow, scatty and organized, rather than the unit just 'fizzling out'.

Step 9: Check supplementary outcomes

Introductory and concluding activities can be written in on the worksheet. Columns can be checked (ticked) for supplementary outcomes to which each activity is intended to make a major contribution.

Step 10: Select activities for working sessions

Additional activities for working sessions can be selected from the list generated in Step 6. These are the major learning activities and may be planned for as long as one wishes the unit to take. Each should make some contribution to the major teaching purpose and to some of the supplementary outcomes. These activities are entered on to the worksheet and the supplementary outcomes to which each should make a major contribution are checked. There may be some alternative or optional activities to allow for differences in interest and ability, but each of the outcomes should have a reasonable amount of attention.

Step 11: Review worksheet

Reviewing the worksheet ensures appropriate sequence, variety and adequate coverage of the topic and the outcomes. Activities can be modified where necessary. Often the same activity can contribute to different outcomes if, say, an ensuing discussion is handled differently.

Step 12: Monitor effects

As Maria teaches there will inevitably be changes as pupils respond in unexpected ways, or as unforseen situations occur (the film which was ordered didn't arrive on time; a relevant television programme is videotaped and discussed in class, the overhead projector blew its bulb just before Maria was intending to use it). The *effects* of changes can be readily seen by reference to the worksheet, and compensating changes can be made in later activities so that the full range of intentions is still achieved.

The chief advantage of the sequence outlined above is that, if it is used in conjunction with the worksheet (see p. 67) it provides a way of continually relating curriculum intentions to curriculum realities. The worksheet is not just a planning document but can also be used to record changes as plans are implemented as well as to record the effects on pupils of the curriculum as it is experienced by them. The columns of supplementary outcomes provide a ready visual reference for the teacher to check the extent to which intended outcomes (predicted effects of activities) match actual outcomes, and to make further changes to activities if necessary. The major focus is not so much on the teacher monitoring the pupils' achievement of desired outcomes as on continually testing the teacher's hypotheses concerning the effects of the planned learning activities. The worksheet, therefore, is essentially an aid to reflection on classroom action.

Curriculum development through effective deliberation

Some of the problems faced by Maria and her colleagues include an apparent lack of effective deliberation among those concerned, and uncertainty about the range of influences which should be brought to bear on curriculum decisions. Let us consider the second question first: what range of influences *should* be brought to bear on decision-making?

It is not much more than a decade ago that school curriculum in Victoria was determined to a large degree by external authorities by the prescription of content in externally examined subjects, often under the influence of subject 'experts' (such as university staff) on the examining panels in those subjects. Schwab's 'practical' approach to curriculum not only highlights the complexities of curriculum decision-making, but also forces us to consider *who* makes the decisions. For example, are subject specialists the best people to make key decisions about curriculum content in schools?

Subject specialists may possess academic knowledge and experience indispensable to curriculum-making, but they may well lack other kinds of knowledge and experience which are equally essential. Other specialists are similarly handicapped. But curriculum-making is far too important a task to be left to any one person (or group) with restricted knowledge and experience. Defensible curriculum decisions arise from the deliberations of persons who represent *all* of the bodies of knowledge and experience essential to the task.

According to Schwab, successful deliberation requires persons with knowledge of subject-matter, of learners, of milieux, of teachers and of curriculum-making itself. In their deliberations these persons must learn something of the concerns, values, and operations, which arise from each other's experience, to honour them, and to adapt and diminish their own values enough to make room in their thinking for the others.[20] A closer look at the five bodies of knowledge suggested by Schwab will reveal the significance of the teacher's role.

Familiarity with the subject matter should include both knowledge

and experience. That is, if biology is to be taught, there must be someone planning the course who has experienced what it is to be a biologist.[21] There must also be someone familiar with the particular learners
who are to benefit from the course under construction. This experience
should include general knowledge of the particular children concerned,
knowledge which is best achieved by direct involvement with them.
There must be someone familiar with the milieux (i.e. the settings) in
which the learning is to take place and in which the fruits of this
learning will be brought to bear: the classroom, the school, the family,
the community and the relations of this community to other communities (e.g., of the same religious, class, or ethnic group). The fourth
body of experience is concerned with the particular teachers who are
to teach the course: knowledge of what these teachers are likely to
know and of how flexible and ready they are likely to be in terms of
learning new materials and methods. Finally, experience of curriculum
planning itself is desirable if these four kinds of experience are to be
coalesced effectively in a course that should harmonize with the total
curriculum whether it be subject- or topic-centred. As Schwab says,
'The usual developing behaviour of such curriculum groups operating
without a representative of this fifth body of experience is one of
resentful or resigned submission of three of the group to a fourth.'[22]
In other words, synthesis of the group's deliberations will be difficult
without someone whose prime task (and motivation for the task) is
achieving that synthesis.

This last person (referred to by Schwab as 'the curriculum specialist')
is usually the co-ordinator of the particular groups at work and often
also of the whole curriculum. He may be an external consultant or an
elected chairman from within the group. This person has to maintain
shifting emphases among the various factors which influence the curriculum: subject matter, pupils, teachers, politics and the limitations of
time and money. In Schwab's idealization of curriculum-making, the
curriculum specialist would be sensitive to the progress of the group's
deliberations and decide, for example, when the introduction of further
complexities might wreck the discussion, when simplification might
advance their deliberations or, perhaps, when simplification might
involve distortion. The curriculum co-ordinator might also suggest when
it is appropriate to suspend group discussion in favour of individual
research or study. He is not the only one who performs these tasks, but
he is responsible for seeing that they get done and, consequently, it is
often he who does them.

In the absence of such specialists, teachers like Maria must themselves attempt to perform some or all of these tasks, if only in self-
defence, to avoid being swamped by other participants in curriculum
deliberations. However, it should be clear that in many circumstances

71

teachers are going to be the appropriate representatives of the other bodies of experience, although not all teachers are equally capable of filling all roles.

If defensible curriculum decisions can be reached only by bringing together a number of diverse skills, then it is clear from Schwab's argument that a number of people must also be brought together to deliberate on those decisions. How is such a group established? Five kinds of experience must be brought together, but it does not follow that five *persons* are required. The group may be smaller than five if two or more of the required kinds of experience can be found in one person. There could also be reasons why the group should be larger than five. In particular, in the school situation, we must give up the notion that problems of planning, say, science courses, have no bearing on curriculum issues in English, or social studies, or whatever. The aim here is not to dissolve specialization or special responsibilities but, rather, to bring the various specializations to bear on curriculum problems by communication between specialists. Ideally, each school should have a curriculum co-ordinator (or co-ordinating body) to encourage such communication.

Even a brief consideration of this issue is sufficient to see the merit of Schwab's suggestions for the composition of curriculum groups. A school may, for example, be developing a science programme for year eight: conventionally, the science teachers in the school would be the only teachers deliberating on the proposed course, regardless of whether or not any of these teachers had direct experience of the current year-seven students for whom the programme is being devised (assuming the programme is to be introduced in the following year). It would seem sensible to include a teacher with such direct experience in the group, regardless of his subject specialization. (In this context it is interesting to note that a South Australian science curriculum committee has recommended that non-science teachers in a school should be regarded as important 'people resources' for the development of school science programmes.[23]) In such school-based curriculum developments, group size need not be unwieldy: quite small groups may be sufficient for developing programmes involving specific class levels or subject areas. Above all, the sharing of experiences by staff members is essential if the learning opportunities provided for pupils are to complement each other.

The importance of effective deliberation should not be underestimated since in practical situations no model based on simple means-ends logic can be an appropriate guide to curriculum decision-making.[24] During deliberation both ends and means mutually determine one another (see also pp. 153–4), and participants must attempt to ascertain, with respect to both ends and means, what facts may be relevant in the particular case. Deliberation must also be concerned with identifying the criteria by which solutions to specific problems may be judged, and with generating alternative solutions. An attempt must be made to trace the consequences which may flow from each alternative and affect the criteria, and then alternatives can be compared in terms of their costs and consequences. Deliberation leads to a choice, not of the *right* alternative (because there is no such thing), but of the *best* one.[25]

Clearly, such deliberations cannot be rule-governed, and Schwab therefore speaks of practical *arts* being applied to curriculum-making. The variables of teacher, learner, subject-matter and setting require artful blending in the construction of a defensible curriculum. And it is the desire for defensibility, for the justification of choices, that animates deliberation. Maria wants to be able to say that she was constrained either by circumstances or by her principles to decide as she did. But unless these principles are shared by those others who have to carry out the decisions and/or live with the consequences of them, she will be unable to justify the choices she makes. In other words, when developing a curriculum, Maria — like any artist — must know her audience.

When a curriculum is developed by a number of people their deliberations frequently appear to be chaotic and confused, but recognizing the invariable complexity in deliberation will be a safeguard against undue discouragement. This is well illustrated by Seymour Fox, who presents transcripts of a group's discussions to illustrate how deliberation of the kind described by Schwab works in practice. He notes that the most rewarding aspect of the work was to witness the commitment that developed among members of staff as they negotiated curriculum decisions. Participants were disappointed at first by the discovery that each of them was limited by training and experience. They found it difficult to reformulate problems and alternative courses of action several times, and to discard solutions that had involved a heavy personal investment. Nevertheless, they agreed that the experience of negotiating the curriculum was itself rewarding, and they also concluded that 'models and rationalized procedures' were of 'limited value' in curriculum-making.[26] Since school-based curriculum development must of necessity involve a high level of staff participation and, further, since the dynamics of group interaction may result in some participants feeling personally threatened or discomforted, Fox's observations may be cause for some optimism. The exposure of individual limitations of knowledge and experience may be less threatening if all participants are, indeed, 'enticed by the process itself'.[27]

Further evidence of the value of experience gained in school-based curriculum development is offered by Melvin Freestone, who describes a number of instances of such activities in Tasmanian schools. Freestone concluded:[28]

> Instead of being a sterile exercise comprised [sic] of a series of artificially manipulated tasks which people felt obliged to go through, it [school-level curriculum review and development] is a dynamic process actively engaging the minds of those involved. Hence the emphasis is as much on developing the personal power of participants as it is on finding answers to questions raised by them . . . While the review and development activities were designed with the school's effectiveness in mind, they also provided learning opportunities for participants.

Freestone also observed that the extent to which teachers were prepared to look at their own performance increased with their level of involvement in curriculum review and development and, further, that the degree of self-appraisal was reflected in the depth and scope of changes in classroom practices.[29]

Curriculum deliberations are a kind of professional debate among those involved with the education of children, and a good deal of Maria's (and her colleagues') efforts need to be directed toward improving the quality of that debate. But handling the community of relationships within the learning environment offered by curriculum development activities in a school is as complex and demanding as teaching in a classroom. Curriculum development depends on individual contributions being valued and fostered, yet at the same time it must provide a framework which constrains individual action in the pursuit of co-operative and agreed tasks.

There are no rules for determining what constitutes effective involvement in curriculum development — each situation must be viewed on its merits. Some of the predicaments faced by Maria and her team might appear less problematic if attention is given to the composition of the decision-making group and to the requirement for their decisions to be seen as defensible. At the moment, the group comprises only the four teachers who volunteered for the task of developing an experimental segment of the year ten course, with the deputy principal sometimes making decisions on their behalf. There are at least two ways in which this group might be inadequately constituted for the decision-making it is expected to accomplish. First, the group might be helped if it were to include — possibly as chairman — a person whose prime task was to monitor the group's deliberations and ensure that each other member's contributions were revealed, respected and placed in proper perspective vis-à-vis the group's task. Paul's insistence on a role for English 'specialists', and Maria's own doubts about the competence of the other team members to deal with sociological concepts, indicate that there is a need for such a person. In this instance the *relative* importance of subject-matter issues, as they affect this specific case, should be explored by the group in more depth than appears to have been done so far. The group had earlier decided that a programme of subject specialization which meant that one teacher might come into contact with 200 pupils in a week made any close knowledge of pupils impossible. If this earlier decision was not made lightly, and reflects the group's real priorities, the issue of subject expertise would become *relatively* unimportant, and a frank exploration of the sorts of fears Maria holds might make it easier for each member of the group to accept the diminution of the role of 'specialism' in the programme (i.e., to honour their earlier commitments). With so many variables to be balanced in curriculum decision-making, it is difficult to see deliberation being really effective without the presence of someone whose major task is achieving that balance.

The second way in which the decision-making group may be inadequately constituted is reflected in the attack made on the project by the rest of the staff in the wake of the deputy principal's decision to increase the project's time allocation from ten to twelve periods. To the extent that the group (or the deputy principal on its behalf) is making decisions which affect the rest of the staff, these staff should be represented in the decision-making, and this should be more than a token representation. Even the earlier 'barely concealed silent hostility' of the rest of the staff, whether 'justified' or not, could have been symptomatic of ineffective deliberation in the early stages of the project; certainly, their hostility was an indication that they were ambivalent about early decisions of the group (and perhaps even about the decision to form the group), and it might therefore indicate that both the composition of the group, and the way in which it conducted its affairs, needs to be examined. Nevertheless, one of the advantages of school-based curriculum development is that it can and possibly should allow diversity within a school. In a school like Maria's where poor morale has contributed to a low level of interest in innovation, the deputy principal can argue that those who have not volunteered to try out different approaches should tolerate small groups that have (just as the innovators should tolerate the rest of the staff's conservatism). However, the repercussions of the deputy principal's decision could have been anticipated, and in the light of that anticipation the planning group might have been more willing to try and reach an internal compromise. Teachers have varying roles in shaping curriculum development tasks, and even to categorize people glibly as 'innovators' or 'conservatives' may serve little purpose other than to set up communication barriers and to shape expectations against which achievements tend implicitly to be judged. Curriculum development is both a consequence of and a condition for sharing and building upon available talents to the mutual benefit of all members of the school community.

Conclusion

This chapter has outlined some practical ways in which seeing the curriculum as something to be developed through deliberation and situational research can help a teacher in Maria's predicament. However, some of the most important benefits of these approaches are attitudinal. For example, one habit of mind which is discouraged by these approaches is the temptation to distinguish between process and product. Curriculum development should not be perceived as a process which results in a product (the curriculum) which, because of its − and/ or our − imperfections, will eventually need to be changed by using the process again. This stop-start view implies that there is some desirable − and to some extent static − end point to curriculum development; or, at least, that we should feel some sense of achievement (or relief) when we produce a curriculum specification, and that our product will provide us with a breathing space before the whole process starts again.

Developing the curriculum through deliberation and research means that there is always evolution in curriculum: there are no products of any permanence and, indeed, there are not even any temporary respites from continual change − change is the norm. A means−ends approach gives us a false sense of security when we achieve our ends. The frustrations and dilemmas with which a continually changing curriculum presents us are symptoms of a healthy state of affairs − that the curriculum is, as it were, alive and well rather than moribund. We do not 'solve' problems in curriculum development in the hope that we will eventually have fewer such problems to solve, any more than the crossword puzzle addict hopes that, by completing each crossword, he is reducing the number of puzzles left to solve.

Maria is said to feel embattled: she may feel less so if she perceives the 'battle' as a normal state of affairs rather than as some aberrant condition. It will be even better if she sees the majority of her dilemmas and personal conflicts as positive contributions to the continuing war of minds that characterizes professional educational debate. With this frame of mind, even if Maria persists in seeing the dynamic arena of curriculum action as a battleground, she should at least enjoy the fight.

Notes

1 Elliot W. Eisner, 'Educational objectives: help or hindrance?', *School Review*, 75 (3), 1967, p. 250.

2 For example, the manual for a short course (ten hours contact time) in school-based curriculum development at Macquarie University devotes thirteen pages to defining aims and objectives, and to instructing participants in how to write behavioural objectives and classify them. It is worth noting that this material constitutes virtually the entire information content of the manual, the remainder of it being concerned with guidelines and resources for workshop activities. Rex Meyer *et al.* (eds), *School-Based Curriculum Development*, North Ryde, NSW, Macquarie University Centre for Advancement of Teaching, 1978.

3 Lawrence Stenhouse, *An Introduction to Curriculum Research and Development*, London, Heinemann, 1975, p. 3.

4 Eisner, op. cit., pp. 254-5.

5 Decker F. Walker, 'A naturalistic model for curriculum development', in *Curriculum, School and Society: an Introduction to Curriculum Studies*, ed. P.H. Taylor and K.A. Tye, Slough, NFER, 1975, p. 167.

6 Geography Teachers' Association of Victoria, *SGEP-PAK: a Teacher's Resource File for the Development of Geography Courses and Materials*, Melbourne, GTAV, 1977, p. 28.

7 See 'SGEP Policy Document', Melbourne, Education Department of Victoria, Curriculum and Research Branch, 1977.

8 Ross Hartnell and Gary Pollard, 'School-Based Curriculum Development in the Secondary Geographical Education Project', Melbourne, Education Department of Victoria, Curriculum and Research Branch, 1980, p. 8 (mimeo.).

9 Ibid.

10 Ibid.

11 Ross Hartnell, Project Leader, Secondary Geographical Education Project, Education Department of Victoria, personal communication, May 1980.

12 Eisner, op. cit., p. 253.

13 Stenhouse, op. cit., ch. 7.

14 Joseph J. Schwab, 'The practical: a language for curriculum', *School Review*, 78 (1), 1969, pp. 1-23. See also Schwab, 'The practical: arts of eclectic', *School Review*, 79 (4), 1971, pp. 493-542, and 'The practical 3: translation into curriculum', *School Review*, 81 (4), 1973, pp. 501-22.

15 Stenhouse, op. cit., especially chs 9 and 10.

16 Schwab, op. cit., 1971, p. 494.

17 Stenhouse, op. cit., p. 143.

18 Ibid., p. 136.

19 Modified from Ian Allen, 'Unit planning for multiple objectives', *Ethos*, 7 (2), 1977, p. 5.

20 Schwab, op. cit., 1969, p. 15.
21 This does not imply a view of knowledge structured according to the traditional disciplines, although the selection of a person with the requisite knowledge and experience may appear, superficially, to be easier when dealing with traditional subjects. The choice of a person *or persons* to represent a subject-matter must face the test of defensibility. If environmental education was the subject in question, I would maintain that it is no more difficult to find a representative 'environmentalist' than it is to find a representative 'biologist'.
22 Schwab, op. cit., 1973, pp. 502-4.
23 Secondary Science Curriculum Committee, *Learning in Science*, Education Department of South Australia, 1978, p. 67 (trial document).
24 Curriculum decisions cannot be made inductively because they are decisions about actions in specific situations rather than explanations or generalizations. Deduction is similarly inadmissible because curriculum decisions deal with specific cases, not abstractions from cases, and specific cases cannot be settled by the mere application of a principle.
25 Schwab, op. cit., 1969, pp. 20-1.
26 Seymour Fox, 'A practical image of "the practical" ', *Curriculum Theory Network*, 10, 1973, p. 57.
27 Ibid.
28 Melvin Freestone, 'School level review and development: a learning experience approach', paper to the Tenth Annual Conference of the South Pacific Association for Teacher Education, Perth, Australia, May 1980, p. 26.
29 Ibid., p. 23.

Chapter 4

The multicultural school — or schools in search of their culture
Bill Hannan

Maria's School

If Maria's fictional school is to typify the real thing, she will one day realize with dismay that all the planned courses and all the prepared syllabuses take no notice of the cultural background of large numbers of her pupils, who conceivably could be from Italy, Greece, Turkey, Lebanon, Cyprus, Malta, Spain or a host of Asian and South American countries. The English course is based on anthologies and wide reading from English, American and a few 'Commonwealth' writers — yet fewer than half the pupils have any background in those cultural traditions. A pupil's whole schooling could happen to include no references to the southern Mediterranean or the Middle East after the time of Christ, no examination of immigration as a historical, cultural or economic fact — yet nearly 60 per cent of Maria's pupils were born of non-English immigrant families.

Maria knows from her training that where she teaches is supposed to be the place *par excellence* for a multicultural curriculum. How then did the school get through all its curriculum planning and Maria through all her course preparation without taking the culture of the pupils into account? She considers the staff, and the answer becomes obvious. Because she has some Italian in her ancestry she has some understanding of the question, but even she cannot imaginatively encompass the cultures of pupils of such varied and wide-ranging ethnicity. How much harder for some of the other teachers, with no minority or non-English background. Even if the staff were willing to devise a multicultural curriculum, where would they start?

She raises the issue with David (see p. 13). Why has the school done nothing about multiculturalism? Where can they get information and guidance?

It turns out that the school has done quite a bit. The emphasis on

79

language teaching in the English department is seen as the main stroke. The remedial reading classes comprise largely migrant students, and the remedial centre has several staff trained in teaching English as a second language. Italian has been kept going in spite of the great difficulty in getting staff — twice in the past few years temporary unqualified teachers have been sneaked in with the union turning a blind eye. But what about multicultural dimensions to other parts of the curriculum? On that the school has had its fingers burnt. The year before, a special in-service day had been organized specifically on the subject of multiculturalism across the curriculum. A couple of academics who had published works on the subject were invited to speak to the staff. Most of the staff remember little more than that the academics argued between themselves about whether 'polyethnic' might not be a more appropriate word than 'multicultural'!

The school had managed to get translators for school notices in the main community languages, and interpreters to help with parents' visits and parent-teacher nights. However, David points out without prompting that the migrant parents are pretty hard to deal with: they want the school to be tough on the kids and to load them down with homework, and for the most part they have 'unreal expectations' for them. 'They all want their kids to be doctors and lawyers.'

Let us consider the nature of this immigrant community that Maria is now bound to in duty. For a start it is not one community, but many. Greeks and Italians are not especially alike in background, language or temper. The Middle Eastern people are different again from the Europeans. Yet, curiously, the district for all its vigorous and sometimes exotic diversity has a distinctive character, which some of the staff at least enjoy and express considerable loyalty to.

All these groups, native-born and immigrant, have one thing in common: they are workers. The English spoken is either the traditional working-class dialect of the region or a blend of that dialect with overlays of the original languages. Whatever can be said about the chances of working-class children in the school system can be said with renewed force here. It is true that the drive of immigrants to better their children, usually at the cost of their own oblivion in grinding work, does bear some fruit. In general, a larger proportion of immigrant students get through the system to tertiary education than native-born children in the district. But, at the other end of the scale, they drop out before the senior years, and the failure rates in the examination years fit the depressing and widely known statistics for working-class children and minority ethnic group children.[1]

Thus in Maria's mind the terms of the debate merge. Questions of multiculturalism fade into the problems of working-class education. Especially in the matter of English teaching, the two issues fuse. The standard of English in the school clearly won't do — it is not going to lead to anything like equal opportunities in the certificate race, and hence in the job market. But is that because the students are of non-English-speaking background or because they are of dialectal background even when they know English? The question has never been answered. Prima facie evidence could justify either answer to some extent or a combination of both. If I were advising Maria, I'd incline to push her towards the social-class explanation, but only as a hunch. I could not produce clear evidence on the point.

Maria thinks her moral position is defensible. Students have a right to education in their own language and culture. The proviso should be that it not be exclusively in the home culture. The students belong also to their host culture and need a thorough understanding of its language and culture, not only for large reasons of national cohesion but also for the simple reason that they depend on it for their living. English is unquestionably the language they must master — and that means the standard English that is the language of writing and of so much work and social life. Nor is there any question that they must live in and work with the institutions of the dominant culture. These are not ethnic groups, such as the Welsh, the Basques of Québecois who could feasibly control their own regional institutions. They are spread throughout the society and their hopes for a decent democratic life depend partly on the tolerance and generosity of the host culture and partly on their own power to assert themselves within its institutions. Maria is aware from the headier days of teacher training that some of that power comes through education. She is also aware that idealists, at least, believe that some of the tolerance may be induced in school. She is sceptical. She has a pugnacious view of the problem; but since it is early in her teaching, it is an optimistic pugnacity.

Personal identity

Many commentators[2] pose the psychological issue of identity as the key pedagogical problem for teachers in any school, but especially in ones like Maria's. Self-perceptions common to a sex, an occupation, a class, a nation or an ethnic group become internalized as part of an individual's interaction with his community. Other chapters in this book describe how the growth of thought accompanies the growth of language, and both become interlocked with our particular cultural environments. The ethnic or national dimension of identity is transmitted most strongly of course in its original setting, where it is least challenged; but even in immigrant groups a long way from home, one of the most powerful transmitters — language — is still present alongside other obvious influences such as family and religion. How much the ethnic dimension ultimately influences an individual's sense of identity will vary a lot. In the case of immigrant women workers their ethnicity is usually reinforced by the fact that they work with other immigrants, or maybe at home, and by the restricted role which their own ethnic group allots to them. An immigrant, on the other hand, who has experienced city life and social change in his/her home country, who has been educated in both countries and who has fairly prestigious work is likely to take a rather cosmopolitan view of identity.

Let me illustrate quickly with my own case: second-generation Australian born, but still identifying myself as Irish-Australian. Perversity? Sentimentality? I hope not. My parents spoke of Ireland as home, not with great passion but simply as the place the family came from. In their view of the world no one actually *came* from Australia except the Aborigines. I went to a Catholic school, was a 'mick' – a term which compressed religion and race – and aggressive about it because we fought pitched battles with state school kids on the subject. Priests and nuns were frequently Irish, as were the sentiments of most church publications. Naturally, most of my friends were of the same mind, as would be, it was assumed, spouses and offspring. Socially and politically I have later leant towards Irish-Australian institutions: trade unions, the Labor Party, the family (currently a rather unfashionable institution). And so, family, class, education, friendship, loyalties are all coloured slightly green . . . let's say wattle green.

One integrates at the same time as one feels different, presumably because the opportunities are at least equal enough to make it worth the battle. Maria accepts the view that, in order to approach cultural independence and hence identity, it is first necessary to establish a sense of one's own worth and to purge the group of degradations.[3] The reverse is equally true: if cultural identity is under attack, so is the person's own sense of worth.

From her own Italian background, Maria recognizes that teachers must have a coherent, fairly detailed knowledge of the perceptions children have of themselves and of their society. This is taken for granted in extreme cases of handicap or difficult behaviour, when the public looks to teachers specialized by their training or experience to relate this knowledge to the child's learning. In the case of the normal child of the majority culture, teachers need not perhaps be too explicit about a child's perceptions because they are similar to his own but, when in front of a multicultural class, he needs to be aware of the cultural gap that so often exists between teacher and pupils – particularly those who are foreign born, but also the native-born from different class backgrounds.

Multicultural education is not just a matter of teaching ethnic groups to remain ethnic. Maria's team acknowledges that it is a matter of re-examining the dominant culture with the aim of accommodating within it the healthy integration of many different cultural experiences. It is not a museum exercise. Nor is it a concern only for recent migrants. It is an issue for all schools, indeed all institutions, in that it calls into question the present nature of our culture, and does so at some of its most sensitive points.

The gap between ideals and realities

Ideals do not of themselves produce theories or even consistent practices. All the major political parties profess to convictions like Maria's, but they are only at the stage of dispensing pin-money for pilot projects. The papers and books available on the subject offer few practical suggestions and spend a lot of time defining terms. What clear thought there is on the subject is plainly at variance with general community opinion. The mere fact that the majority of immigrants are unskilled or semi-skilled workers and that their children (and presumably they themselves) are among the most disadvantaged groups in the country is eloquent evidence of their place in society. Whilst educationists debate introducing community languages to schools, linguistic bigots (that is ordinary people) outside school are busy trying to expunge them. The most likely result is that the languages will enter the school when they are effectively dead outside it.

Maria toys with a few hypotheses. Apart from the undeniable moral rights of immigrants to education in their own language and culture, and apart from the moral necessity facing the school to reflect the culture of its actual community and to contribute to the growth of a pluralist national culture (she pauses for breath), multiculturalism may have something to contribute to the central educational problem of schools such as Maria's, which is this:

Her school is probably as efficient as the average. It has much the same curriculum as schools elsewhere. Its teachers move about and probably perform as well here as elsewhere. However, the pupils of this school do not get through the school system as successfully as the average pupil. There is a gap.

One hypothesis would be that the gap might be closed by improving efficiency, by taking the standard courses and methods to an unusually high degree of efficiency, with more staff perhaps, with more aids and equipment, with better understanding of individual learning problems. Another would be that the system itself might be changed. Yet another would be that an entirely new factor or factors is needed to close the gap. Could multiculturalism come in there? Or is the debate about multiculturalism unconnected with the larger cultural context in which the school finds itself so invidiously placed?

An answer to Maria's last question would come clearly from the parents of her pupils. As they see it, the task of the school is to make the system work for their children. If that meant throwing away their language and culture they'd probably do it − the right to success in other words overrides the right to cultural identity in their eyes. But naturally they hope, like Maria, that these two are not opposed. Their ideal is success and retained identity. Both in their eyes are rights.

Others on the staff have stigmatized this parental view as 'unreal expectations'. The phrase is used scornfully to suggest not simply that the expectations will probably not be fulfilled but that they are illegitimate. This is a version of the poor knowing their place. It is perfectly legitimate for anyone, even an immigrant worker, to want success for his children. The problem is that his chances are so very low. Even if we accept that competition must be, he is unjustly handicapped.

All three hypotheses need testing. The first − increasing efficiency − is the one most people, including parents, go for. All that is needed, says the hypothesis, is for schools to do their job properly. As Maria sees it, the school is doing its job in that sense adequately already. It is hard to imagine that the extra effort that would be feasible would close the gap, though it ought to produce marginal improvements.

Changing the system faces similar limitations. In a sense this is what Maria and her team are trying to do with their new curriculum. To the extent that the traditional academic subject-based system may disadvantage students in schools such as Maria's, changes to content and to the methods of teaching and assessment could narrow the gap. But again, since one of the main elements causing the gap seems to be language mastery, especially of the written language, the extent to which the system may be changed is fairly slight. Eventually success is measured by examination passes and progress through further education − systems which change slowly if at all.

And so we are led to the third hypothesis: something new. Could it be multiculturalism in the case of this school?

A multicultural curriculum

At first glance this too seems an unlikely hypothesis. Indeed the very reverse could be argued. Preserving identity with a minority ethnic group might be a fancy way of preserving disadvantage. In English-speaking countries the classic way up for immigrant minority groups has been to assimilate. Only those who have learnt to merge their identity with the majority culture have been accepted by the majority.

The rest, no matter what their material success, have remained Wogs, Pakis, Polacks, Niggers and so forth.

In any case, even if it were desirable, the school staff have no hope of preserving or even respecting the cultures of their pupils. The simple fact is that they know next to nothing about them. Very few even speak a language other than English, and none has any obvious knowledge of what it's like to live in another culture.

Here then is an apparent dead end for Maria. The school could possibly expand its cultural breadth by bringing in more teachers who share the cultural background of the pupils, but that would involve a long programme of recruitment and training, and would have no inbuilt guarantee of success. Such teachers, too, could be on the margins of school affairs, tolerated for some small contribution to the curriculum but not very influential in changing the general approach.

The only way out of the dead end that Maria sees is to treat multiculturalism as an issue for the whole school and the whole curriculum. Clearly, the concept implies some special approaches to language and some deliberate provision for teaching of minority cultures, but the main drive should come from a view of culture that permeates the entire curriculum and touches every child.

A multicultural curriculum, in brief, rests on the foundation of a sound definition of general culture: on what it means to be an Australian, an American, a Canadian, a Briton.

Put as broadly as that, the issue is a gob-stopper, but it can be elaborated and eventually translated into practice. A less ambitious way to express the point is to say that the general curriculum needs to be revised so that it is democratic, pluralistic and free from bias.

Put this way, the issue of multiculturalism across the curriculum merges with the general issue of curriculum reform. Throughout the western world the content, structure and processes of the curriculum are under attack. There are reactionary pressures to bring it back to 'basics' and there are radical calls to make it more democratic, more adapted to individual need and more in tune with the cultural aspirations of the mass of working people and of minority groups.

The curriculum in Maria's school is still narrow despite its recent revisions. It has very few answers to the problem of social-class bias in content and in methods of assessment. It takes little account of the ethnic minority cultures represented in the classrooms. It has therefore an equivocal approach even to the definition of the majority culture which it depicts somehow as the universal standard rather than as the largest among many. And it probably gives its blessing to a lot of race- and class-biased material in books and assignments.

Maria is fortunate in being a humanities teacher, since it is there that multiculturalism most clearly applies. She is also fortunate to be with a team that is attacking the authoritarian nature of schooling, and is trying to offer achievement to all. Such reforms are basic to any multicultural curriculum because they are basic to democratic curriculum.

Maria is confident too that her team of teachers will try to keep ethnocentricity out of their courses. While this is only the negative side of multiculturalism, it is important since ethnocentricity in materials is virtually the norm. The ground, then, has at least been cleared. What are some things that might now be planted in it?

A democratic humanities curriculum like Maria's, based both on general concepts and on pupils' experience, contains some important assumptions. One obvious one that the team has discussed is that generalizations help us to think about reality, and enable us to absorb what would otherwise be an overwhelming mass of fact and disordered experience. Some of these generalizations are everyday and unremarkable — for example, about family relationships, or simple notions of good and bad. Others also in common use and formed from experience have broad social consequences: class, work, God, freedom, sex-role. All of these have been included in the team's planning. Yet others, though equally powerful, may be more remote: atomic theory and cultural relativism would be examples. Such generalizations have led to our present knowledge explosion and they will enable pupils to cope with it. They simplify, they explain, they predict, they raise fruitful questions, and ultimately they are changed, modified or replaced by our reflection on them. This final characteristic, of changing, has important implications for teaching methods. We are not talking about established truths, but ideas that are made and re-made by people. If teaching methods don't take account of that central quality, they are clearly inadequate.

A second assumption to be made without discussion, because it is developed at much more length in other chapters of this book,[4] is that our learning develops as the generalizations we have made for ourselves from experience meet those formed by the intellectual culture of the times. Learning, in other words, grows out of concrete experience and abstracted reflection. Schools have the task of presenting organized knowledge in such a way that pupils can relate it to their own experience and develop in themselves the same habit of critical reflection. Schools, as is evident in Australia, tend to offer disproportionate success in tertiary entrance to a small minority of poorer pupils or fortunate migrants who then become part of the dominant culture out of touch with those at the other end of the spectrum, be they English-speaking or foreign born.

In a multicultural society, an ideal school would equip its pupils both to understand and to create their own society. The school's course would reflect in its content the multicultural nature of the society, and in its methods would require pupils to define and to criticize the nature of the society. The content is reality, the method critical reflection.

In practice, such a prescription contains a contradiction – one that threatened to defeat Maria's team. Reality is unpredictable and undefined; yet an orderly course presupposes planning and selection. The course, then, is necessarily a compromise. On the one hand it is false to imagine that there is a set of concepts in the bank and that schools have the chequebook. On the other hand, pupils rightly expect guidance and visible progression. Out of the tension a course is developed. Teachers initiate the process of investigation and reflection. Through dialogue then with their pupils they help create the concepts which lead to seeking more evidence and recognizing more problems.

Thematic, concept-based courses jointly planned by teachers, pupils and, to some degree, parents, are appropriate, Maria thinks, to the whole range of the humanities. Of course, the social sciences – history, geography, economics, sociology – come first to mind when Maria thinks of cultural content. The arts, however, are not very different pedagogically. They may seem to be more concerned with form, style, technique and skill but to make them exclusively so is to deny their relevance. The various stylistic divisions of music, for example, into jazz/rock/classical/folk/pop and so on correspond to age, class and ethnic divisions. Each style carries its own load of concepts and assumptions as well as its more manifest skills and rituals. At present, school music largely follows the cultural assumptions of people who regard classical music as serious and most other music as inferior, 'commercialized' and destructive of their musical criteria.[5] They are in fact apt to admit some ethnic music into their courses but generally as light relief with some condescension (illustrated for me by several music teachers who have described non-harmonic, melodic conventions as 'simple', despite the audible fact that their own very impressive instrumental technique could not cope with the 'simple' style).

The first move for a democratic, multicultural music course would be to admit the music interests of pupils. The basic traditional aims of teaching instruments, organizing instrumental groups, learning to listen, read, arrange and compose would continue, but on new material. Sometimes traditional methods would have to be modified for certain styles – in the case of styles normally learnt by ear, for example, the reading is not necessary and should be only an option. In so far as each style has a history that illuminates its present, it would be taught with the same critical seriousness of method applied to any historical theme. Ireland, for example, teaches traditional instruments, music and styles in the state schools of music and admits them as studies for the final year secondary examinations and in tertiary courses. Teachers of

87

classical music in Ireland claim that there is a national tendency for musicians to rely uncommonly on ear because of their traditional background.

A democratic course is automatically a multicultural course. Imagine a Greek girl in Maria's class who is interested in her country's musical tradition. Technically, the course could make her quite accomplished. It could also provide opportunities for her to play in groups. It could introduce her to related forms – other ethnic traditions, or fusions with jazz, rock or classical forms. It could introduce her to the maintenance and/or construction of instruments. It could set her to reflect on the place of the tradition in her homeland and country of adoption. None of the these is an unreal aim. On the contrary they could be achieved, beginning at an early age, with virtually any interested pupil, given appropriate resources and adequate teaching. Nor is there any reason to see such musicianship as separate from the majority jazz, classical or rock traditions. A course could cope with a multiplicity of styles.

The example, I hope, makes the general point. The teacher draws upon the pupils' knowledge and interests for teaching skills and enlarges that knowledge by providing wider contexts. I hope also that the example suggests both the virtues and the limitations of having folk clubs and occasional dances. Such events help make a given style acceptable; but in not developing skill and reflection on the uses of skill, they are by definition extra-curricular.

The example illustrates, too, that change in curriculum entails not only new courses and methods but also new materials and (sometimes) teachers. All these interlock. If, as would be the case in language teaching, we have to allow for substantially different time-scales to accommodate the different tasks faced by bilinguals, dialect-speakers, and standard-speakers, then we need different materials and resources to meet these differing needs. In the various social sciences the provision of materials, already daunting, is trebly complicated if we want the course also to be multicultural and multilingual. In languages we face an almost total lack of teachers, as well as a famine of materials. In the arts, we are often not much better off.

Teaching resources

When one considers the magnitude of the task that Maria and her colleagues are undertaking, it is clear that they need access to up-to-date and suitable materials that are well catalogued.

In general, she might expect them to be (i) varied in medium, (ii) readily comprehensible at the relevant level, (iii) of a good standard in presentation, (iv) concept-based, (v) open, in that they require student activity and reflection, and (vi) under the control of the schools rather than pre-packaged. Clearly, materials that are designed to rob teachers of the sort of initiative shown by Maria's team are undesirable.

Specifically from a multicultural perspective she might add that they be (i) purged of ethnocentrism, nationalism and the like, (ii) culturally comprehensive and (iii) available in the languages the school uses.

Some of these general criteria sound very commonplace; but the worksheets handed out in experimental courses make it obvious that it is still worth talking about basics, such as legibility and comprehensibility. Schools are still in the wasteland between the mass commercial text, and decent, flexible materials suitable for individual and group learning in open courses. Often, when I look at my own spirit duplicator products I wonder whether it mightn't be better to go back to texts. But go back for a while to texts and I find myself supplementing them from the same dispiriting duplicator.

Classroom teachers can reasonably be expected only to supplement existing material, and then sparingly. Anything more ambitious is beyond their knowledge and well beyond their technical resources. In individualized courses they have their time cut out guiding pupils, teaching skills and selecting material. Most don't have the time or insight to do even that — to a considerable extent pupils depend directly on materials. The materials, therefore, need to be produced and distributed by central libraries over which schools should have close control. Such centres need to be both big enough to function efficiently, and small enough to be under co-operative school control. They should combine teachers and specialists in the work of producing material according to the kinds of criteria I've mentioned.

Much, much more could be said on the subject of materials, methods and their mutual compatibility. Our particular concern here is with the multicultural criteria I've suggested below.

To provide multilingual material to fit into humanities courses is clearly a job for a central organization. Marta Rado, at La Trobe University in Victoria, fortunately has provided a valuable example. In La Trobe's scheme, the school nominates or prepares its material and La Trobe basically provides the technical service of translating into the required languages. Such a service could of course also supply other relevant material from its own stock, if it had any, and could be part of the resources co-operative I have just described. The essence of the service is that it respond quickly and accurately to school needs.

Other centres are now beginning to select, catalogue and distribute specifically multicultural material.[6] With these, the systematic work has begun of (a) sifting existing material from a multicultural viewpoint, and (b) hunting out or commissioning new material to fill the gaps. While it could be argued that work of this kind should be part of normal production and supply of materials, the fact is that, without special centres and associations, nothing is done on an organized scale.

Since it is highly unlikely that ethnocentrism could be purged from our historical, sociological and artistic sources, teachers of a multicultural course need to make their pupils constantly aware of the issue. In the USA, Amerindian literature and black studies are setting somewhat to rights the customary ethocentric bias of materials. In Australia, works such as Geoffrey Blainey's *Triumph of the Nomads* are breaking Aboriginal history out of the confines of anthropology.

The need for a multicultural education pushes schools to deliberately seek out other cultural perspectives. Education thereby becomes more culturally comprehensive. Let me illustrate with an example from a schoolbook published in Italy about the campaign of metalworkers in 1972 for a new award – a triennial event in Italy, spearheaded by the metal industry. The book is intended for late primary or early secondary pupils. It is copiously illustrated, partly in comic-strip form. Its language would be accessible to native-speakers aged eleven or to older pupils with two to three years of Italian as a second language:

> *Nell'autunno del 1972 i rappresentanti eletti dai lavoratori di tutte le fabbriche italiane si riunirono a Genova in una grande assemblea nazionale.*
>
> *In questa occasione furono precisate le richieste dei lavoratori di tutte le fabbriche (. . .)*
>
> *Le richieste piu importanti erano:*
> *l'aumento del salario uguali per tutti gli operai*
> *l'eliminazione delle differenze fra operai e impiegati*
> *l'aumento dei giorni di ferie*
> *50 ore all'anno retribuite dal padrone per permettere gli operai di studiare.* (from *Una Lotta Operaia: il contratto dei metalmeccanici*, ed. gruppo 'io e gli altri')

(In the autumn of 1972 elected representatives of workers from all the factories in Italy met at Genoa in a great national conference.

On this occasion the demands of all workers were listed.

The most important demands were:

equal wage rises for all workers

scrapping of wage differences between blue- and white-collar workers

increase in holidays

50 hours a year of the boss's time to allow workers to study.)

This clearly contrasts with the subject-matter usual in language courses. In fact it deals with a subject-matter very much in contemporary

Italian consciousness, and as a piece for study in a social science course it is rich in conceptual work by any standard. My purpose here, however, is solely to demonstrate that in presenting the material *from an Italian viewpoint* we find certain novelties arising – novelties in that they would not arise necessarily in a similar topic based on experience elsewhere. In particular we note the intention to eliminate differences between blue- and white-collar workers, and the demand for 50 hours (now risen to 300 in some cases) of study in the boss's time. These are rich themes for reflection, and would be stimulating, even disconcerting, contributions from the Italian group to the common study of social themes. To make existing material bilingual is one thing. To clear material in general of bias and ethnocentrism is yet another. To enrich ourselves actively with the insights of cultures other than the majority one is yet another thing again, and beginning to sound like what we hope for from multiculturalism.

Does relevance entail staying close to home?

It is sometimes argued that subject-matter in a concept-based course is arbitrary, and even more effective perhaps when it is distanced from the learner. Jerome Bruner's much used and discussed *Man: a Course of Study*[7] is a case in point. The concepts it aims to establish are eminently apt to a multicultural course. It focuses on anthropological material about Eskimos and African bushmen, and on zoological material about East African baboons. It takes, moreover, an internationalist-American view of the material. This almost extra-planetary approach is not an oversight, but a deliberate distancing so that the concepts involved become sharper and more accessible. Similar arguments have been put by teachers of English in favour of fiction and drama – the form, in this case, and the conventions of criticism being the distancing factors.

I don't think that my emphasis on content as a reflection of the culture of the participants is necessarily an opposite approach. The designers of *Man: a Course of Study* envisage eventual application of concepts to everyday life but the materials allow teachers and pupils to make the appropriate links. Relevance comes from comparison and contrast. Some subjects are probably too close to home and too sensitive to approach directly. Youth culture comes to mind. So does the family. And sex-roles. Their very centrality makes them hard to approach directly in a critical way. The same may well be true of some ethnic themes. The hot ones, and there are plenty of them, have to be handled from a cool distance. The aim, after all, is not to resolve old conflicts with simplistic analyses but to equip people first of all to look at culture and society critically. I suppose a course has to be as distant as

91

it needs to be and as close to immediate reality as it can be. The exact balance, it seems to me, can only be judged on the spot.

If conceptual sequences alone don't guide the humanities course, and if the detail of topics and themes is a matter for teacher–pupil–school decision, what can be said of the binding thread of a multicultural course? To me, the basis, at least, is a sense of national identity that carries implicitly within it a critical awareness of what it means to be a part of that culture. For want of better expressions, Americanism, Britishism and Australianism require an awareness that the character of each is a synthesis of many constituent cultures. Such an awareness is the basis of integration as opposed to assimilation.

The school divorced from its local community

Re-examine our origins. Re-examine our present. Immigration into English-speaking countries continues as part of a world-wide pattern of urbanization which is attended by drastic changes of attitude towards the family, women, education, wealth, religion, the state, international relations. Educationally, the need to maintain and reinterpret a nation's contributing cultures is beginning to be defined and up to a point accepted. In helping to crystallize the content of curriculum, the apparent complications posed by multiculturalism may turn out to give focus to a lot of curriculum reform; which is a far bigger question than one of merely revising course content.

Maria in her school is learning fast and hard that quite simple curricular changes far less drastic than those I am proposing here can cause great upheavals within the whole school administration and can have noisy repercussions in the wider community. A democratic curriculum such as I have tried to sketch for Maria and her colleagues is the creation of a whole school (or even school system) which in its turn has to be democratic, both internally and in its community relations.

The problems which Maria faces within her school and with parents highlight the need for democratic processes. Far too many of Maria's reforms, great or small, are in danger of turning into conflicts or confrontations without much hope of resolution. Her whole experiment could be simply shut down by authority in the person of the principal or an education department official. Parents, completely isolated from any decision-making, see change as a threat to standards and hence to their children's success. And problems such as Fatima's arranged marriage (see pp. 18–19) come up only at the point where they look insoluble.

Far from being a place where pupils' needs and aspirations can be looked at methodically and practically, the school is a meeting-place of prejudices and conflicts. It is all very well to try, through an integrated unit, to diminish some of the pupils' inbred prejudices and racism. Maria daily sees not only the community but also the school sharing an assimilationist mentality in which minority children remain problems until they are absorbed into the general behaviour − teachers seldom know at what cost − and in which parents never gain acceptance. Parents, as schools see them, are a lost generation, possibly a barrier to their children's progress. The more the ethnic group is associated with cheap labour and poverty, the more it is seen also as culturally deprived. In classic exploiter fashion, the 'deprivation' serves to rationalize the oppression.

Reformers within schools can only try to devise ways in which school staffs can be sensitized to the facts of multiculturalism and the action they imply. It is not enough for a school merely to tolerate the enlightened souls and leave them to conduct their own courses. In fact, it may be counter-productive if the 'multicultural' groups (some bilinguals for example) become isolated within the school. The totality of the school's behaviour, in and out of class, has to be democratized.

New attitudes cannot be created by brain transplants or salary increments. As we do in the case of pupils, so for teachers, we have to put our faith in organized courses and cultivated consciousness. In my view, one of the important gains made by ten years of curriculum change in Victoria, Australia, has been the habit in schools of developing curriculum committees which keep relating classroom change to general school organization. These have shown time and again that the hidden curriculum, enshrined in assessment policies, administrative principles, power structures and an array of school rituals is also capable of being changed by determined and continuous review. It is at that level that many of a school's attitudes to cultural groups have to be examined.

Among its values there has to be a commitment to the community outside the school, primarily to parents. Parents would be represented in the school's structure of government, and the content of the curriculum, among other things, would be a subject of continual discussion with parents − decisions and directives no, except perhaps of the most general kind. Whether we like it or not, operative decisions about learning from day to day are mostly made by pupils. Parents, like teachers, are best employed guiding learning constructively. They ought to be involved in school government as a matter of democratic right, but not in order to reinforce their authority or to be wheedled into accepting change.

True, true, thinks Maria, and wonders (a) where you'd start on all that and (b) what it's got to do with a case such as that of Fatima.

What could Maria do about Fatima? In a general way, she shares the

93

responsibility for creating Fatima's dilemma. The chief cause obviously is the fact of Fatima's migration but, as I have argued already, this migration cannot be seen as entirely voluntary. The wealth of Maria's society depends in part on the exploitation of Fatima's family's labour. It is very likely that Fatima's parents aim to return home when they've made enough money to set themselves up in the village. Hence in their minds the dominant culture of their temporary home is one to be ignored, by-passed or resisted. Rather than have Maria and her kind teaching their children, Fatima's parents would probably prefer teachers of their own cultural background. Indeed to immigrant parents of many nationalities, the local teachers seem to be too easy, too casual, too lacking in what it takes to command respect. It would not surprise them — neither would it impress them — that Maria supported Fatima in her refusal to follow established cultural ways.

I am sure that Maria can do nothing much about Fatima's problem, except to give her moral support. If Fatima avoids an arranged marriage, it will be because she manages to persuade her parents to relent or manages to get support elsewhere within the family. But what is the moral basis of Maria's support? Feminism lays claim to universal values of equality. Liberal democracy recognizes a right, presumably held to be universal, to freedom of choice in marriage. This universalism, however, is only ideal. In any historical context, ideal values are only partly realizable. The sexes do not achieve equality no matter what the marriage system may be. Freedom of choice turns out to follow almost predictable patterns. There is no demonstrable correlation between marriage systems and the way people are treated within them.

Culturally, Maria's support of Fatima is partisan. It relies not on self-evident truth but on the fact that Fatima's choice not to enter an arranged marriage coincides with Maria's own cultural values. I would not dispute Maria's right to expound and defend her own values to Fatima or any other child or parent, but only on condition that she continually does everything she can to know and understand the values and ways of thought of other cultures remote (ideologically) from her own. The case of Fatima, in other words, is but a dramatic reminder of the duty of teachers in a multicultural society: to understand as much as possible, to leave alone whenever possible and to help immigrant communities to understand the institutions that do cut across their lives.

The most obvious barrier between Maria and the parents of Fatima is that they do not speak the same language. Of course it might be argued that, even if Maria were fluent in Turkish, she and Fatima's parents would not speak the same language of values. Perhaps so. Language study is certainly not in itself a means of reconciling cultural differences. None the less it is impossible to consider multiculturalism in any context without considering the language question.

Language as a means of cultural expression

It is now a commonplace among linguists that a person's home language has a lot to do with establishing personal identity.[8] We use language not as a disembodied code able *à la rigueur* to be replaced by any other comprehensible code, but as a means of relating ourselves emotionally to our social community and as a vehicle for turning experience into concepts which added up together give us a particular view of the world. To some extent, then, the language we are born into conditions our world view, our emotional relationships, the way we articulate our own ideas and the way we communicate with others. Educationally, these assertions make a case both for maintaining home languages and for widening our insights into culture by learning other languages.

Some linguists take this argument beyond our everyday categories of languages — English, Italian, Greek and so forth — to include dialects and class varieties whose status, *for non-linguistic reasons*, may still be disputed.[9] Hence, in America, black English vernacular has been a hot issue. William Labov's studies, in particular, have shown that black English has the same logical power as any other language, and is markedly different from standard American. If the link between home language and identity is accepted, there is good reason for bringing black English constructively into the schooling of its speakers, say as the initial medium of instruction. And there is good reason for accepting black English as a valid medium of communication at any stage, provided it is intelligible to those communicating. Historically, however, American schools have treated black English as a low, inadequate form of English, and have either by-passed it or suppressed it, thereby adding language oppression to the well-known wider pattern of black oppression.

The language issues that arise in a multicultural school have been very concisely encapsulated by the Canberra Curriculum Development Centre in their report on the first year of the Centre's Language Development Project. Of language development generally, the report maintains that an essential condition for all language development is that the school should accept and respect the child's own use of language. Only then can the school successfully engage the child in learning experiences which aim to foster language development.[10] Language, however, is not uniform:[11]

> different groups in the community use different forms or dialects
> of the language. The status of the form of language used by the
> child is a reflection of that status ascribed to the users of the dialect

. . . It is a mistake to think that children who have not learnt to speak the prestige dialect are therefore linguistically incapable.

If students have a language other than English as their mother tongue, the report asserts that 'schools must provide opportunities which allow the speaker of English as a second language to develop the same sort of resource, if possible, as the native speaker'.[12] Further,[13]

there are two compelling reasons for schools to play an active role in language maintenance. First of all no child should be kept at an educationally lower level while learning the language of instruction. Bilingual programs would allow students to learn at their true intellectual level while learning English as a second language. Secondly, from what has been said about the inter-relationships of language and thought, language and cognitive development, and language and self-concept, it follows that the child's intellectual, emotional and social development depend upon the development and maintenance of his or her mother tongue. Beyond these reasons, every . . . child should have the opportunity to benefit from the heterogeneity and richness of [his or her country's] linguistic and cultural resources. Community language programs ought to be provided for all students.

This sounds fine. Probably many teachers of Maria's age would have heard of such ideals in training. Maria, as we have seen, is no linguist. Even so, in teaching her own pupils she tries to develop what she believes to be valuable. Her pupils do not write for her alone, but have their work either published in a class magazine or presented as papers to discussion classes. She also makes sure that topics and problems are thrashed out first in discussion before she sets written tasks. None the less, as she looks round the class and the school she realizes that what is being done doesn't begin to measure up to the ideal. She lists a few categories, thus:

Alberta, the daughter of an educated family, who has taken in the standard prestige dialect with her mother's milk.
Brenda, another local, but born and bred to the district's working-class, low-prestige dialect.
Rita, born here, a working-class dialect-speaker, but with Italian as her home language or, more precisely, Calabrian.
Soula, who arrived in her infancy and whose family speaks and writes standard Greek.
Tina, a not so recent arrival who has been put in the English as a Second Language (ESL) class, too, and whose home language is a regional language remote from the national standard.

Maria soon begins to realize that the list could stretch on, each category merging with its neighbours. The linguistic variety among the non-English-speakers is genuinely bewildering, not merely because so many regional and national languages are represented but also because no one on the staff appears to have the knowledge about languages or linguistics that would be necessary if the school were to attempt a multicultural language programme. And that in itself is a very big 'if'. The school has always had a battle to keep up a supply of teachers of English as a Second Language. Maria has a very distinct impression that a proposal to recruit a teacher of English as a Second Dialect would simply not be believed by most of the staff. The majority view among staff is that only standard English will do, in speech and in writing.

As for community languages, the school has made honourable enough attempts but with very limited success. Italian — the language of the largest non-English group — was taught for a few years, but at the beginning of this year no new teacher was appointed to replace the one who had left. Other languages have not been attempted at the school. Some are, however, maintained by private ethnic schools and by special Saturday morning classes at a nearby school.

In a word: chaos. Where does a multicultural language curriculum start?

A multicultural language programme

A multicultural language programme would try to cope with this complexity both by finding a method of teaching everyone standard English, and planning for growth in the home language. I put the two aims in this order not for linguistic or psychological reasons, but simply because I believe the first to be more practicable and in general more in demand (for example, from parents) than the second.

The problem comes when we try to find equal methods. Baldly stated, the idea of teaching everyone standard English gets nearly universal acceptance from left and right. Possession of the standard, runs the legend, guarantees access to the whole society. I think behind this acceptance lie also other ideas that the standard must spread as the schools teach it and the media use it, and that sooner or later immigration must peter out.

In fact, none of these propositions is demonstrably true. There cannot be equal access in a stratified society. If pupils come from families on the way 'up' they will probably seek the *cachet* of standard. If, however, access is downward, other dialects may be more appropriate. The equal-access-through-language idea went out with Eliza Doolittle. Nor does standard spread, despite the schools and the media. And

97

migration shows no signs of disappearing.

Simply to urge teaching standard English is, in other words, the linguistic equivalent of the assimilationist argument, and it fails for the same pragmatic and ideological reasons: language and ethnic (or class) loyalties survive, and ethnically-connected disadvantage persists.

Since a long-standing policy of teaching only the standard has reinforced the situation where educational disadvantage can be charted against language groupings, with dialect-speakers and non-English-speakers coming out worst, we must assume two fairly obvious and related things: one, that language is mirroring social forces outside the school's control, and two, that language in school is not being approached in a democratic way. Presumably if schools did approach language in a different way, their policies could be widely influential.

As linguists often point out, the most obvious change we can make in language teaching is to recognize the validity of home language. Trying to eradicate a person's dialect only provokes bewilderment, resentment and often resistance. It is linguistically, psychologically, socially and pedagogically foolish. The 'standards' of English are not preserved by this kind of teaching; they are merely identified with privilege and priggishness.

Generally, the same linguists advocate a 'bidialectal' approach: teach in both, starting with the home and working on to the standard. This is substantially the same argument as the bilingual argument for non-speakers, though I suppose to many readers it must still seem a bit far-fetched. Aren't the dialect and standard pretty close? To sophisticated eyes maybe they are. But we are talking about young learners. To them a change of dialect, like a change of language, can be quite baffling. Even if the school dialect is intelligible, because of the media and whatnot, it may not yet be a basis for learning to read and write. It really is more than a case of not denigrating a child's home language. Special allowances have to be made in approaching reading and writing, and oral instruction has to be able to build on dialect differences. And, of course, given that dialects don't crumble easily before the majesty of the standard, we have to be able to accommodate them, and use them, at all stages of schooling.

The fact that dialects persist in all kinds of favourable and unfavourable circumstances leads some linguists to say that it is a waste of effort trying to replace them at all. All that is at stake, they maintain, are social attitudes and in the long run it may prove easier to change the attitudes than to superimpose a single universal dialect.

Looked at in one way these are common-sense arguments. Of all Maria's types of speaker, Alberta is the only one in a state to launch into reading and writing in straight standard English. All the others need some variation of approach, even if we envisage them all ultimately as fluent speakers, readers and writers of standard. For Tina we must make enormous variation, because no variety of English is really intelligible. Brenda presumably needs less variation, but in our present state of knowledge, *no one knows* how much. We do know that well into her school life, often right up to the time she leaves, the standard causes her trouble. It doesn't take long teaching in working-class schools to know that dialect effortlessly survives ten years' counter-instruction, and that fluency in standard is never achieved by many. In that category there will be many recent immigrants.

The difficulty is that as teachers we're in the business of hopes rather than present facts. We hope that all our students will have at least the cultural advantages of knowing standard. Not necessarily the posh jobs and the power and all that, but access to decent stuff in print and to organizations where they can participate actively and intelligently without having to fumble for the verbal forms. As teachers we battle for our particular pupils against the fact that the schools are still the agents of social selection, and that language is one of the means of that selection. We come up with the conclusion that we will do our best to get our pupils as near to standard English as we can. We fail in that aim on an impressively large scale.

I dwell on this unresolved issue at length because it is one way of pointing out the weaknesses inherent in what I regard as a primary tenet of multiculturalism, namely that everyone should have good command of the common language of the dominant culture. I raise it also because it particularly concerns those students we first think of when we speak of multiculturalism, and it occurs most acutely with recent immigrants from non-English-speaking cultures. It concerns them because their informal acquaintance with English is usually not with standard but with a series of class-ethnic dialects. How much this particular aspect of their language affects their future learning, we do not know.

For argument's sake, let us take two of Maria's simplistic categories: those who will not have much trouble with standard, and those who will — Alberta and Rita, for example.

With Alberta, the trouble will not be interference from her home dialect. At primary school she will accommodate readily to the few differences between her standard and the school's, and possibly may not experience much trouble until she runs into certain registers used by academics, technicians and so forth, though teachers would be well employed all the time watching for language habits particular to her sex.[14] The trap for Alberta is that once she's getting along in the school language successfully, there is a danger that some of her narrow linguistic attitudes will ripen, not to say rot. This is especially dangerous, as Alberta is of the class likely to become a teacher. Early in life she needs to confront differences in language due to region, social class and ethnicity so that in later life her instincts will incline in the direction of tolerance and reason. Her language course, therefore, as well as strengthening her native dialect, should be one that aims to give her an understanding of the validity and strengths of other dialects and other languages. She automatically uses the all-powerful standard English. Her language teachers have a formidable task. For reasons I will explain later, I don't think that task should be left to foreign language studies. It should be tackled from grade one, in the context of learning English. It is the multicultural equivalent of a health course.

Rita requires very different teaching. Her period of bi-dialectism will be much longer, her paths much thornier. The time put into opening up Alberta's inborn narrowness goes into more intensive and more controlled language work for Rita. Her teacher has to know much more about language than Alberta's when it comes to the details of analysing the significant differences of vocabulary, pronunciation and syntax between Rita's dialect and standard dialect. (Which does not rule out the possibility that Alberta's teacher could have the tougher assignment.) The point about Rita is that it is much harder to plunge into the standard English of reading and writing. She is closer to the situation of the non-speakers.

The logic of Rita's case is to teach via the dialect, as we find it. We should remember, however, that her dialect may not be quite the same as the local working-class dialect. If it differs from the regional dialect, we might try to find out whether some of Rita's experience has been in yet another language. Possibly her mother and grandmother speak very little English.

Teaching reading (of standard) via a dialect requires a great deal of oral work. It therefore requires small groups and plenty of time. The teacher's task is to know the differences between dialect and standard well enough to ease the learner over any possible interference of the dialect with standard. Oral work, based on pictures, painting, drama, walks and informal chats, can be recorded by the teacher to provide a quantity of appropriate reading texts. Or, if already published readers are suitable in content, the reading is preceded by much oral work and rehearsal of likely difficulties. In matters of vocabulary the new words in standard have to be learnt in addition to the dialect terms. In syntax, new structures are drilled by the methods developed for second-language learning.

None of these techniques is novel, nor, with practice, especially difficult. More than usual, they need time, resources and linguistically rational teachers — all in short supply in Rita's kind of school. The problem, therefore, is to have these resources and techniques within the grasp of most classroom teachers, to whom they may not be merely novel but actually repugnant. It is not a programme, obviously, to be imposed from above by a keen multicultural principal or inspectorate. Rita needs sensitized, trained teachers working to a coherent year-by-year plan if her own knowledge and the time available are going to be effectively used.

Though each needs a different approach, Alberta and Rita are both English-speakers, one no more proper than the other. Let us turn now to those whose home language — that is, the one they speak and understand best when they start school — is not English.

As with the English-speakers, we are really talking about a continuum, with at one end usually the kid who has picked up a deal of English from being born in the country, and at the other the completely new arrival with not a word of English. These are what schools generally call the migrant problem, but which multiculturalists, we hope, would see as seams of wealth beneath our flat linguistic plains.

The degree of knowledge of English is not the only complication here. Many immigrants come from highly complex language situations, some of which could teach us a lot about how to cope with multilingual, multicultural problems. Yugoslavia recognizes three major languages — Slovenian, Macedonian and Serbo-Croatian — five dialects of Serbo-Croatian and several minority languages such as Albanian and Hungarian. It provides amply, by way of publications, schooling and so forth for its great diversity, and does so from markedly fewer material resources than many richer countries which by comparison scarcely provide for language minorities at all.

Let us take Italian migrants as an example. Following the great demographic trend of modern times in leaving the land for the industrial cities, many have moved into Italian cities or to near-by European countries, especially France, Germany and Switzerland. Migration to Australia and the Americas is a far-flung arm of the same movement, and Italians form the largest group among Australia's non-English-speaking immigrants. It is a forced migration, of people needing to find work and wanting to improve their children's future. Almost by definition, migrants are not highly schooled people (see reports of the Commission of Inquiry into Poverty in Australia), and they come from regions considered in their home country as the most backward economically and the most traditional culturally. In countries where regional dialects and languages are strong and numerous, even in cities, migrants will almost inevitably be dialect-speakers.

In the Italian case, to continue the example, regional dialects are on the whole mutually unintelligible and very different from standard. Standard Italian developed from one of the dialects (Tuscan) and besides having the stamp of that dialect, by now it also has the various characteristics of a language used as an official medium by a wide variety of speakers. Hence, to many Italians, the standard is not only different in accent, vocabulary and syntax, but it is also seen as opposed in some ways to the home language, the language of intimate, everyday life. Thus not only country people but also many educated city people prefer to use dialect in many situations.

Perhaps it's worth illustrating how different dialects may be from standard. Here is a sentence in standard Italian:[15]

Non puoi portartelo via con te quando te ne vai.

(You can't take it with you when you go.)

In the dialect of the Veneto, a northern region of great emigration, the same sentence would read:

No te pol miga portateo via quando che te va.

In Sicilian, also the language of many emigrants, it reads:

Nun tu po purtari cu tia quannu ti ni vai.

To the eye, these are clearly related languages. To the ear, the relationship scarcely matters. It is possible to be fluent in one and be baffled by the others. For practical purposes in teaching young children, these are separate languages.

Variations on this Italian example could be repeated for other Mediterranean countries, and for the Asian and African countries from which increasing emigration is to be expected. Until the recent unlamented passing of the colonels, Greek schools used a high variety, Katharevousa, barely comprehensible to demotic-speakers. Arabic, too, has a literary as well as many popular varieties, again mutually unintelligible even to sophisticated speakers. It is safe to say that quite a few home languages of immigrants scarcely exist in written form, and very, very few have materials suitable for teaching.

How do we navigate these linguistic archipelagos?

Let us go back to Maria's types again. I have already said something about Rita, who has some English, but I have yet to discuss maintaining her language. In addition, we have Soula who knows a standard, demotic Greek, and Tina who knows only a rather rare dialect. Neither Soula nor Tina has much English.

Soula appears to present the straightest case for initial bilingual schooling. She has a language we should be able to find teachers for. She could therefore be taught initially in her home language and steadily introduced to spoken and written English, provided teachers could be found. At some time during primary schooling she should become effectively bilingual, and able to pursue secondary and tertiary studies in either or both languages, at will.

The educational virtues of such an approach are still argued about. Does it help maintain the home language? Certainly — the point hardly needs making. Does it prove effective, even perhaps more so, for the learning of English? Impossible to say. Bilingual schooling on any scale scarcely exists in the conditions we are concerned with, and where it does the number of variables makes tight research impossible. Does bilingual schooling perhaps give kids a better grip on other school subjects by enabling them to get into maths, social studies and so forth straight away in the medium they are most at home in? Again, it is impossible to say for initial learners who do after all learn to speak English pretty quickly. For older learners, however, there is probably some gain in bilingual teaching.

I think all we can answer to these questions is that *politically* bilingual schooling is eminently justifiable, and educationally it still looks a reasonable bet. Indeed, in situations where a regional group is claiming the right to schools in its own language – the Basques, for example – the issue is only political, and the effectiveness of teaching in both home and official languages is not measured against progress in the official language. The fact that so much of our thinking about using ethnic languages in school is dogged by worries about how the kids will get on in English tells us a lot about the status of English- and non-English-speakers and next to nothing about human learning. The English-speaking world suffers from glossophobia – a state of believing that a second language, like alcohol, can be tolerated by the educated classes but does more harm than good to the lower orders. Not everyone finds multilingualism so forbidding. The Somali for instance deliberately keep their own language, with its large poetic literature, oral; and use an entirely foreign language (Arabic, Italian or English) for official transactions.[16] Multilingualism is a very common human talent.

To me, to make Soula's schooling bilingual from the word go seems only common sense. We must of course satisfy the necessary political condition that she does so with her parents' and community's general support, and that from the teaching end her whole progress through school is seriously conducted. In particular we have to recognize that Soula will probably be in an unusual situation. Even if she is in a migrant area, there will probably not be a majority in the school taking a fully bilingual course. For reasons I will go into shortly and which apply to Tina, most will probably be starting in English. Those taking Greek bilingually are likely to be a minority and if they are not, it will probably be because Greek students have been bussed into a central school, which itself poses some problems of isolation, maybe a certain ghettoism. Further, Soula will have eventually to cope with two teachers – one Greek, one English – both of whom could have pretty uppity views about the quality of Soula's linguistic background. These are all obvious dangers, but I would risk them because the return seems to be worth while. Some ghettoism seems inescapable, and even desirable, if we are interested in the survival of minority cultures.

Most of these circumstances mean that Soula's linguistic education is going to take up a lot more time than usual. No harm in that, perhaps, since the rewards are double. But it does impose on schools the obligation to make her whole curriculum as coherent and efficient as possible. No doubt that should be true for everyone, but in practice we put up with a fair bit of repetition, and gaps and wandering about in courses for the sake of allowing teachers independence and pupils room to express their interests. The danger for Soula is that her special courses will separate her a certain amount, maybe a whole lot, from her natural age grade, and that her acquaintance with the ordinary curriculum could become scrappy unless it is well co-ordinated from one year to the next and covers similar ground to other classes. Above all, people will worry if progress in English looks slow.[17]

Naturally we welcome any evidence which suggests that bilingual programmes improve English performance a bit.[18] We could logically also welcome evidence that they made not much difference to English performance, because improving English is not the primary aim anyway. What we can never welcome is the comparatively weak linguistic levels (especially in reading and writing, but often also in discussions) that we perceive daily in many children and which we assume must reach back into their families and communities.

Soula, of course, represents a certain large segment of an important community. Living from infancy within a mile of her school she nevertheless arrives unable to speak English. Asked at a conference in Melbourne some years ago how he would teach such children, Paulo Freire asked back: 'Why do they arrive at school speaking no English?' The group then swapped a few pointed stories – of the Greek woman who soon learnt a second language in Australia, but it was Italian, not English; and of the executive who let slip that his company preferred to have mixed nationalities on the assembly line so that they could not communicate with one another.

To a large extent, Soula's progress in English, as in Greek, depends on family and community. In this she is no different from any other children. We have fallen into the habit of writing off the first generation of migrants and we compensate for our neglect by promising to do something for the second. For some kids it works; for most it's an illusion.[19] The exploitation of the first generation blights the chances of the next. To respect Soula's home language by providing bilingual programmes is a major rapprochement of the school to Soula's community. Who knows where it could lead? Not, I suspect, to Soula's immediate translation to the great wide world of educational opportunity. More likely to a greater solidarity and understanding between school and community. The question then becomes, solidarity for what? For the right of the whole community to education in English and

Greek? To the civil right to use Greek without being molested or subtly discriminated against? For employment rights in Greek?

Tina presents a radically different case – in my opinion a real problem. The argument for bilingual teaching is based on very important assertions about identity and rights. But Tina's regional dialect defies all practicable solutions – or more precisely, its status does. It is a dialect little known to scholars and regarded even in its homeland as rustic and inadequate. Asked if she speaks her national language, Tina echoes her parents in answering, 'Only a dialect.' Far from there being a literature in her dialect, there is not even an agreed method of writing it down. Tina may by chance find a teacher who speaks it, but still not be able to learn reading or writing through her home language. In fact, I have usually found that teachers who speak a regional dialect are not willing to use it in school because of its very low status.

It is impossible, unfortunately, to imagine a programme able to cope with the hundreds of such low-status languages and dialects. Some regional languages are very well studied and do support a vigorous written culture. Both of these conditions are necessary, I think, to make a language accessible from afar. In a large Spanish centre, for example, it would be possible to provide a Saturday morning school, and it would be just as logical to offer Galician and Catalan as to offer only Castilian to Spanish immigrants. But in most cases we are dealing with neglected languages, and our practical choice is really limited to starting teaching English with an ESL approach. With that at least we can hope to guarantee a permanent trained group of teachers. Without that guarantee, we're only mucking about. Yet even with adequate ESL provisions, the minor minorities have not had fully equal treatment. A richness in them has been by-passed. Something obviously distinctive in their culture and intellectual skill has been ruled out of order. The 'only a dialect' inferiority they arrived with has been officially confirmed. Linguistically, they are from nowhere.

It seems to me that the only real chance of reinforcing Tina's cultural identity through language is by introducing her to the standard most closely related to her dialect. So far I have emphasized the difference between her dialect and standard because I was concentrating on the all-important question of initial teaching of reading and writing, to which the dialect seemed inappropriate, and the standard even more so, since as well as also being a foreign language it is limited in usefulness compared with English. However, when she is older – towards secondary school, say – she will be more conscious of her nationality and hence of any relationships that may exist between her home language and its nearest national standard. Probably, within her community, the standard national language will serve as a lingua franca as it does in the homeland. Tina therefore stands to gain culturally from a knowledge of it. She will, however, be studying it as a foreign language, not bilingually. Her home language, unfortunately, appears to be incompatible with any feasible school system.

I don't know whether these remarks apply to all minority groups. It is likely that some will have emigrated out of disaffection with their homeland, and not see their own culture adequately represented in any of the accessible standards. Language differences are after all one of the prime causes of rivalry, bitterness and open warfare. However, in the case of the two large emigrant groups I have exemplified — Italians and Greeks — it is perfectly reasonable to offer the standard because it is widely used within the ethnic community and opens the way to thriving and vigorous national cultures. To increase the host country's openness to these cultures in any way at all could only do good.

Linguistic optimists would welcome developing the cultural depth that can come from fusing the insights of many diverse cultures. Schools could deliberately extend migrant pupils' bilingualism and extend the foreign language teaching of English-speakers. As well, we have good reason to broaden every pupil's conception of the variety of English and the social dimensions of language.

Unfortunately there are not many such optimists around, and little reason why there should be. In most of the English-speaking world bilingual programmes in primary school are still extremely rare, scarcely sufficient to give us an idea of the problems, much less the solutions. The problem indeed is the simple basic one of convincing anyone that it's worth trying. And second-language teaching is in a state of decline. The traditional studies of French and German in secondary school are falling away, and though community languages are occasionally introduced, the total number of language students reaching any appreciable level of competence is declining.

Both the narrowness of English teaching and the demoralized state of second-language teaching have clear social origins. The majority group's perception of language — that standard English is all that is needed to get on in the world — finds its way into school via the prejudices of pupils, teachers and teacher-trainers. It is enshrined in examinations and hence in qualifications and conditions of employment. On a very wide scale it is reinforced by the international ascendancy of Anglo-American English.

There are also plausible in-school reasons for the flaccidity of second-language teaching. The tradition has been to teach 'major' languages from a middle-class English viewpoint. In the most traditional methods this has resulted in translation being the chief activity. In modern methods the spoken language has been put first but the perspective remains middle class or academic Anglo-American. Learners are asked to identify themselves with a tourist or overseas student as a central character. Necessary language is defined in terms of the everyday needs of such a character. Progression in structures and in vocabulary is rapid and requires a high level of abstract analysis. Certainly, since the growth of audio-lingual methods, teaching techniques have become much more effective and the aims, to some extent, more realistic. But teaching materials still reflect the restricted academic role of language in the curriculum. We are indeed still close to the time when universities were apt to require a foreign language for selection, and foreign language was the distinguishing subject of the A stream. This aristocratic tradition, combined with unevenness or even total lack of material outside the 'major' languages, throws a big load on teachers. A language course has to be very systematically structured over a long period, and to be interesting needs to bring in topical, local material. Very few teachers would have the time or training needed for such a formidable job. Normally, a teacher can only hope to supplement ready-made materials. The more unsuitable the ready-made, the harder they are to supplement. Well-produced, flexible, democratic materials (and teachers) in a variety of languages would need to be produced in an organized way before some languages could be satisfactorily studied at all.

Let me sum up the language question:

English, democratically studied and taught, I have argued, is the common element of a multicultural language programme. Given that, a multicultural curriculum first looks for students who are potentially bilingual. For them, it provides initial instruction in their stronger language, in tandem with their second language. The aim is to have them literate in both English and their home language as early as possible. In the suburbs where we would be likely to find Maria's imaginary school – be they in Australia, Britain, Canada or the USA – we can visualize a network of language teaching that could provide a bilingual education for the children of at least four different foreign-language-speaking groups. But, ideally, this should begin at primary school and be serviced by richer programmes of teacher education.

In rural areas or city districts with few immigrants, a bilingual policy would usually be impracticable. In that case a multicultural curriculum aims to provide for pupils who have a second language in their cultural background, but one which, for reasons either of its obscurity or our lack of resources, cannot be adequately taught, that they be taught in English, if necessary as a foreign language, and later in their school life offered teaching in the national standard closest to their home language. Both these and bilingual pupils are offered not only direct language instruction but also normal curricular subjects (and assessments) using their non-English languages as media.

Finally a multicultural curriculum is tolerant of dialect variations in English and uses the pupils' home dialects constructively in teaching

English. And within its language courses it aims to cultivate linguistic tolerance in children whose only language is standard English.

To achieve these aims, language teachers have to be prepared to examine not only the varied backgrounds and skills of the pupils but also many of the present assumptions made about the languages to be taught.

Conclusion

I have many times emphasized that both in the detail of curriculum and in its total organization, a multicultural school is a co-operative, democratic institution. It remains to repeat, by way of concluding, that this is an ideal statement. Our present society is stratified, competitive and intolerant of cultural difference. While it remains so, the multi-cultural school will struggle to emerge. Multiculturalism is ultimately an aspect of equality. Intolerance, discrimination and stratification are tools of inequality, used to divide people or reinforce existing divisions among them. Immigration itself is an aspect of the unequal distribution of international wealth and the unequal division of the national labour force. The relationships between ethnicity and social and educational disadvantage are inseparable from our social structure. Schools unaware of these forces and unprepared to confront discrimination and inequality where they see it, in or out of the classroom, are in no position to bring their pupils to grips with the realities of their society.

I have tried to suggest that a broad view of multiculturalism could not only lead us to re-examine the curriculum all over again, but also give us a sharper focus on the content of a national curriculum. A narrower view of the issue, I think, obscures the causes of our present problems and consigns multicultural education to the exotic fringes of curriculum.

Notes

1 See, for example, *Poverty and Education in Australia*, fifth main report of the Commission of Inquiry into Poverty, Canberra, Australian Government Publishing Service, 1976, particularly ch. 2.

2 For a very interesting explanation, see Barbara Falk, *Personal Identity in a Multi-cultural Australia*, Hawthorn, Australian Council for Educational Research, [1978]. She argues that 'members of both dominant and dominated groups would, in a State that lacks [democratic, multicultural] integration, be insecure in personal identity' and 'personal identity is an internal moral rep-

resentation of who I ought to be, formed by participation in a specific ethnic group.'

3 See, for example, Paulo Freire, *Education: the Practice of Freedom*, London, Writers and Readers Co-operative, 1976, and Frantz Fanon, *The Wretched of the Earth*, New York, Grove Press, 1966.

4 See in particular Gwyn Dow's chapter in this volume (pp. 147ff.). Douglas Holly's *Beyond Curriculum: Changing Secondary Education*, St Albans, Paladin, 1974, develops these points forcibly, and I am much indebted to him.

5 My musical example owes much to the ideas expounded by Graham Vuillamy: 'What counts as school music', in Geoff Whitty and M.F.D. Young, *Explorations in the Politics of School Knowledge*, Driffield, Nafferton Books, 1976.

6 See the resources listed in *Radical Education Dossier*, 7, 1978, p. 28. There is a Multicultural Curriculum Resources Project at 123 Church St, Richmond, Victoria. A list of London-based bookshops specializing in multiracial and ethnic materials is published by the Centre for Urban Educational Studies, 34 Aberdeen Park, London N5 2BL (send a stamped, addressed envelope). The same Centre also publishes *Practical Guidelines for Assessing Children's Books for a Multi-ethnic Society*.

7 This too is discussed at length by Holly, op. cit.

8 For an accessible account of the main linguistic arguments, see Peter Trudgill, *Sociolinguistics*, Penguin, 1974.

9 Notably William Labov, but see again Trudgill, op. cit., for a summary. Labov's important article, 'The logic of non-standard English', is widely anthologized.

10 *Language in Education*, Language Development Project Phase 1, Curriculum Development Centre, Canberra, September 1979, p. 329.

11 Ibid., p. 316.

12 Ibid., p. 336.

13 Ibid., p. 338.

14 *New Society*, 12 October 1978, reports research into 'chauvinist talk' which claims that sex differences exist not only in the content of conversation but also the structural forms used. Women, for example, ask more questions, pass more compliments of the 'that's interesting' kind, and throw in more attention-holding phrases such as 'Y'know'.

15 The examples were kindly supplied by Professor Cali and Giancarlo Rizzardi of University College, Cork.

16 B.W. Andrzejewski, 'Poetry in Somali society' in J.B. Pride and Janet Holmes (eds), *Sociolinguistics*, Penguin, 1972. In the same volume, A.P. Sorenson describes South American groups in which it is normal for a person to have control of five or more languages.

17 In a paper presented to a conference on bilingual education sponsored by the National Institute of Education in Washington DC in February 1977, Lily Wong Fillmore, an experienced supporter of

bilingual teaching, picked out some fundamental problems of bilingual teaching as practised in the USA. Among these were: that bilinguals get cut off from the main school programme and do not profit from the skills and concepts embodied in the main school curriculum; that teachers and classes consequently try to take on too much and become exceptionally anxious that they will not be be able to cover everything expected of them, especially in English; that the use of the two languages is insufficiently planned; that the home language taught at school is not the same language actually used at home; that native-speaking aides are inadequate teachers, and not always proficient in the actual home language of the learners; that the cultural attitudes of teachers and aides can clash with those of the students; that in general teachers are inadequately trained to exploit the learning styles peculiar to different cultures.

18 See L.R. Claydon, Tony Knight and Marta Rado (eds), *Curriculum and Culture: Schooling in a Pluralist Society*, Sydney, Allen & Unwin, 1977.

19 *European Communities Supplement, Bulletin,* Brussels, 12/76, p. 38.

Chapter 5

A core curriculum — a political solution to a social crisis

Doug White

The curriculum — from certainty to doubt

In the 1960s and early 1970s, particularly in Victoria, control of the curriculum passed to some extent from the central authority to the teachers. In response to new responsibilities many teachers' thinking and teaching were revitalized. We shall present Maria here as typical of many young teachers with whom she came through university who are motivated by a striving for equality. Her anger is directed at those social practices and structures that inhibit the development of equal relationships between people She is opposed to sexism and the oppression of women; she is opposed to discrimination against people from non-Anglo-Saxon origins; and she is opposed to class distinctions. In short, she believes in a classless society. However, old-style socialist thought, particularly that which emanates from the left of the trade union movement, does not interest her very much. While she feels sympathetic to the authors of these ideas, she does not think of herself as a member of the working class.

State socialism strikes her as being necessarily bureaucratic and requires too much subordination of individuality. Her notions of equality are accompanied by a belief in personal autonomy, and she favours an equality of entry into a common life — an association of independent persons who are equally valued rather than an equality which requires a sameness of ideology and belief. In school terms she does not favour the equality imposed by a uniformity of content and behaviour, but an equality accompanied by and achieved through a variety of interests and personalities.

Maria's thinking has evolved, and is no longer what it was when she first began her post-graduate course in education. Then, like most of her friends, she vaguely thought that autonomy, independence and equality should be made directly available to the pupils. A quick reading of Ivan Illich and Paulo Freire supported her beliefs that ordinary schooling restricted the autonomy of the person and reproduced the division of classes by dividing certificated professionals from the rest of the people. And, although being inducted into her professional role presented her with something of a dilemma, it was not unresolvable or long lived.

It was resolved for two reasons, as she could see now looking back on the past, so recent in time and so distant in experience. One was her experiences in the feminist movement, which had shown her the significance of consciousness-raising − for, while it was true that women were oppressed, it was also true that formal changes alone would not remove their inequality. Reforms such as the introduction of equal pay or changes in the laws of the family and divorce needed to be accompanied by a change in the psychology of women themselves. The man-in-the-head, as one of her friends used to say, had to be done away with along with the man in the principal's chair. There was therefore a reason for being a teacher, and a recognition that while everybody can recognize unequal pay, the recognition of women's cultural position comes less easily. In applying one of the classical dicta of teaching − teaching for cultural understanding − Maria found herself challenging the given structures of society.

The other experience which affected her early views on the proper approach of the teacher was the emphasis in her teacher training, an emphasis reinforced by her first year of teaching, on the need for an organizational structure if any teaching was to occur at all. She occasionally relapsed into settling for her earlier ideology that freedom, independence and equality could come to the classroom by proclamation and immediate practice. She soon learned, and relearnt, that the result was chaos. For both pragmatic reasons, and on the basis of a more clearly worked out strategy, she no longer regards teaching to a pre-organized plan as a denial of her most strongly felt beliefs. This of course makes her specially irritated with Betty's celebration of spontaneity (see p. 15).

Maria, that is, has by now found a teaching role without falling for elitist professionalism; and she has found a way of being organized without falling for a belief in structure as an end in itself. Now she faces new problems, and as the habit of reflecting upon the sources of her own activities is more developed, the crisis is more apparent.

Fatima's position epitomizes her worries (see pp. 18 ff.). The communal life of the Turkish village is obviously inadequate for finding a way through an urbanized society; the communal life also includes ways of treating women which Maria finds repressive. Yet it is some form of communal life that Maria and her friends yearn for − a life which has meaning and purpose renewed by the direct association between people. By contrast, the relation between the pupils and the content of the year ten integrated studies course seems superficial and of only passing interest. Nor does the school's 'multiculturalism' as a programme of Turkish cooking, Greek dancing and Lebanese cultural evenings satisfy her. The variety put into the life of the school is enjoyable enough, and useful in enhancing tolerance and appreciation, but Maria sees it now as something akin to the empty nationalism worked up to sell World Series Cricket. That is, bits and pieces of culture are displayed and used for purposes which have little to do with the life that produced them. Multiculturalism, as usually practised, Maria now thinks, is a sham, and yet the preservation of village cultures in an urban society is also doomed. In more pessimistic moments Maria wonders whether the effect of her own teaching is not the destruction of a social life which gained meaning through being lived rather than through consciousness and theorizing. She knows that a theoretical understanding of social life is necessary, but is unable to see how to act on it in or out of school. Her thoughts tend to nostalgia and fantasy, and the practices she takes up are far short of what she thinks desirable.

Unemployment and the curriculum

The other source of Maria's crisis is the existence of growing youth unemployment. She knows that not all of her classmates from her teacher-training year are in as fortunate a position as she is. She has a teaching job. It is becoming increasingly apparent that the pupils she is teaching are to leave the school, and go — nowhere. Structural unemployment indicates that the society has no place for many of the people she is teaching. The cultural understanding that she has attempted to make the basis for her teaching makes sense only if there is a society in which it can be used. Like others of her generation she had assumed that the society, and its economy, could be taken as a functioning entity, even if not a very satisfactory one. Now it is clear that this is not the case. A year or two earlier, Maria would have argued that jobs should be of a kind that meet the needs of the people. She still thinks so, but that thought now seems something of a luxury when there are few jobs of any kind. Having worked through her earlier difficulties of finding a teaching role and a structure of teaching practice, Maria now confronts larger problems. These are the relations of the school to a larger culture. She is one of many who have challenged the values and human relations which once underlay the old curriculum. Now the problem is that of the relations betwen the curriculum and the social structures of work, and social organization generally — issues previously inadequately considered. Maria's curriculum cannot proceed very far without solving the problems which the movement for a core curriculum is also attempting to solve; but she enters into the consideration of these problems in a quite different position from that of the powerful conservative and narrow interest-groups associated with the promulgation of the official core curriculum.

Maria rejects the idea that the cause of unemployment lies in a failure of the schools. David's new-found enthusiasm for operationally defined objectives is not convincing to her, and those members of staff who have found new reasons for the tired restatement of the principles of hard work and basic training seem scarcely worth answering. Nevertheless, Maria feels responsible for her pupils. At least they should not be disadvantaged by comparison with those in other schools. The notions of equality and the autonomous person become more distant, and she finds a pragmatic response to the problems of social survival overtaking her efforts. It is in this spirit that the proposals for basic and core curriculum, made to the school from a variety of sources, come to her attention.

Why the popularity of a core curriculum?

The moves for a core curriculum come with a variety of support. There are of course those who think that teachers and pupils have got out of hand in recent years, and that it is time to reassert control. Spokesmen of the Employers' Federation, for example, have stated such opinions. There are those who are concerned that some natural consensus among the people is breaking up, and it is time that the elements were brought together in an atmosphere which co-ordinates local initiative and central control. Increasingly, such views are expressed by spokesmen of the major political parties. There are others who are concerned that individualism and variation have gone too far in encouraging unrealistic attitudes towards work and the organization of social life among young people. And there are those who, fearing that all the certainties of life are going, feel that schools and school teachers have had something to do with this. It is safe to say that many parents, particularly migrant parents, are among the supporters of this view. In so far as their position is not articulated, the speakers from the political right appear to speak for them. Teachers are divided in their response, but many still defend their right to take responsibility for the curriculum, claiming that the school is the best place to determine the appropriate curriculum for its population.

The various proposals for a core curriculum do not deal with any of the educational or social issues which lead to present social ills. Instead they are, at best, attempts to achieve a superficial consensus. The curriculum changes of recent years were partly a response to a new situation, but they were also attempts to reform some outmoded conceptions and practices. A new basis for conflict has emerged. On the one hand there are attempts to stop a process, to consolidate and hold things as they are, even to reverse the direction of development. On the other there is the possibility of extending understanding and developing appropriate practices. The official moves for a core curriculum are all more or less of the first kind; whereas a programme of social reform could also produce a core curriculum which would entail in practice a reformed school–society relationship.

We have already seen that Maria and her deputy principal are highly suspicious of the local plan to impose a core curriculum on schools. One very important reason is that a core curriculum could vitiate all the attempts by Maria's group to design a new curriculum that might offer the pupils a more satisfying education – a point that I shall return to later in greater detail.

More immediately, Maria is worried by the emphasis presently placed on testing children's performance throughout the length and breadth of the country before anything really constructive has been said about the what-should-be-taught that is being tested. This sort of a programme in England, for example, is attracting massive funds at a time when massive economies afflict the schools. As far as Maria can see, nobody questions the importance of the basic skills that are to be tested; but perhaps the investment might be better put into finding out how to impart them. The testing, apart from being a waste of public money, seems to her an attempt to reassert central control.

The coincidence of the core-curriculum platform with the testing programme gives rise to the fear that only the trivial, measurable things count politically, and that the core curriculum will be a soft sell. But this view could be unjust to some of the supporters, who are no doubt as conscious as Maria is of the vagueness of all the propositions so far. Is it significant that, in all the plans, scant attention has been given to content? Is it significant that so much attention is paid to testing that cynics wonder if the exercise will not end, where it began, in devising methods of control? Is it significant that a careful attempt is being made to indicate that reforms will be democratic even though they appear to entail stronger central directives?

These blanket alternatives posit an interpretation that oversimplifies the issues (as most public statements tend to do too) in order to present the possibility that a show of populism could be offered to conceal political naivety at best or chicanery at worst.

Of course education is always political, and so the specific statement that recent moves are political rather than educational needs further analysis and argument. It is helpful to examine the old and new notions

115

of curriculum and the reasons for the differences between the two. The curriculum of a school system holds together a number of social necessities: the renewal of the common symbols and beliefs which the population of a nation has in common; the division of the people of that nation into a number of groups and social classes in a manner that appears natural and given; the regeneration of a group of culturally influential people (secular intellectuals in our time, priests in some other societies) who are able to examine, elaborate and renew the general beliefs without damage to the continuity of social organization; and the provision of a means of entry into social life which has for a hundred years or more meant an entry into the workforce. The content of the curriculum is so related to the structure and the culture of its society that it escapes public notice — that is, it is seen to be not at all politically controversial.

Some proposals for a core curriculum

Later in this chapter I shall attempt the analysis of why, although political intervention is seen by many to be necessary, a laid-down core curriculum is no longer so easily feasible. There appears to be a contradiction between the idea of education favoured by many teachers and the functioning of the society. Although no society can function if personal wishes and freedom (in the sense of absence of restraint) are valued over all else, this argument for a compulsory core curriculum is more of a propaganda point than a real representation of teacher opinion. Innovative teachers tend to favour the development of social relations that will enlarge their pupils' understanding of the meaning of their life — in a way which will help them develop as autonomously active persons within those relations regardless of apparently unequal intelligence or aptitude. These teachers take a 'cultural' approach, in the sense that they give pre-eminence to valuing their pupils equally, and they try to ameliorate the inequalities of entry into social life.

The old curriculum, in contrast, was devoted primarily to repeating the structural inequalities in society — the relations of employer to employed, of mental work to manual labour, of men to women. The values of the old curriculum were expressed in the practices associated with differentiated intelligence, competitiveness, possessive individualism, the curriculum for the boys and that for the girls, and the like. However, the teachers are themselves victims of the present distinction between culture and structure; for it is not possible to have a society without work and some equivalent of the family. Schools which were in the first place set up to serve the social organization, and to maintain the beliefs and values to justify it, have developed differently.

The integrated studies programme planned by Maria's group places culture to the fore. But schools cannot realize their hopes without resolving the relationship of the school to social life. While those in power would like to resolve that issue in a conservative fashion, it is not possible for the teachers acting alone to resolve it by more penetrating solutions.

The question for teachers such as Maria, if they are to accept a core curriculum at all, then becomes that of finding a content which is appropriate to a democratic culture and capable of being integrated with it. This amounts to a proposal for a core curriculum prepared by the teachers in alliance with parents and others who accept, on whatever grounds, a democratic and egalitarian way of life. In many cases this is expressed as equal access to material rewards or to pleasant and well-paid jobs, a desire which is impossible to achieve without a reconstruction of both the meaning of equality and the structures which prevent its fulfilment. That reconstruction, of course, cannot be completely carried through while the structure of social life, and the sources of political power, including work, remain authoritarian and unequal. It also requires a re-evaluation of some of the steps taken in recent years in the name of alternative and progressive education. Obviously any practicable core curriculum designed in opposition to unequal and authoritarian social structures cannot be total in this opposition – it must take account of political and economic realities. Neither can it be merely freely chosen – that is, on both political and cultural grounds it must be constrained by the limitations of what is practically possible and by such considerations as the pupils' and parents' demands for credentials. Moreover participation and democracy are not sufficient unless they are inherent in a project which will play a part in remaking culture and creating new structures.

Some of the recent proposals for a core curriculum indicate the tension between the maintenance of social power and the need for participation. In 1976, for example, the Ministry of Education informed teachers in the Canadian province of British Columbia that it had sought professional and public opinion on what was expected of schools. The reactions received led it to revise the 'goals' and 'learning outcomes' sought in the educational system, and teachers were told they 'must' teach all children according to the consequent new document.[1] This directive referred to a discussion that had preceded it when the Minister of Education had circulated a document entitled *What Should Our Children Be Learning?* in which three levels of curriculum were identified: 'that which *must* be learned, that which *should* be learned, and that which *may* be learned.' The core curriculum was defined as 'that which must be learned'. The booklet contained a response form, and by June 1977 over thirteen thousand usable responses had been returned to the Ministry.[2] Participation here was used to maintain old structures of social power. Maria knows enough of the history of populism to be wary of such moves.

In England, a Green Paper, *Education in Schools: a Consultative Document*, of 1977 proposed that there should be a review of educational authorities to establish a broad agreement 'on a framework for the curriculum, and on whether part of the curriculum should be protected because there are aims common to all schools and pupils at certain stages. These aims must include the achievement of basic literacy and numeracy at the primary stage'.[3] While the discussion, carried out in a much less directive manner than in British Columbia, seems to have been inconclusive, various kinds of monitoring tests have been devised which may be used by schools to compare the effects of their teaching with what are thought to be reasonable national standards.

In Australia a Core Curriculum and Values Education project for junior and middle levels of the secondary school is under way, sponsored by the national Curriculum Development Centre (CDC) and with Australian government funding (although primary and secondary education is the responsibility of the six state governments).

The CDC's proposal, circulated as a document called *Core Curriculum for Australian Schools*, reaffirms the principle of school-based curriculum to the extent that it opposes 'a national or state testing program' as 'retrogressive'. It recognizes that schools must 'adjust curricula to local circumstances, community interests and the differing learning requirements and characteristics of students', and that testing programmes have been shown 'to narrow teaching unduly'.[4] Maria and her deputy principal, of course, welcome this explicit statement of the dangers of external testing.

They are less satisfied with the document's approach to content in that, as presently stated, it seems to offer something for everybody, implicitly placing on an equal footing the teaching of car-driving with scientific and technological understanding, the study of English literature with clay-modelling; but at this stage the document is merely an outline that divides curriculum into nine areas about which further research and recommendations will be centred.

The proposal appears to meet popular demand for participation and negotiation of the curriculum, and to leave aside the distinctions between parents, teachers and pupils in entering the curriculum process. Given the problems that Maria has come to see − the problems of unemployment and the breakdown of the traditions of social class, family, neighbourhood and nation − the CDC appears to offer appearance without essence, democratic form without content.

While it repeatedly points to the necessity of anticipating change and producing a map that allows for dynamic change, it avoids fronting up to the nature of cultural change, and the means by which decision-making can be effected. Its failure to confront the conflicts endemic to modern societies may be seen as a retreat into moral agnosticism.

In short, it is difficult to assess the practical significance of these moves for a common core curriculum. Their intention is clearer, and is shown by their varying and common characteristics. There is in all cases an appeal to popular opinion and a direction to teachers, but the direction is not particularly restrictive because most of the curriculum remains untouched. Schools are to guarantee the acquisition of basic skills but otherwise the curriculum specification says almost nothing about content. The exercise, however, is a reminder that central authority exists, and that a society outside the wishes of the teacher (or pupils) is significant. Unlike those curricula which depend upon class, national feeling or truth – such as those in which history books set out the greatness of the Empire, school readers dwelt on nationalism and the Protestant Christian virtues, and science books told the story of nature – the only significant sources of curriculum design which exist outside the person spring from concern for social functioning. The society which believes in itself indoctrinates its pupils in its mysteries; that which merely functions has to elevate functioning itself to be the highest goal, hence words such as 'literacy', 'numeracy', 'oracy' and 'survival' litter curriculum discussion. The common content of education is arrived at by deciding what will enable students to take part in surviving – a word with a different meaning from living. Even the glorification of progress as measured by material products is not called upon as a cultural good to justify the social functioning. Rather, social life as it exists is its own end, and this social life appears to have neither history nor meaning.

The idea of a cultural map, mentioned earlier, at first sight, may appear as a gutsier notion. As Malcolm Skilbeck, (then) Director of the CDC, who is perhaps the chief advocate of the cultural map as the basis for a curriculum, put it in an earlier document:[5]

> A cultural-map curriculum ought to consist of both a way of identifying and analysing the principal features of culture which are of interest to us educationally, and a set of procedures for learning about, assessing, and, where desirable, modifying or re- constructing culture.

He went on to list among the principal tasks this one. 'The central themes and groupings of subject-matter in the curriculum need to be so defined as to correspond to the tendencies and features of contemporary culture which we are able to identify.' Maria would like a clearer idea of the culture to which the school curriculum could relate. She comes

119

to think, however, that nothing much has been actually said; the cultural map describes the surface features, and she wants to know both where it's all going and how its course may be changed. Relating the curriculum to the temporary names on the map sounds a bit too much like a flexible form of David's behavioural objectives. Perhaps she should have been warned by the language – the juxtaposition of culture with map could indicate the technocratic mind at work. Though, when questioned as to whether, by a map, he had in mind a model or a metaphor, Skilbeck admitted to a distrust of models.[6]

The societies of all nations have a core curriculum, in a sense, although the term is not normally used to describe the curriculum when it is not overtly common. A core curriculum in the broad sense refers to common values, and commonly accepted relations between people, even though people may be in opposition within the commonly accepted framework. A society, that is, may be divided on the basis of class, race, sex and religion and yet share a great deal, even a belief in the inevitability of these divisions.

When the term 'core curriculum', or 'common curriculum', is used and advocated, as it has been lately, we may infer several possible historical reasons. Among these, there is the possibility that a common framework has disappeared and must be recreated, that equality of entry into social life has been achieved, and hence there is no longer any social differentiation to be established by the schools within a common framework; that differentiation, though it will continue to exist, is no longer to be established by the schools, but is to be brought about by other means; that schools still produce differentiation, but do so in different ways. When we examine the reality, it is not very difficult to exclude some of these possibilities. Equality in fact has not been established, schools still play a large part in establishing differentiation, and the moves for a core curriculum appear to be a means of re-establishing both a common framework and a means of differential entry into it, but by new methods.

The moves for a common core curriculum that we have referred to usually come from governments or government-sponsored bodies. It is quite conceivable that a core curriculum could come about by the actions of teachers or of other groups of citizens, but this has not so far normally been the case. Given a recognition of what is a fairly obvious reality, that none of the government bodies concerned is anxious to establish a classless or equal society, the moves for a core curriculum can be seen as attempts to reconcile the maintenance of social cohesion with the continuation of social differentiation. For reasons that must be discovered and examined, if we want to know what is happening and to act sensibly, the moves for a core curriculum can be taken as attempts to resolve the problems of designing a curriculum when the very nature of its content has become a matter of differing opinions and doubt, when older modes of social stratification and differentiation no longer have support among many teachers, and when consensus must be established by a new means.

The dissolution of content; the reforms of the sixties

The rhetoric of classical liberalism, with its emphasis on individualism and division of labour, fitted well the requirements of industrial society. A division of people and schools developed to suit this prescription. In all the industrial countries, no matter what the apparent differences in school structures and organization, ways were found for offering courses with a professional, commercial or industrial orientation; but there were tensions over the balance between a liberal and a vocational education, a national or international outlook, and competitive or co-operative practices.[7]

An important change came in the mid–1960s, announced in educational terms as an emphasis on the structure of the disciplines, on historical and scientific method, on intellectual skills rather than particular content. The development of science in industry transformed the demands from particular content to general skills and formal theoretical knowledge which could be exerted on many contents. The changing world relationships appeared to make national content jingoist. The fluidity established by an apparent social mobility damaged the previous solidity of social structures and the educational institutions that supported them. In Australia, Victoria gives an example of teacher militancy that was both a response to, and a further cause of, the development of this fluidity. Within a few years an education based on a fixed or slowly changing content was devalued (most markedly in the first four years of secondary education). If the new situation had any common thread it was the concern with the process of intellectuality, and this threw the old content and structure into disorder; but a process cannot by itself provide content and structure. Intellectuality has itself become differentiated. On the one hand the creative act is seen as part of a relationship of people held together as an intellectual culture; on the other hand those relationships may be seen merely as 'communication', which becomes the process without content. These trends, which are most marked in Victoria, were evident in Europe and North America. In this sketch of the ideological background that Maria encountered, several observations have been linked. A weakening of emphasis on content and pre-ordained structure was associated with a new emphasis on intellectual skills and on pupils' acquisition of a sense of self-determination in areas that are important to them.

Established authority was questioned, if not put aside, as teacher militancy grew against a background of changing power structures both nationally and internationally.

Intellectuality, the intelligentsia and the curriculum

Maria was conscious of where she stood, historically speaking, in the changing scene. She saw the strengthening of the demand that a more general and more intellectual education be extended to all secondary school pupils not only as a response to technological developments but also as a response to teachers' growing awareness of the inequalities inherent in the traditional curriculum.

In the rapid changes which arose from the interpenetration of abstract thought with industrial process and social life the educational institutions and teachers took a leading part. Looked at more broadly, Maria conjectured that the intelligentsia's role, so far as it is possible to generalize, has been to interpret the symbols and ideals which govern relations between people while remaining in some respects outside these relations. Intellectuals have additionally formed communities extending beyond their particular nations or localities.

Paradoxically, however, this separation has also assisted in the alienation of the people in general, who are not conscious of their own meaning or roles. Intellectuals have historically provided a basis and justification for a class society, and generally gained secure existences in some niche provided by the ruling class, while remaining outside it. The ancient professions of law and medicine are notable examples.

Where intellectual communities once could serve to interpret society and transmit knowledge, the pressures in the modern world for intellectual elites to make new knowledge and thereby to shape societies has increased greatly.[8] Theory has become not only reflective but also directive: abstracted theory linked with multinational capital (also abstracted from local and national context) becomes a practical force which further blots out the old historically-formed national and community units.

It is this process which leads to the dislocation of the school from social life. In practice the school is asked to do quite contradictory things: to establish a particular place in society for its pupils, and to introduce them to the current intellectual/social forms which in their movement wipe out the stability upon which traditional social life and particular lives depend. Perhaps it is this which explains the listlessness and disorientation of her pupils. Maria wonders where she fits into such a picture.

The changes that she is trying to analyse, she concludes, delocalize social life, weaken if not dissolve the structures of social life, and make direct relationships increasingly rare. She enjoys the freedom to think, work and make human contacts that transcend local cultures and structures, all of which makes her think proudly of herself as cosmopolitan; but the price has also been an emptiness resulting from the destruction of those elements of life which require direct personal involvement and exchange. Maria's steady look at her options makes her conclude that she has an advantage over her pupils, and so she can try to help them towards understanding the analysis she has been undertaking. This view implies that she actively prizes the autonomy and insight that she has been lucky enough to develop. It leads her to see, as a teacher, the importance of fostering the pupils' critical self-knowledge and social awareness. She has to distinguish very carefully, she realizes, between the pressures on the intelligentsia to become a part of greater power agglomerates (with the concomitant greater complexity of new knowledge), and the possibilities of enjoying membership of less powerful and less elitist intellectual groups that, while creative, like artists and the best teachers, can fight against mystification and the temptation to enjoy manipulative powers.

Modern society allocates power to many groups that have to be reckoned with in the search for personal independence. One large group which has formed because of the development of technology — a social as well as a material technology — is an offshoot of the work of theorists. The most important of these technological developments is the electronic medium, in which a form of universality is developed without the re-creation of communal life. Television productions manufacture stories which have little relationship to a life anybody could actually lead, although with some relationship to everyday fantasies. They are not in principle different to the attempts to manufacture new organisms by processes of genetic engineering, or the activities of sensitivity trainers in the manufacture of social relations. These creative groups which have formed as a consequence of scientific and technological development do not stand in the same relationships to the people as did earlier intellectuals; they do not elaborate, explore and give meaning to communal life and practice, but rather make the conditions of social life via industrial technology and the manipulation of popular taste. In so doing they are constrained by the level of scientific development and to some extent by the character of nature (including human nature); but they are not constrained by the needs and values created by the interaction of people in a community. These intellectuals construct social life, rather than interpret its meaning and significance.

123

Doug White

Restoration of community

Maria's pupil, Fatima, seeks a freedom in human relationships that puts her in conflict with her parents and with the traditions of her local ethnic community. The price of her achievement in a new society is a re-adjustment of values entailing a diminution of her involvement in the traditional forms of life upheld by her parents. On the one hand greater individuality, fluidity and equality have been created for Fatima; on the other hand she may feel so lost that she becomes prey to manipulation and subject to identity crises. This emptiness has been filled, in part, by communal contemplation, encounter groups, and other trendy forms of 'togetherness'. The core curriculum is a political response. Its emphasis on literacy and numeracy — which both bring about and allow people to handle the changes in social structures — indicates a recognition of the social reality; its populist character exploits the realization enjoyed by parents and many others that people cannot live without structures. The only structures it can offer are those of the old authorities; and its content is subordinated to the apparently participatory — but, more likely, manipulated — forms of decision-making.

The problem of the curriculum needs restating. The core of the traditional curriculum, whether the term was used or not, linked together an historical and national past, and served the structures of society into which young people were to be fitted. That curriculum thus had the authority of tradition and of the state in maintaining the social structures. Nowadays the proposal for a 'core' is a way of maintaining the *status quo* — via state power with a populist additive in some cases, and via a dynamic consensus limited to what is immediate. The alternative which seems necessary, but is not mentioned, is the development of a core which draws from tradition and accumulated knowledge in the creation of a *new* social life. Hence the core must be intellectually-based, for there is no other way of understanding fully the situation we are in; and it must lead towards the formation of a social life which is both enjoyed and understood. The old curriculum has been destroyed by the interpenetration of intellectuality with social life. Likewise, what replaces it needs to be derived from an intellectual understanding of the situation we are in; but the relationship of intellectuals to society has changed so that they are not fulfilling their traditional role of interpretation and clarification.

These changes are not due to any act of will on the part of intellectuals, teachers or anyone else. Many intentional acts are taken, including the active destruction of the old forms of bureaucratic authority, of patriarchy and the like. Such acts are responses to the wider world of freely made association that has become visible to us all

124

in recent years. The vision became possible, however, only when a large part of production, gaining a momentum of its own, long ago ceased to be related to the most important wants and needs of communities, and became part of a world system. The larger vision was paradoxically coupled with increasing loss of control to act on it.

The computer and its programmes – the software – are the electronic-mechanical association of the parts of the world. The craftsman, a part of a community, was long ago replaced by the assembly line in the factory; now the assembly lines are co-ordinated on a world scale and instructed by abstract technique, and the nation is dissolved as the community once was. Our wider world can be seen on the one hand as a network of freely-associating persons, on the other as the market of transnational corporations and the recipient of satellite-transmitted entertainment. First the old cultures are wiped out, and secondly a part of the population becomes redundant. The old communities cannot be reconstituted. As Marx and Engels said long ago:[9]

> Constant revolutionising of production, uninterrupted disturbance
> of all social conditions, everlasting uncertainty and agitation
> distinguish the bourgeois epoch from all earlier ones. All fixed,
> fast-frozen relations with their train of ancient and venerable
> prejudices and opinions are swept away, all new-formed ones
> become antiquated before they can ossify. All that is solid melts
> into air, all that is holy is profaned, and man is at last compelled
> to face with sober senses, his real conditions of life, and his relations
> with his kind.

To return from this prophetic vision to the more limited view of this chapter, it seems that the core curriculum is a poor attempt at a holding operation.

To Maria and her colleagues, as the problem becomes clearer, the task becomes more daunting. The notion of the core curriculum, when looked at more closely, appears as a problem of the relationship of school to society. The questions of basics (what every child should know) and of who should define them do not lead to ways of understanding and appropriate action; they are distracting issues. The school has taken part in its own dislocation – in changing its old relationship with society. It has done so in a manner about which there was little choice, for the demands of a more intellectually based flexible education have cut across the traditional ways in which people have been held together in families, religious groups, ethnic communities, neighbourhoods and industry-based association.

The specific contribution of schools to the evolving industrial society lay more in their hidden curriculum than in recorded syllabuses. The tripartite division of the school system, sometimes of the individual school, into professional, trade/commercial, and general (thinkers, intelligent doers and the semi-skilled/unskilled) grew to fit what was seen as the class system. Although the rationale was seldom verbalized, except for some naive and crude attempts like those in the Norwood Report,[10] it was nevertheless tacitly developed and accepted by teachers as a sub-group of the intellectual culture. In a similar manner they more recently became disenchanted with the model which they recognized as too static in its production of elites and too ineffectual in educating the masses. Many teachers, like Maria, put those two things together as arising from anachronistic inequalities.

In many countries teachers have introduced reforms that are attempts to repair the old model. In school they have tried to replace individualism and isolation with interactive grouping and shared responsibility, and they have been guided by the same principles in the associations forged with the local community and with parents. In both of these things they have responded to an intuitive recognition that people need to belong to groups that will give them a sense of identity as well as the feeling that they have a place in a world that they can help to construct. The community school is one response which, at its best, is pioneering a new approach to learning. It is not surprising that Maria was invited by such a school and was tempted by the invitation; but she felt that the challenge was greater in an ordinary school. She also knew that, at their worst, community schools could be doctrinaire, using pastoral care and T-group-type counselling as subtle (and often unrecognized) means of manipulation. She chose one battleground rather than the other.

In thinking of the choice this way Maria recognized that, like the proponents of the core curriculum, she was preoccupied with school structure and organization rather than content, with the covert rather than the overt curriculum. It is no accident that informal policies seem to take pre-eminence over formal ones, for this is how institutions are most effective. Ultimately it is desirable that, as a teacher, one should speak and act consistently. Those who propose a core curriculum that is vague, and merely stipulate that basic literacy should be taught, indicate that they see only a formal universality and no worthwhile content. If schools' failure to date has resulted from mass alienation which is a reflection of profound cultural ills, legislating for minimal literacy will be a hopeless gesture.

The British Columbian 'musts' and 'shoulds' seem like a desperate exercise in mock democracy − if we don't know what to select as having the highest priority, let us make a decision by the methods of market research. But there are political reasons behind the educational fraud, in that populism is used to control the teachers.

The Australian 'cultural map' perhaps indicates an intention to find a metaphor as a guide to constructive thinking about content. Of all three, it is the only one that in any sense pays respect to content as an expression of culture. But it too uses the market research model, although in a much more sophisticated fashion. Culture is used as a description of the present, in an anthropological sense. Another meaning of culture, as the source and practice of judgment and decision-making, is not examined. The curriculum proposed allows access and encourages participation; but it does not promote moral and social judgment or nonconformity.

Maria finds a basis for her actions in reconsidering her personal history and in her extended understanding of recent events. The traditions of the past cannot be re-created, and the nostalgia of the back-to-the-basics movement is not for her. Those varieties of core curriculum which reassert old authority as if it should never have been questioned are to be opposed. The participatory modes of core curriculum have some appeal to her, as providing the conditions under which it is possible to continue curriculum development. The thought of a high-cultural basis to give a moral direction to everyday action tempts her, but it is, she realizes, an impossible basis for practice. What is left is the combination of a participatory curriculum process centred on the establishment of understanding of those matters necessary for the life of all societies. The ways in which the world is understood and acted upon entail a recognition of the necessity of organizing material production (but not a blind adherence to particular ways in which this is now done) and of the necessity of an organized family life (but again not of any particular form of the family): these become the meat of the curriculum to which she is committed. While this is a core curriculum, it does not lead to a rigidity; while she does not think that one can do as one likes, she is quite sure that this does not imply the automatic acceptance of the prevailing authority.

Notes

1 *What Should Our Children Be Learning? Goals of the Core Curriculum*, Ministry of Education, Victoria, British Columbia, 1976.

2 J. Bottomly and P. Bates, *An Analysis of Public Response to the Core Curriculum*, a report to the Minister of Education, Ministry of Education, British Columbia, 1977.

3 DES, *Education in Schools: a Consultative Document*, Cmnd 6869, London, HMSO, 1977.

4 Curriculum Development Centre, Canberra, *Core Curriculum for Australian Schools*, North Blackburn, Victoria, Dominion Press, 1980, pp. 15–16.

5 Malcolm Skilbeck, 'Ideology and Values', in Malcolm Skilbeck and Alan Harris, eds, *Culture, Ideology and Knowledge*, Milton

Keynes, The Open University Press, 1976, pp. 83–7.

6 Conversation with Gwyn Dow, 1980.

7 Lyn Yates, 'The History of Australian Education and the Question of Core Curriculum', discussion paper, School of Education, La Trobe University, 1979.

8 Geoff Sharp and Doug White, 'Features of the intellectually trained', *Arena*, 15, 1968, p. 31.

9 Karl Marx and Frederick Engels, *Manifesto of the Communist Party*, Vol. 6 of *Collected Works*, London, Lawrence & Wishart, 1976, p. 587.

10 Board of Education, Secondary Schools Examination Council, *Curriculum and Examinations in Secondary Schools* (Chairman, Sir Cyril Norwood), London, HMSO, 1943.

Chapter 6

'Human nature' and educational practice

Rod Foster and Gwyneth Dow

9M — Maria's form*

When Maria took over her year nine class in her first year of teaching she soon recognized that a large proportion had survived six years of primary school and two of secondary school without acquiring minimal literacy. In her innocence early in the year she had two or three times tried to give lessons in which the pupils were asked to read aloud. Her astonishment was equalled by the pupils' humiliation as they fumbled over apparently unfamiliar words and carried on regardless of any marks on the pages that better tutored pupils knew to be punctuation signs. She quickly abandoned the practice until she knew her class better, for she was sharp enough to recognize that the tomfoolery that some of the children turned to was an ill-concealed attempt to make ineptitude look like blasé contempt for the task.

When she knew the children better, she became convinced that there was nothing wrong with their perceptual faculties; and their thought-processes, while erratic, were well developed in some situations. They had learned very effectively many skills of 'tuning-out' or 'turning-off', and some had ready access to an impressive array of strategies for rebellious classroom disruption. A few, who had an even greater problem (or so she thought), sheltered behind unobtrusively 'good' behaviour which camouflaged (they hoped) their deceitful secret. Something like three-quarters of them thought of themselves as failures and were well aware of their likely future. The increasing depression and resentment thus engendered led Maria to see her first battle as one in which she must help them to build up their self-images.

* In keeping with the school's policy, Maria took her form for six periods weekly — four for general studies, one for extra English, and one for class matters and counselling.

As a beginning, she had to discover those pupils who really did want to learn and to work, though she had to bear in mind that even in those pupils the desire not to have their incompetence or ignorance exposed to public ridicule was a powerful disincentive to contribute to classroom activities. One step that she took as soon as she felt some trust had developed was to ask all the pupils to consider the weaknesses in their English that needed her most urgent help. On the basis of their self-assessments they worked out with her a programme in which those who thought they had similar problems worked together on a specific project that she designed. She kept this programme going during two periods a week so that, by the end of a month, she had worked at least once with each small group and more often with most of them. She herself undertook such writing as the pupils were doing, and she was especially careful on this point when they were writing anything personal or of an exploratory kind. This showed that she took the tasks seriously and understood how it feels to reveal oneself to a reader. No one-way glass for Maria.

Since imperfection is universal, this sort of method enables the teacher to stress need rather than ability, and Maria felt that it established her as a helper rather than a judge, thus to some extent clearing the air of the extreme nervousness many pupils felt at the prospect of a new teacher's discovering their weaknesses. Maria's work with the small groups enabled her to recognize the pupils with the most severe problems and to devise work for them that guaranteed them some initial success. The discussion that it gave rise to, both in ordinary lessons and in small-group work, helped to develop some fellowship in the class. One symptom of poor morale is classroom feuds. There was enough tale-telling and spitefulness in the class for Maria to realize that she had to discover the cliques and power structure before she could work out effective strategies. By the end of the month she was beginning to get the feel of things, helped as much (probably more) by her informal contacts with pupils outside the classroom as in it.

In some cases, of course, the battle to break the old habits of tuning-out and disruption was a real battle, and Maria had to 'out-tough' some 'toughs'. She knew that this was risky, but she managed it without intensifying personal feuds between pupils, and without adding to them a struggle in which teacher and pupil are 'out to get each other'. Many a teacher has come off second best in that sort of battle, which usually results in mutual mistrust. For a pupil who feels defeated, often the only pride left is in dignified withdrawal or in manifestly 'one-upping' the teacher.

Maria recalls her despair and finally her anger as she watched the class around her collapse on one of her really bad days. She realized that the culprit's devious behaviour was a rebellion against a system that had failed him. She had no doubt that he was entitled to save face and give vent to his feelings. Her exasperation and momentary loss of temper were probably preferable, she thinks in retrospect, to indulgent pity for the child. She caught herself out several times evading confrontation so as to avoid unpopularity, and she recognized that such behaviour on her part could do nothing for the child, who saw it as weakness — the kind of weakness that strengthened him as an adversary rather than a learner. Maria's first year was one in which she gradually gained the necessary detachment to deal with a class that contained so many troubled children. By now there is more than a truce. The pupils trust her because they believe in her respect for them — a respect that enables her to risk unpopularity when pupils deserve rebukes.

It had taken her time to learn the children's games for what they were. Playing dumb, baiting classmates, baiting her, 'accidentally' banging desk-tops, throwing things (including classmates!) were some of their tactics for avoiding concentrated effort, and for diverting Maria's attention from the pupil as learner to the pupil as troublemaker. In their bid for care, attention, and even for status, some pupils have few means at their disposal other than 'stirring'. About half-way through her first term, Maria thought she knew who was her key troublemaker. Earlier she had thought it was Paddy, who was always clowning around apparently looking for attention. Then it dawned on her that Paddy was dancing to the tune of a much more sombre, more formidable boy, Lennie, who mysteriously carried a lot of weight with the class. She knew that she must not confront him to the extent of testing the class's loyalty. If it came to a show-down she knew that Lennie would win and she would lose.

She decided to treat Paddy's clowning as a joke that was sometimes genuinely funny but sometimes fell flat. She gambled in treating his disruptive behaviour as mischief rather than cheek, and the gamble came off because he was good-natured and welcomed the help and attention Maria gave him. In a sense, by legitimating his role as class jester, she lessened his dependence on Lennie and increased his status. Lennie's surly hostility, however, was another matter. She rode it out for the first two terms until she was more confident of her class's trust. Several girls were moonstruck in Lennie's presence and there was little she could do to compete for their attention, but she gained their goodwill by giving them a great deal of help with their written work.

By third term Maria felt confident enough to try to penetrate Lennie's armour, but there were no chinks that she could find. His bitterness and resistance to her and to all that school stood for were beyond her. Once, when he had been away for several days, she called at his home and had a long talk with his mother, a widow, who claimed to be as nonplussed as Maria by Lennie's coolness. He had already been caught 'joy-riding' in a stolen car, and he was on a good-behaviour bond, which, she said, was the only hold she had on him. She never knew where he was, but she was sure that he was up to no good. Shortly after this the police visited the school looking for Lennie. When eventually he was brought before the court for shop-lifting, Maria went with his mother and did all she could to help him. He was once again let off with a good-behaviour bond. He showed Maria what thanks he felt by refraining a little from stirring up the others, but he remained impenetrable, and Maria was realistic enough to be somewhat relieved that no power that she or anyone else could wield would persuade him to return to school after the year's end, when he would be sixteen, jobless and illiterate, though no doubt still powerful in his influence over his peers.

Thus her biggest problem would be removed in the coming year. But there were others that ran Lennie a close second. She had insisted, with the class's agreement, that the classroom had to be one in which those who wanted to work could do so. To bring this about she had been prepared not to be liked by a number of the pupils. She had found a number of activities that most pupils really enjoyed: making and listening to tapes, playing educational games, producing photographic exhibitions, to name a few. There were also periods when a buzz of discussion was in order, though she waited until she was fairly sure of herself before she admitted that type of lesson. To begin with, patterns of concentration had to be built up by those who were easily distracted, and in lessons or parts of lessons set up for that purpose she dealt firmly with disruptions. Because of after-school jobs, lack of a quiet place, family tensions and other obstacles, the children had little chance of working properly at home, at least not until their motivation drastically changed. The very most, therefore, had to be made of their hours at school. Maria had found it a great burden having to be heavy-handed with troublemakers, though most of the class welcomed it, and she consoled herself that it was better than resorting to ineffectual nagging. When pupils were asked to nominate the group they wanted to join for the coming year, she was surprised that most of the pupils with whom she had been severe gave her their first preference.

Another problem that Maria had to overcome was a tendency to pitch the level of her lessons to roughly the middle of the range of abilities present in the class. It was, she came to see, a guaranteed recipe for losing the lower group. She noticed that much naughtiness was a sort of frenzied fussing ('What heading d'yer want?', 'Should we leave a space?', 'Do we have to hand it in?'), which she knew had to be calmed before anything constructive could be done. She unapologetically gave tasks such as copying out and even drawing and colouring in, which gave her room for manoeuvre and enabled pupils to save face instead of becoming conspicuous by their inability to carry out a more difficult task like making their own notes. These were merely stopgaps while she learnt to avoid their fussing by being better organized herself.

Once the class settled down she could move among them, look at their work, talk for a while to each pupil and hear them, one by one, read what they had done. With the weakest pupils she would sometimes write down some of their answers and get them to read what she had written, thus giving them sure success in the dreaded activity. She came to call these her 'reconnaissance' sessions in which she gained time to suggest some realistic tasks both as regards level of competence and time-span involved — 'This term, let us concentrate on improving your handwriting', for example. To her horror she found that sometimes it was a matter of 'revising' the alphabet before moving on to something else. She always had on hand extra and more difficult assignments for the fast workers so that she could take time to diagnose the difficulties of the poorest achievers. The school, she discovered, had excellent reading schemes with teachers' handbooks that helped her considerably in gaining confidence. Also, after overcoming her pride and a strange sense of guilt at her inexpertness, she gained a great deal of help from other members of the team and from the near-by Resources Centre.

Small-group work became an indispensable part of her teaching. It was the only way in which she could give individual attention to pupils, it enabled her to break up the most difficult and demanding cliques, and it encouraged pupils to help each other.

The search for a theory

Maria's handling of 9M, she thinks, has been rather 'by guess and by God'. Or has it? (There's a distinction, she suspects, between good hunches that take time to be explained, and unexplored assumptions.) It is very hard for her to justify her practices in detail to the staff: indeed some of her reactions in the worst classroom crises have been so intuitive that she wonders if she can remember them in any detail, let alone explain them without being wise after the event — in short, without rationalizing. Her fear of abusing personal power involved her in something of a paradox. It suddenly dawned on her when 'the kids' were almost on top of her that her reluctance to exercise her power simply gave them the power over other pupils as well as over Maria herself, and that was bad news. Not that she verbalized it all like that at the time. It was only later that she began haltingly to explain to herself why she had done what she did.

While Maria seemed to live from one crisis to the next in her first year, she had little time to stand back from it all and subject it to some sort of order in her own mind. At times she felt that she could not possibly understand what was happening until she could stop still and think — and read — without distractions. This was one reason why she felt great relief and a sense of challenge when her team started its planning; but the early difficulties only intensified her sense of inadequacy as a theorist. There seemed no clear-cut justifications either for how she was handling her own class or for the team's approach to curricular planning.

Even in her training year Maria had been well aware that the educational theorists provided no easy answers to classroom problems, and after a year's experience all the talk of 'conditioning' and 'freedom' and 'rationality' seemed so remote that she would have ignored it altogether but for the fact that such terms and various associated slogans are part of the rhetoric of education, and kept cropping up even in staffroom debates. Sometimes she was fully aware that they were used in high-falutin justifications of various proposals and policies; at other times they were used as weapons of attack and tools of demolition as, for instance, in the demand for the precise specification of the 'behavioural objectives' of some curriculum proposal. She saw David's demand (see pp. 14–15) during the team's planning as a somewhat defensive bid for scientific respectability.

Even so, she feels that it is not good enough to dismiss such arguments simply as tactical digressions. She wants to develop her own analysis more positively as a basis for meeting her classroom problems. Perhaps she is even asking the wrong questions in what other people might call an immature search for *the* one foolproof theory — a point dealt with at some length by Noel Gough in chapter 3.

The considerations raised in the following discussion we offer not as a panacea, but as something more like a partial corrective to some of the very one-sided views of 'human nature' which implicitly or explicitly inform some of the most influential educational philosophies.

In her search for some tools to help in her analysis, Maria, we believe, might look to Ethology, the comparative study of behaviour, which draws on field studies as well as laboratory work, and which has begun to map the complex interrelationships between components of behaviour — the innate, the learned and the higher inventive capacities variously referred to as 'insight', 'reason' and 'intellect'.

'Small is beautiful'

If one considers the possibilities raised by Ethologists concerning population density, group size, personal territory and the kinds of social organization in which man evolved, one is hard pressed to imagine a more unnatural way of organizing people than the set-up in some large urban schools. If Ethologists are right about some of the innate factors in human nature, then it would almost seem that some schools are expressly designed to maximize tensions, resentments, loneliness, bullying and various destructive forms of rivalry, and to minimize the co-operative aspects of human nature, the spirit of local community, and the desire to explore, invent, etc. No doubt this is an exaggeration and oversimplification, particularly when one thinks of the efforts made by some of the staff members within these schools; and, of course, staff and children with more dominant personalities can thrive in such situations, as there is wider scope for the exercise of power, for 'empire-building' and for various kinds of showing-off and 'ego-tripping'. But it is just this very thriving of the minority which could mask some of the problem since, just because of their more dominant personalities, the members of this minority tend to hold positions of influence, both official and unofficial, and to be relatively happy with the large-scale, centralized organization. Even if the division of large schools into several smaller ones and other similar kinds of decentralization were to the advantage of an overwhelming majority, there would still be many administrators, head teachers, teachers and even pupils for whom such moves would mean a significant loss of status and/or power. Almost inevitably, then, many of those enjoying positions of power and influence would oppose such moves, and obviously enough, just because of their personalities and positions, theirs are the voices most likely to be heard.

Of course, it would be easy to be romantic and quite unrealistic about decentralization and organizational possibilities in general, especially in a mobile, competitive, industrialized society. But the grim realities should not blind us to the fact that there is some room for manoeuvre, nor should they be used as an excuse for the kinds of 'efficient' planning which fail to take into account the inevitably dehumanizing effects of large organizations. For instance, the closure of small schools is sometimes justified by an appeal to economic considerations; but if truancy, vandalism and various kinds of stress, demoralization and 'dropping out' are taken into account, even this economic efficiency may turn out to be a very short term matter indeed.

Maria was acting on more than a good hunch in the way she grouped her unruly class. She sensed that she had both to get closer to her pupils individually and to break the power structure that had developed almost unnoticed in a largish class in a big school, a power structure that determined the classroom ethos. It would be possible to document the fact that small community schools and 'mini-schools' within a larger institution (both of which developed as innovations in Victoria, and usually consisted of about a hundred children) do not count among their problems the fostering of *invisible* power groups. Nor in such organizations is it so easy for teacher and pupil to become adversaries. Of course, school size is only one manifestation of modern organizational problems.

Ethologists suggest that some of the stress of modern urban life may well be due to the fact that our social organization is now, so to speak, out of adjustment with our basic emotional equipment. Urbanization has brought with it not only crowding, but the formation of very large anonymous societies, 'a far remove from the small in-groups of early Man'.[1] Also the work of countless thousands in industry has become monotonous and the very antithesis of the meaningful and more immediately satisfying occupations of the craftsman, let alone those of the primitive hunter-gatherer. Because so many people now spend their whole life in industrialized cities, we tend to forget that man's abilities and emotional needs evolved to suit a very different pattern of life.[2]

> Cultural man has been on earth for some 2,000,000 years; for over 99 per cent of this period he has lived as a hunter-gatherer . . . Of the estimated 80,000,000,000 men who have ever lived out a life span on earth, over 90 per cent have lived as hunters and gatherers; about 6 per cent have lived by agriculture and the remaining few per cent have lived in industrial societies.

Large-scale organization has not only tended to dehumanize many kinds of work, it has also constricted our living space. If we think of the conditions and ways of life and social organizations for which man's behaviour originally evolved, it seems likely that, in Niko Tinbergen's words, 'we now live at a far higher density than that in which genetic evolution has moulded our species'.[3] Paul Leyhausen believes that the zoo behaviour of wolves may perhaps throw some light on the behaviour of humans in high-density cities.[4]

> The members of a family of wolves in the wild are friendly towards one another, the ranking order is recognizable but seldom em-phasized, biting bouts virtually do not occur, food is willingly shared with others. The animals kept in a confined space in captivity, however, behave quite differently. Here the strictest ranking order was observed, which allowed only the top animal unrestrained

activity. Almost continuously there were serious biting bouts, and scarcely one of the animals could ever relax completely.

Even if all the remaining wolves in the wild were to be wiped out, that would not make the behaviour of the tense, captive wolves any more the normal or natural behaviour of wolves, except in a trivial statistical sense. Or, to put it another way, in a case such as this it can be seen that the meaning of 'normal behaviour' or 'natural behaviour' need not be confined to 'the behaviour of the majority' or some sort of 'statistically average' behaviour which takes no account of the conditions involved.

Of course, in schools where stresses and tensions run high, the introduction of any self-directed activity can be an invitation to riotous chaos or to an almost total inactivity. No doubt some would interpret this as showing the uselessness and unpracticality of such activity: to others it would suggest that changes and reorganization at more fundamental levels will be necessary if some of the vicious circles of modern society are ever to be broken.

However, such ideas are probably of little use to Maria with her immediate classroom problems. In some circumstances she might perhaps be able to make use of information from Ethology concerning 'individual territories', since it seems likely that attachment to individual territory has some natural basis in humans, especially when we consider that strong emotions are often aroused by 'invasions' of a person's desk, private seat or corner, emotions that seem not fully to be explained by conditioning or rational considerations.[5]

Every teacher knows, too, with what tenacity the pupils in a class usually adhere to a seating plan once it has been worked out. And here the vital factor is not always personal links between children sitting in neighbouring seats. Frequently it is simply a matter of holding onto the 'place'.

Herbert Kohl and other teachers have reported the remarkable difference in atmosphere and productivity in their classrooms once the pupils have established secure 'territories' of their own, something which in most secondary schools is virtually impossible, at least at present, for organizational reasons.[6]

It is important to build private spaces into existing classrooms . . . Material is magical. A few muslin dividers hanging from the ceiling can create private space . . . Even rugs on the floor can mark private spaces . . . Portable Japanese walls or ingenious room dividers can be used. The classroom can be changed into a complex environment accommodating and respecting private as well as public experience.

One alternative school of a hundred or so pupils in Melbourne is held in an old church hall which has a number of small rooms running off a semi-circular gallery. Each room 'belongs' to a small group of pupils for special interests — pets, fossils, biology — and is a source of intense pride.

According to Ethology, if we take into account man's recent phylo-genetic history, it is quite possible that even in a stable system man could be a misfit in his own society. If man's adaptability is stretched too far by unnatural conditions and ways of life the mental health of the individual could be in danger. 'If this happens to enough individuals to constitute a sizable proportion of a community, then that community ceases to be stable, healthy and fit for humans to inhabit.'[7]

And even though no one can precisely state the limits to individual adaptability, there is mounting evidence that some environments and social organizations can appropriately be called 'more natural' than others. We might be dealing here with a gradual shading-off or tran-sition from clearly natural set-ups to others involving increasing tensions — transitions without sharp cut-off points, border-lines or definite, quantifiable limits.

This 'stress and nature' theme is brought directly into the educational arena by Tinbergen as follows:

> To the ethologist it is clear that we will have to do some hard
> thinking about both the aims and the methods of education lest we
> increase, in this sphere too, social stress to beyond what is tolerable.

Schooling necessitates the bringing together of peers, which is no doubt a good thing in many respects, and would seem to be 'in harmony with the "deeper structure" of human social life',[8] as well as providing an antidote to the isolation that results, paradoxically, from the crowded conditions in high-rise flats, for instance, and from that most common form of urban social organization, the small family group. For some, however, it would seem that loneliness is actually increased by school attendance, or at least the awareness of it is.

Maria and most other teachers will probably be well aware that large classes are not just quantitatively different from small ones as regards atmosphere, tensions and the kinds of problems that arise. To put it in modern jargon, the 'group dynamic' of a class of thirty is of a different kind from that of a class of fifteen, and this too may have some natural basis, and not just be a matter of what the pupils are used to.

Learning by conditioning

Just as the most common justification of the large school is one of economic efficiency, so, too, extreme proponents of Behaviourism readily resort to an 'industrial' (input–output) model of learning. Maria encountered this 'hard-headed' approach first during her training and then among colleagues, and again she may feel less discomfited in defending her position by considering some of the main ideas of Ethology.

Maria is deeply suspicious of the claim that all behaviour is the result of conditioning, with its implication that educational problems are to be seen largely as a matter of increasing the efficiency of conditioning techniques. B.F. Skinner puts the case with seductive simplicity:[9]

> If you can discover how behaviour is related to the environment
> you can use the environment to predict behaviour and control it.
> We've done this with psychotics, with retardates, with juvenile
> delinquents, with students in the classroom, and so on. You
> simply arrange a better environment and you get a better behaviour.

Is that all that Maria's efforts to reorganize her class, 9M, amount to?

According to that picture of human nature, stress could result from *changes* in the environment – that is, changes that occur during an individual's life, changes that would cause the conditioned responses (shaped earlier in his childhood) to 'misfire' or be inappropriate in the new conditions. But there is little room in the Behaviourists' account of human nature for the idea that some environments and social patterns may be, as it were, *intrinsically* more natural to man than others are, or for the consequent idea that great stress may result from life in less natural conditions, even if they are kept constant throughout an individual's lifetime.

Ethologists do not deny the existence and importance of conditioning in human behaviour, but they claim that to see conditioned responses as the sole components of human behaviour is roughly equivalent to seeing nuts and bolts as the sole components of a motor car. Skinner and other Behaviourists fail to do justice to the inventive, problem-solving abilities variously known as 'insight', 'reason' and 'intellect', as well as to many different kinds of innate factors in human behaviour. Of course, nothing like an exhaustive list of innate behaviour can be given, because, for obvious moral reasons, it is not possible to perform the kinds of 'deprivation experiments' that are permitted with animals. (To discover whether the song of a particular bird species is innate or not, young birds are *deprived* of the chance to learn it by being reared in a soundproof cage, for example.)

However, there do occur, tragically, what might be called natural or accidental deprivation experiments involving humans. Some children, for instance, are born deaf, some blind, and some both deaf and blind.

Eibl-Eibesfeldt and others who have worked with such children report that smiling, laughing, crying, pouting and the expressions of anger, fear and sadness, looked the same in blind-born children, although they could not have imitated anyone:[10]

> a whole array of even quite complex behaviour patterns, which are typical for human beings, have developed also in the deaf-blind and are therefore present as phylogenetic adaptations. Some characteristics of social behaviour developed, even contrary to the educational efforts, such as, for example, the fear of strangers.

If a Behaviourist were to insist that such motor patterns could have been learned by the child as a result of touch (e.g. by exploring the parent's face with its fingers), then cases could be cited in which even this source of experience is closed (thalidomide babies born deaf-blind and with feelingless stumps for hands). More details and more cases could be given, but even these examples suggest that human emotional responses and needs have an important innate basis.

In the absence of various kinds of 'hard data', it might be said, we are just not in a position to make claims about 'human nature' and what kinds of innate factors it does or does not have. But, in a sense, this is just the point, or part of it, for any ignorance in this area cuts both ways. Obviously enough, to the extent that we do not (or cannot) know whether some features of human behaviour have innate bases, to that same extent we do not (or cannot) know that the behaviour is wholly the product of learning. Such admissions of ignorance, however, are never conspicuous features of the writings of Behaviourists like B.F. Skinner.[11]

> Fortunately recent advances in the experimental analysis of behavior suggest that a true technology of education is feasible. Improved techniques are available to carry out the two basic assignments of education: constructing extensive repertoires of verbal and nonverbal behavior and generating that high probability of action which is said to show interest, enthusiasm, or a strong 'desire to learn'.

Although the heyday of Behaviourism is long past, views such as Skinner's continue to be influential and are still enormously attractive to many, especially to those with faith in the idea that all social and educational problems must have a technological solution.

It is interesting to note that Ralph Tyler, the father of the classical model of curriculum, in recent tape-recorded discussions with John Goodlad has pointed to the need for a corrective to modern tendencies to treat educational technology 'as though it were a "robot teacher" rather than a source of certain tools that teachers could employ'. He makes a place for the 'active role of the learner' instead of the attitudes revealed in terms like 'educational delivery system' and 'teacher-proof materials'.[12]

He also accepts the criticism that 'formulating objectives' will not show 'how the question regarding what goals the schools *should* have is to be answered'. To meet this apparent dilemma, however, he has to create a dichotomy:[13]

> two screens must be used: the psychological view of learning which is favoured and a philosophy of education which will help determine what the curriculum builder considers to be a 'good' life, a 'good' society, and a 'good' person.

It should be pointed out that Ethologists have distinguished a number of different kinds of learning apart from conditioning. The details are perhaps not so important for this discussion, but the message for the teacher is that a variety of styles and approaches should be used. The idealism of many a first-year teacher takes the form of trying to perfect a particular teaching style, or *the* teaching method, where a much more varied and eclectic approach might well be more effective and, indeed, natural. It is known, for instance, that in 'primitive' societies, learning depends partly on exploratory play, partly on social imitation, and partly on deliberate instruction by adults. Tinbergen suggests that in our present society we may have disproportionately increased the part played by social instruction,[14]

> and that in doing so we are likely to hamper, indeed to stunt and distort development in two ways: we are quite possibly *suppressing* exploratory learning; and we are undoubtedly calling up serious *resistances* against social instruction.

Yet this is not to deny the importance of social instruction in a child's language development — a point well made by the psychologist Lev Vygotsky and taken up by Gwyn Dow in the next chapter.

There is no simple solution to the problems raised by these considerations, however, since exploratory learning flourishes only in conditions of security, minimum adult interference and where there is sufficient time and opportunity in an environment that invites exploration. No doubt no classroom is the ideal place for exploratory learning, but there would seem to be matters of degree involved: for instance, a classroom in which there are no clear limits to tolerable behaviour, and in which various 'trials of strength' between teacher and pupil are waged more or less continuously makes for maximum tension and insecurity, and probably for minimum learning, as Maria's even scant experience indicated. The very pupils who are most disruptive, she noted, often later complain about the conditions and the atmosphere in such classes.

According to Ethology, then, the Behaviourists see only a part of human nature, and this is inevitable since the original theory is largely derived from laboratory work with rats and pigeons. The demand that all curriculum proposals be specified in terms of precise 'behavioural objectives' is a dogmatic legacy of this blinkered outlook. Of course, this is not to say that the teaching techniques advocated by Skinner are never appropriate. On the contrary, for some pupils especially, and for some kinds of learning, even the use of various machines would seem to be highly appropriate, since to a machine one does not 'look a fool', and some students will attempt things where otherwise they would have 'tuned-out' in self-defence.

The noble savage?

From what has already been said it will hardly come as a surprise that some of A.S. Neill's pronouncements on human nature, at the other end of the spectrum, could also be accused of providing us with only part of the story. 'My view is that a child is innately wise and realistic. If left to himself without adult suggestion of any kind, he will develop as far as he is capable of developing.'[15]

Of all animals, man would in fact seem to be the most dependent on 'adult suggestion', though obviously this does not mean that the whole of a child's life should be organized and directed by adults. Emphasis should also be given in the context of Neill's 'freedom philosophy' to the vast difference between a school of Maria's type and a boarding school where the children have to live continuously with the consequences of their group decisions (or lack of them). Although Neill underestimates the importance of adult influence, he provides a corrective to mechanistic views which ignore man's natural curiosity and inventiveness. Even pre-verbal children are capable of surprisingly sophisticated exploration and experimentation, and yet observers of children,[16] as Maria well knows, despair at the waning of their curiosity and interest, especially during secondary education. Perhaps part of the explanation lies in the increasing pressures to which secondary pupils are subjected. In competitive systems the emphasis on ranking increases dramatically during secondary school. The desire for good marks or to avoid looking a fool, or in some other way being found wanting, is also intensified by the heightened self-consciousness of the adolescent.

Even in non-human primates the use of 'external' rewards can radically and detrimentally alter an activity, as is illustrated by a test done on a chimpanzee 'artist'. (Painting and drawing can be a self-rewarding activity for several kinds of ape, their work being indistinguishable from pre-representational phases in the work of human children.) Desmond Morris relates:[17]

> a chimpanzee was once subjected to bribery with a food reward to
> encourage it to draw more intensely . . . The ape quickly learnt
> to associate drawing with getting the reward but as soon as this
> condition had been established the animal took less and less interest
> in the lines it was drawing. Any old scribble would do and then it
> would immediately hold out its hand for the reward. The careful
> attention the animal had paid previously to design, rhythm, balance
> and composition was gone and the worst kind of commercial art
> was born!

A heavy emphasis on external rewards, on marks and ranking, may contribute to the 'drying up' of natural curiosity that occurs in so many schoolchildren, and the atmosphere of competitive individualism inevitably involved with ranking may be one of the factors contributing to the loneliness so acutely felt by so many, especially by some of those 'at the bottom of the pile'. The headmaster of a large secondary school recently noted in a personal conversation that if things run true to form there will be about eight attempted suicides by pupils during the year. The two periods of greatest danger are at the beginning of the school year and at the beginning of spring. He quoted some research which explained these peaks as the times when the lonely are made the most acutely aware of their condition. The problem is at its worst when a youngster is surrounded by active peer-groups but ignored by them for whatever reason. Groups are formed early in the school year, hence creating a period of great stress for the non-joiners, for some of whom loneliness was barely tolerable during the holidays. In early spring the groups become active again, having been greatly restricted during the winter months. Of course, there can be many factors involved in such problems, but our experience and that of many others suggests that isolation and the consequent stress are aggravated for many by 'unnatural' social organizations in which the individual gets lost.

As a result of an ethological study of lack of socialization in one of its extreme forms, Early Childhood Autism, or Kanner's Syndrome, Tinbergen and his wife tentatively conclude: 'we believe that at least some forms of autism are the consequence [of], and indications of certain forms of increased social stress, and that autism may well be an "early warning" of harmful effects of ... [our recent] cultural evolution.' In examining these children's 'complete withdrawal from, and even violent rejection of other persons', and their underdeveloped speech, the authors had tried to analyse non-verbal expressions of emotions. Though they found the syndrome developed in naturally timid children, they concluded that 'it may well be caused to a much larger extent than is generally recognized by shortcomings in the social environment'.[18] Such an analysis is saying far more about the importance of environment than we find in the writings of Behaviourists: it is pointing towards environments and social patterns that may be, as it were, *intrinsically* more natural to man than others are.

To sum up then, although the heyday of Behaviourism is long past, views such as Skinner's continue to be influential and to be enormously attractive to many, especially to those with faith in the idea that all social and educational problems must have a technological solution. Ethologists can see no grounds for such faith, but neither are they in full agreement with the more romantic notions of A.S. Neill, for instance, as can be seen by the following speculations on 'human goodness' by Konrad Lorenz:[19]

> We fundamentally disagree with the biblical thesis defended by some child psychologists and psychoanalysts, that man is utterly 'wicked from childhood on'. Our primitive ancestor . . . was — at the very least — just as 'good' as a wolf or chimpanzee, in both of which youngsters and females are spared from harm and in which even a jealously fought male society member is protected against an external enemy without hesitation and with all possible vigour. I should like to paraphrase the biblical text to read: Man is not wicked from childhood on, but just good enough for the requirements which were made of him in the primitive human group, in which the small number of individuals were personally acquainted with one another and 'loved' one another after their own fashion. He is not good *enough* for the requirements set by the enormously expanded, anonymous society of later cultural epochs, which demand that he should behave towards any completely unacquainted fellow human being as if he were a personal friend.

Ethology has been done a disservice by some of its popularizers who, having thrown Tinbergen's exemplary caution to the winds, have produced some dubious theorizing and some explanations which may well be simplistic or one-sided. Even in their most dogmatic moments, however, such popularizers do not have the blinkered outlook of Behaviourism in the Watson–Skinner mould, in which a whole theory of behaviour, animal and human, is based largely on studies of laboratory rats and pigeons.

The pedagogical implications of Ethology are still to be worked out. Until recently, Anthropologists and Ethnologists (as opposed to Ethologists) have restricted their enquiries almost entirely to human societies. Wittgenstein reminds us about our overlooking of important general facts because they are before us all the time. 'The fish would be last to discover water' is an oriental proverb much quoted by Jerome

Bruner to stress the importance of broadening the base of comparison if we are to increase our understanding of ourselves. A similar point is made by Goethe's dictum that he who knows no other language knows nothing of his own. Obviously this is a grand overstatement, but we suggest that the important element of truth might well apply to *species* as well as to languages.

We started with the problems Maria had with her class and the efforts that she made to turn the classroom into an educative one. At times when she feels most troubled by the damage already done to her most difficult pupils, she needs to be reminded that human beings can adapt and adjust themselves to a variety and range of environmental and social conditions. But, as Tinbergen asks: 'Are there intolerable pressures, and are there, conversely, gaps, pockets of missing outlets for behaviour patterns that have strong, perhaps compulsive internal determinants? Ethologists believe that there are such signs.'[20] Maria cannot be wrong in trying to reduce loneliness, to offer success, to curb the stultifying exercise of power. As we have seen, irretrievable harm has already been done to one of her pupils, Lennie. School, of course, did not cause that failure; neither did it ameliorate it.

There are no simple recipes to be followed in such cases or, for that matter, in educational problems generally, though some people handle them better than others. Of course, in her daily dealings with her pupils, Maria draws on a vast intuitive knowledge of human nature; but in planning, analysing and reflecting on educational policies and practices there is also room for considerations of a more explicit kind. Those drawn from the wider perspective offered by Ethology suggest that Maria is right to reject a simplistic either/or approach to Behaviourism on the one hand, and romanticism on the other. Both contain some partial truths, or truths about parts of human nature, and in discarding their more dogmatic generalizations she is not committed to the view that 'human nature' is necessarily a vacuous term or that it refers to something indefinitely plastic. Indeed, the considerations raised by Ethologists suggest that nature and culture are closely interwoven. No doubt matters of degree are involved, but the point should be emphasized that cultural potentials are not fulfilled under social and educational conditions that are incompatible with our nature.

Notes

1 Niko Tinbergen, *The Animal in its World*, vol. 2, London, Allen & Unwin, 1973, p. 220.

2 Quoted in Henry Phelps Brown, *The Inequality of Pay*, Oxford University Press, 1977, p. 124.

3 Heinz Friedrich (ed.), *Man and Animal: Studies in Behaviour*, London, MacGibbon & Kee, 1972, p. 132.

4 Konrad Lorenz and Paul Leyhausen, *Motivation of Human and Animal Behaviour*, New York, Van Nostrand Reinhold, 1973, p. 108.

5 Leyhausen in Lorenz and Leyhausen, op. cit., pp. 104–5.

6 H.R. Kohl, *Writing, Maths and Games in the Open Classroom*, London, Methuen, 1977, p. 26.

7 Paul Leyhausen, 'Social organization and density tolerance in mammals', in Lorenz and Leyhausen, op. cit., p. 138.

8 Tinbergen, op. cit., 1973, p. 223.

9 Quoted in Alec Nisbett, *Konrad Lorenz*, London, Dent, 1976, p. 181.

10 Irenaus Eibl-Eibesfeldt, *Ethology, the Biology of Behavior*, New York, Holt, Rinehart & Winston, 1970, p. 405.

11 'Why we need teaching machines', *Harvard Educational Review*, 31, 1961, p. 378.

12 Ralph W. Tyler, 'Two new emphases in curriculum development', *Educational Leadership*, 34 (1), 1976, pp. 62–3.

13 Frances Klein, 'Tyler and Goodlad speak on American education: a critique', *Educational Leadership*, May 1976, p. 566.

14 Tinbergen, op. cit., 1973, p. 224.

15 A.S. Neill, *Summerhill*, Penguin, 1962, p. 20.

16 See, for example, John Holt, *How Children Fail*, Penguin, 1969.

17 Desmond Morris, *The Biology of Art*, London, Methuen, 1966, p. 158.

18 Tinbergen, op. cit., 1973, p. 223.

19 Lorenz, *Studies in Animal and Human Behaviour*, vol. 2, London, Methuen, 1971, p. 186.

20 Tinbergen, op. cit., 1973, p. 221.

Chapter 7

Yin and Yang

Gwyneth Dow

The traditional/progressive split

The terms of the argument between those who demand that schools induct children into the best of the culture and those who demand that they interpret and respond to pupils' needs are so familiar that they qualify for inclusion in the list of speech night platitudes. The counterpart in pedagogy is seen in polarizing the process and products of learning: the pupils' powers of analysis on the one hand and their empathy, insight, inspiration on the other; their thinking and their doing.

Maria is at the stage in her teaching when she needs to be alerted to and forearmed against such dualism — to see it as untenable and therefore unprofitable. I want to suggest to Maria how she might keep her cool by recognizing such platitudes for what they are and so, by question and comment, she might turn discussions in more productive directions — as she could have tried to do with David (see pp. 14ff.). But more than that, unsound practices result from unsound thinking, and if Maria becomes quick at spotting 'either–or' thinking it will help her in the classroom as well as in the staffroom. To polarize components that are interdependent in a learning activity is to cripple the learner — and to stultify knowledge.

I find a helpful corrective in the pre-Confucian Chinese notion of Yin and Yang with its thesis that the universe is controlled by the interplay of opposites:[1]

> These twin forces were known as Yin and Yang. Yin was wet,
> female, dark, cold and the moon; Yang, dry, male, light, heat and
> the sun. But the Chinese did not think of these forces as conflicting
> and at war with each other. They pictured them (as they still do) in
> the diagram made up of a circle, equally divided by a curving line

typifying the idea that these forces constantly acted upon each other, fluctuated, but remained in equal strength and should be in harmony.

Traditionally, western education has been 'male chauvinist' — that is Yang in Chinese terms — analytical, rational, theoretical, and disciplined

I went to a progressive school in the 1930s and taught in two in the 1950s. By the fifties I could see these schools as reactions to Yang but I could also see them as sometimes too content with Yin in their romantic faith in children's creative powers and innate goodness. This mistake, I felt sure, could never be repeated. But to some extent it was repeated in the late sixties and early seventies, when the western world luxuriated in a brief spell of affluent optimism. The new progressivism welcomed 'yak yak' (spontaneous outpourings from pupils in discussions), laissez-faire classroom management (of the 'wait and it will happen' kind — the 'it' presumably being the 'great leap forward' in learning), and pupils' doing their 'own thing', including uncomprehended transcription from encyclopaedias. The new movement became the easy victim of an equally mindless backlash. When mistakes are repeated in practice that is bad news: it means that teachers have not learned enough from their own history. This is true of both the revival of progressivism and the reaction against it.

In concentrating first on the soft underbelly of modern progressive pedagogy we must be careful to keep in mind that, just as the release of innovations that we witnessed during the late sixties and early seventies was made possible by a period of economic and political optimism, so the backlash that followed was an expression of fear and gloom from sources far more influential than the schools, but for which the schools were sometimes unduly held accountable. It is not my purpose here to examine the political scene so much as to examine how and why educationists made themselves vulnerable, and how we might be forearmed in the future.

Maria was born in the sixties when expansiveness, amounting at times to effervescence, was shared by many teachers, administrators, children and their parents as the rigidities in many schools were stripped away in organizational and curricular changes, and as new experimental schools sprang up. Yet the innovators, knowing that they were on trial and that the more fearful and conservative elements in the Establishment (wherever it was) were waiting to swoop at the smallest false moves, naturally tended to close ranks and to be hypersensitive to criticism. Hostility to the very mention of 'evaluation' was an indication of the fear of making evidence available to the critics In the early stages of innovation, teachers became so preoccupied with organizational and clinical problems that they tended to let curriculum

148

and lesson planning recede in importance. This problem was examined fairly closely in chapter 2. In that chapter we attempted to help Maria and others like her to recognize that danger. In this chapter I want to suggest the *pedagogical* implications of 'either/or' thinking. The tendency of many progressives to think that schools could remedy the sicknesses of society as they affect children's learning, and a permissiveness designed to foster Yin at the expense of Yang often led to cynicism in teachers and pupils which added force to counter-reformation.

During Maria's teacher-training year the emphasis given to A.S. Neill indicated that he was back in fashion with his catch-cry 'hearts not heads' (take care of the heart and the head will take care of itself). Maria took note of the surprise of some of the older staff who had lived through an earlier period of Neill's fame, and who reminded the students that it is one thing to say that our schools have been harshly cerebral, but it is quite another to make the heart absolutely superior to the head. In fact, why it is difficult to generalize from Neill is that he was so loving (though not soft and indulgent), and such an influential personality (though often wrong), that many pupils did learn from him in a way that was unforgettable, and perhaps had little to do with why he thought he was successful.

Another 'either/or' slogan of the thirties or perhaps earlier is, 'I teach children, not subjects.' No one these days, I think, would dare to put it the other way round, though many teachers do go on and on teaching their subjects to practically no one. The modern version of the slogan in reverse might take the form: 'No matter what, I must uphold standards', or the beautifully vague and high-sounding slogan, 'We are here to transmit our cultural heritage.' The progressive, on the other hand, tends to make the equally vague assertion: 'Our first duty, our first consideration, is the child.' Of course there is no learning unless someone learns: on the other hand, the child has to learn *something*. How he learns and what that something is are inseparable questions, just as how one teaches and what one teaches are inseparable. What is at issue is not a semantic game but the profoundly disturbing beliefs that underlie such loose talk. Perhaps it is best expressed by quoting what one teacher said to a student teacher he was supervising in my teacher-training course. 'If you understand my kids and something of their lives I'd give you 95 per cent as a teacher as against 5 per cent for having all the teaching skills and knowledge in the world.' The sad part is that that supervising teacher *was* highly skilful and scholarly — perhaps so much so that he did not even realize it. Like Neill, he apparently had little notion of where his success lay.

A much newer slogan that crops up in progressive educational talk is, 'It's process not product that matters.' It is sometimes put this way: 'I follow a process, not a means–end model.' It is not at all clear what people mean when they say this. If they mean that process is how things connect, interact and form patterns in various branches of knowledge that is fine. If it also means that studying, say science, entails examining the nature of things but also learning some of the skills of the scientist, that, too, is fine. It is certainly preferable to aiming at one static, precisely defined behavioural outcome or fragment of information. But all too often the context of the discussion shows that the slogan is given much the same meaning as the title of a popular song in my youth: 'It ain't what you do, it's the way that you do it' – you can do anything so long as you do it well. Dangerous advice in the days before the pill, and none too sound at any time.

These are homely examples of 'either/or' slogans, which are likely to be misleading half-truths, to be doctrinaire and thus to have a blinkering effect. It is the underlying beliefs which gain the status of pseudo-theories that have to be explored; but once our ears become attuned to picking up 'either/or' statements we can press them hard and get some more precise formulations of the propositions. Maria, a child of the sixties, had thrived in a trendy high school, had allied herself with the idealistic left at university, and had sympathized with the progressive ideology of her education lecturers. She found herself thinking in the language of the progressives, and it was Betty's exaggerated stance (see pp. 15-16) that brought this sharply to her attention. Although she had always been too tough-minded to argue in platitudes, she was beginning to reflect on the possibility that there might be more than a little sentimentality embedded in some of her assumptions and, worse, her practices.

The reality, she knows, is that for many children life is corrosive, harsh and consequently alienating to the point of dwarfing their sense of identity. In schools like hers teachers have to battle to convince pupils of the worth of the education offered, for the most socially valued educational rewards are rarely within these pupils' grasp, as they know full well. Sidestepping their abrasive hostility or demoralized resignation in school by offering nothing but patience and understanding is dangerously paternalistic. Of course, Maria thinks, little can be done until the children are convinced that they are genuinely respected and cared for, but it is easy for the teacher to settle for permissiveness and to mistake this for respect for the child's freedom.

I have seen student teachers seemingly so afraid of imposing themselves on their pupils' (often negative) value system that they retreat into paralysed inaction. It is as if, to take an everyday example, they regard asking a child to pick up a pencil and write, or helping a child to pronounce a new word correctly, as a form of rape. By neutrally standing back and refusing to thwart, criticize or influence the child, the teacher reinforces the child's sense of unimportance – of lack of

150

social meaning. This is further reinforced by robbing the child of the sort of meaning that knowledge of the teacher can give. Children learn through their curiosity and fail to learn when it becomes blunted. The teacher who does not become part of a pupil's world of curiosity is failing indeed. Though he would not use the term, the child wants to know something of the teacher's identity and how she thinks. Withholding oneself is as damaging as asking too much.

Paul, Maria thinks, is very sound on these things, and it is as a result of some of their discussions that Maria had come to recognize how easy it is for the teacher's forbearance with pupils to become a disguise for the fear of losing popularity. 'Teachers can be crawlers too,' Paul had remarked recently about how some staff indulged their pupils. Yet both Maria and Paul had to admit that they were often in doubt about when and how to correct pupils without doing harm.

The work ethic?

Maria, too, is conscious of the temptation to be what she calls 'soppy with the kids' out of a sense of guilt. Fully confronting her own privileges for the first time she feels overwhelmingly helpless. Can she really offer to a whole school the advice that succeeded with her — 'Work hard at school so that you can qualify for higher education and a professional job'? Where would we be if all teachers in her position succeeded? The answer, she thought wryly, would be to persuade all the boys at Manchester Grammar or Groton that they must work harder for self-enrichment, for university and the professions were beyond their grasp.

So much, she thought, for social mobility as the answer. But even the left, she thought, were indoctrinated. How often has she heard her leftist friends recently bemoaning the sorry fate of their PhD and MA friends who were wasting their education by having to become waitresses or taxi drivers or go on the dole? The implication was that their educational success entitled them to leave the rotten jobs to lesser men. Had they not noticed the numbers of semi-literate dropouts who had failed in East End or Harlem blackboard jungles and would have considered themselves lucky to become truckdrivers or waitresses or an assembly-line worker at the nearest factory if that choice were offered them?

Teachers, Maria thought, were more sensitive to these dilemmas than most groups. Some of them turned to a political analysis that was more earthy than that of the armchair leftists she had mixed with at university. Taken to extremes, perhaps by the most sensitive of her colleagues, some were apt to immolate their own advantages in a blind

151

attempt to wipe them out and start afresh (as if they could!). In its most simplistic manifestations it resulted in teachers trying to adopt the pupils' language, manners and tastes, failing to see, though their pupils do not, that this is phoney and patronizing, and therefore demeaning. In more grandiose terms, it took the form of cultural relativism, which all too easily can lead back to one fashion that bedevilled the United States progressive movement − adherence to a curriculum based on the 'democracy of all subjects'.

Back to Yang?

By the end of the sixties Cassandras were calling a halt to the new progressivism, and were winning new adherents. Late in her schooling Maria sensed the growing concern with permissiveness and self-indulgence that some critics attributed to the counter-culture. The realization that universal secondary education did not automatically result in universal literacy and numeracy came as a shock to many well-intentioned people, and Maria shared their concern; but there was a lot of hullabaloo too, she concluded in her year of teacher training, about the need to intensify competition, to increase the number of external tests and exams, to confine schools to basic training, to restore drilling and rote learning, to revert to streaming and other highly selective devices.

At the school, Maria and her deputy principal were on guard against these extreme reactions, believing as they did that some progressive schools had demonstrated that pupils can work keenly and diligently without the incentive of marks; that children can take initiative and responsibility for their own and each other's learning; and that there are more illuminating ways of reporting on children's progress than the bare marks that rank the child and are followed by some inane cliché. Many teachers and pupils who had tasted autonomy, Maria believed, would fight to retain it. Back to Yang, moreover, meant going back to a world in which cheating is seen as a more heinous crime than serious academic misdemeanours like sadistic arrogance or hypocritical bluff. What light *that* particular value in the hidden curriculum throws on our values, Maria thought to herself, to the pre-eminence given to winning a credential.

She had often puzzled over how an Ivan Illich with his throwaway hyperboles and heady rhetoric could catch the western world's imagination and prick its conscience for its excessive consumerism. In caricaturing education as offering a marketable commodity that we buy, if we're shrewd enough, from our schools, he drew savage pictures of teachers, educationists, guidance officers, parents and even children buying and selling 'knowledge' and certificates as if learning were a possession. Thus we say we 'have' matric., or we 'have' Spanish, or we 'have' a good education like having a car or having a shopping-bag full of goodies. Illich's influence, once the flurry of excitement passed, Maria felt, lay in part in what he revealed to us about our language usage. She noted for herself how many teachers used value-laden words such as Intelligence or Knowledge or Sensitivity as if they were a possession that some of us 'have' and others lack. Teachers and parents see that it is more accurate, less damaging, and therefore more effective to say 'that was a bad thing to do' than 'you are a bad boy', but they don't see the same point applying when they say things like 'she has a high intelligence' instead of 'she handled that difficulty most intelligently'.

Maria never ceased to be astonished during her year of teacher training at how many supervisors took the spotlight off her lessons by comments like, 'You couldn't expect to have done more with *that* class.' She was, she was grateful to say, spared the ignominy of one of her most vulnerable friends, whose lesson was dismissed with a curt, 'Well, the class ran rings around you, didn't they!' Instead of concentrating on features of the lesson that might have been improved, the supervisor was saying, by implication, 'You have a this or a that about you, and that's all there is to it.' Since a lesson is an interaction between pupils and teacher in a particular setting, at a particular time, no one of these elements can be singled out in isolation without distorting the reality. I shall return to the question of the importance of this in acquiring self-knowledge, which both pupils and student teachers are trying to acquire and which entails the very difficult and often painful act of trying to 'get outside oneself' in order to see oneself through others' eyes.[2] A blanket judgment can make this seem so hopeless and painful that it is truly damaging. But the present concern is that such judgmental labelling solidifies elements that should be seen in flux and as susceptible of constant adaptation.

Recognition of this makes it impossible for teachers to teach rigidly to other people's specific plans. It also underlies why baldly clear statements of aims and objectives and methods of attaining them cannot work, as Noel Gough has shown (see chapter 3). No one of the elements can be held constant in a real classroom. If it can, that entails static teaching. This is what Maria was trying to say to David when he pressed the group to plan their course within a fixed framework of agreed objectives (see pp. 14-15). For the moment she can only think of how, when some of her own plans had become unstuck, her lessons were much the better for it.

She recalled a set of lessons that she had observed during her training year in which the syllabus set out the aim of teaching about overpopulation in Third World countries. The specific objectives were to train children to analyse and interpret certain statistics of demographic distribution. The pupils were to learn how to give them graphical representation and how to read graphs. The teacher whom Maria observed was so intent on this task and making sure that the pupils could do the test which all the classes were to be set that she ignored the urgent and widely shared interest in a child's unexpected question about why free contraceptives and abortion don't necessarily stem population growth. Surely, Maria had thought at the time, a good teacher would seize on the obvious curiosity of the class and reformulate her objectives to pursue the line of enquiry that had arisen. Perhaps, in the process, there might develop greater interest in the significance of some of the statistics and graphs by showing the light they could throw on the broader question. Thus the objective (learning about graphs) might have changed from an end to a means, and even if for the time being statistics and graphs were deserted it would be in a worthwhile cause.

Maria also recalled reading a report on pupils who, while studying poverty in Latin America, were suddenly 'grabbed' by the discovery that children did not have enough room to play soccer. By seizing on this the teacher was able to reduce the remoteness of the study and to turn it profitably to an investigation into land use.[3] It should be noted that this teacher had sufficient knowledge to exploit an apparent diversion.

Maria, herself, the previous year had set out to examine the effectiveness of humour in propaganda. There were good materials at the school, and the class began making comparisons between different kinds of humour in the propaganda before them. They kept bringing into class new examples of jokes and funny situations, even writing some propaganda themselves because the topic engrossed them. It ended as a far more ambitious project than she had started with, and, in the process, the means had become the end.[4]

There was no doubt in Maria's mind that too much Yang, if it entailed tightly prescriptive programmes and teaching to external tests, had to be resisted. We noted that she decided to bide her time with David until she could put her case more clearly; but there is no doubt that, during the team's work, she would be able to point out where deviations from the set intentions improved greatly the quality of the education given. She would come back to some of the other parts of what she had called the 'hullabaloo' later; but her thinking, during the teething problems in planning with her colleagues, was concerned with the interdependence of all the parts that constituted learning and teaching. There must be adaptation and fluidity all along, and somehow she had to show David how he was undermining this. To change the allusion, they had to discover how to steer between the Scylla of classical discipline and the Charybdis of progressive spontaneity.

In their attitudes to curriculum teachers tend to veer to right or left, rather than finding the middle course that is not a compromise but a new, if ever-changing, synthesis.

Yang and Yin

In reacting against the rigidities of traditional education, some progressives, like Betty, have assumed that learning will occur willy-nilly and that the teacher's role is to be no more than a 'facilitator' or 'resource person' — a therapist who has merely to remove as many inhibitions as possible and the child will discover meaning for himself. Traditionalists, by contrast, elevate analysis, some of them going so far as to act on the assumption that learning is a passive accumulation of simple concepts that we built doggedly, bit by bit, into a generalization that is the mere sum of its parts.

One piece of advice that stuck during my teacher-training year came from the lecturer in Method of English (W.V. Aughterson) who repeatedly said in both the lecture theatre and when observing trainees in classrooms, 'Never dissect a piece of literature under any circumstances and never deal with its details until the pupils have some grasp of it as a whole. Always start with its unity.' It was the same sort of thinking that led earlier in this century to dropping parsing and analysis. It was no doctrinaire dismissal of the importance of grammar; it was rather that teachers did not see the learning of grammatical terms, the analysis of grammatic structure or the memorization of rules in isolation as improving children's grammar in speech or writing.

We may also note that similar influences were affecting history. History, once so dominated by chronology (pupils in years seven to twelve, moving relentlessly and superficially from 55 BC in Britain to the First World War), started to be taught thematically, with depth studies of important episodes that could be examined as 'slices of life' in which classes explored as fully as they could the relationships and interactions of man and his environment. Ancient history teachers argued, with force that deserved more attention than it usually was given, that the study of an ancient civilization could be encompassed more dynamically and with greater understanding of context than the bewildering complexity of modern questions. Similar arguments were offered about science — that it was more within the child's competence to trace vicariously some earlier scientific discoveries than to be blinded with the daunting background knowledge that was prerequisite to a glimmering of understanding of modern science. These reforms were pragmatic. We can now begin to grasp the reasons for their success.

As early as 1929 A.N. Whitehead warned teachers of the harm they were doing by insisting on unrelieved analysis and logical exposition. As he put it, the desire for wisdom (meaning) arises from 'natural cravings of the human intelligence'; 'there is no comprehension apart from romance', but when this has been savoured there is a further craving for 'precise knowledge'. Romance is the background to the 'disciplined' stage, but 'to write poetry you must study metre; and to build bridges you must be learned in the strength of material . . . The untutored art of genius is − in the words of the Prayer Book − a vain thing, fondly invented.' He chided schoolmasters and university dons for failing to see that romance and precision are in constant interplay; instead they regarded the stage of precision as 'the sole stage of learning in the traditional scheme of education', resulting in a 'plentiful array of dunces, and of a few scholars whose natural interest had survived the car of Juggernaut'. Whitehead had in mind premature memorizing and theorizing. His example shows that he sees analysis as part of meaningful or meaningless theorizing, depending on the way it is introduced.[5]

It is perhaps not surprising that educationists are turning back to Whitehead as a great thinker who earlier this century pointed out the need for increased harmony and humanity in our teaching. In mulling over her difficulties at school, Maria turned to the notes she took during her teacher training. She was seeking, above all, some guidelines to support her as she began to piece together all the ideas that she had encountered on learning theory.

She realized now that her Methods lecturer had introduced ideas like those of Whitehead to counter the views of the experts on programmed or computerized learning. She also realized now that the argument was about more than merely teachers' fears of becoming redundant. The size of the investment in new devices almost guaranteed that they would be self-perpetuating (just as expensive packages in schools tend to be retained even after they have been proved unsuccessful). Once a programme was hooked up to a telephone network that covered thousands of miles (as at Stanford University, for example) and could be used in hundreds of schools, the chances of unhooking were slight; but, far worse, there was a danger that it would become the dominant mode of teaching.

Many teachers cried out in dismay. 'But children are not automatons: they cannot be programmed and reduced to statistics!' Progressives took up the cry and perhaps swung to the other extreme. Maria recognized as she reconstructed the debate that part of the appeal of research like Piaget's or Chomsky's lay in its emphasis on the human being as the active agent in his own cognitive structuring.[6] She also acknowledged that the contribution of imagination, empathy, intuition − the immeasurables − to learning *and* knowledge was seized on in a desperate attempt to show the limitations of the machine.

She saw a renewed recognition of the inner spark in learning further exemplified by the way in which Edward de Bono's lateral thinking as a problem-solving device caught the public imagination. His ideas expressed a popular reaction against unrelieved linear, analytical, vertical thinking. We don't want more 'straight-down-the line' people, his followers declared, and Maria agreed: we want people who will move around problems, explore them in search of the unexpected. He has shown how children will find inventive solutions to specific problems, and he chose to get them to express their solutions in pictures, having found that children can often express their inventiveness more readily in pictures than in words.[7] Even so from an incredibly early age infants put together their own inventive (in the sense of untutored) phrasing of verbal communication. They do this without piecing together one word after another. They make exploratory statements before they have any capacity for analysing them.

Maria began to tie these ideas in with the notion of the *Verstehen* encountered in her reading of early sociologists. Added to these popularizers of the *Verstehen*, Hilary Putnam has recently thrown a good deal of scholarly weight against the 'scientizing' (as he says, 'a barbarous term I have invented to fit a barbarous idea') of human behaviour and human affairs. In human affairs our understanding depends on our ability to identify ourselves with others. This *Verstehen* he defines as 'the ability to imagine what it would be like to be, say, a knight in the army of Richard the Lionheart, or a follower of Savonarola'.[8] We may, he says, discover regularities, even laws, about human behaviour, but we can never find an 'explanatory model' as we can in some kinds of physics, for example: yet, he sees occasions in which physics needs *Verstehen* too. His plea for the 'human view' has great significance for us as teachers:[9]

If we are doomed to have neither a computer's-eye view nor a God's-eye view of ourselves and each other, is that such a terrible fate? We are men and women; and men and women we may be lucky enough to remain. Let us try to preserve our humanity by, among other things, taking a view of ourselves and our self-knowledge.

If Putnam and the others referred to are right, this has great importance for curriculum and teaching methods. We must cease to 'scientize' history, the social sciences, and to some extent the sciences. This does not mean, in any of them, that there is no place for empirical or statistical methods, nor does it mean that all scientific models are useless. It does, however, mean that they cannot be the whole story.

The 'tacit dimension'

Maria knows that the staff, apart from her team, regard her as a senti-mental idealist who has not yet sloughed off the ivory-tower influence of her teacher-training year. There are a few who are so indoctrinated into the thought and practices of what the other staff call the rats and pigeons men that she can find no meeting place with them. She resists the temptation to counter-attack by reminding them that *they*, more than she, retain the ideologies of their teacher training.

But what worries her more are the staff who, in general talk, share her views while in practice they dehumanize their content and bore their pupils. They have never had practice, she thinks to herself, in working out the implications of their views in their day-to-day teaching. Betty, on the other hand, is a good enough teacher not to act on her romantic, messy so-called progressive ideas. She thinks that her pupils totally dictate their own course, but Betty almost unconsciously chooses telling examples, and while drawing on the pupils' own experiences, she leads them out of blind alleys. She is a bit like Neill (see p. 149) in not diagnosing her own strengths correctly.

Maria ponders over why what people say and do can be at such variance. Her efforts with her team, as described in chapter 1, were, she realized, part of a bigger task of trying to verbalize her own position so that she could be surer in practice and more influential in debate. She sometimes wonders if there is any point. Isn't what Betty does more important than what she says? Does it matter that Robert, the most stubborn hardliner of all the rats and pigeons men at staff meetings, is the teacher who makes his pupils, even the weakest of them, love maths? She puzzles over that and decides that she would rather have Betty and Robert than the teachers who agree with her but can't teach. Betty and Robert, she thinks, must have some sort of know-how that they have imperfectly analysed or characterized in words. At this point in her thinking she turns again to Putnam's chapter that modernized her thinking about the *Verstehen*.

Putnam points to 'practical knowledge' as embodying the mastery of skills rather than theories. The skills may be physical, verbal or intellectual and they are not susceptible of scientific experiment. Nor, he maintains, are psychological explanations. Our knowledge of people is 'implicit ... not something we can state explicitly',[10] and such checking of our knowledge as we do is largely intuitive.

This feature of some parts of our knowledge[11] has bearing on learning and therefore on teaching. We rely on intuitive judgments in formulating hypotheses even in science, and, as Putnam says, no one has ever been able to 'formalize' them. This ability to form useful hunches depends on a 'well-stocked mind'. It is only then that we can advance our own knowledge in the erratic leaps that characterize much enlightening learning. Maria, in thinking about her team, concedes that David is right in his repeated reminders of this point; but what escapes him is the place of intuitive synthesis in the process. David seems to think that learning proceeds almost exclusively by building up from additive analysis. Many teachers, like David, certainly lean too heavily, too often and too exclusively towards Yang.

A child may accumulate a great deal of information that is very useful, but when important things click into place conceptually, we do not know how it happens and we may not even know that it is happening until after the event. Sometimes we experience the 'Eureka!' excitement of relief after puzzlement: sometimes we suddenly recognize that we have unknowingly grasped something that we hadn't understood before. In either case, there is a tacit dimension to our understanding, and for the teacher to ask the oh-so-common question, 'Why?', at that time, is inappropriate and may even be inhibiting.

Again, if our leaps are tacit, unconscious, and undescribable in precise words, our mania, as teachers, for verbalization all the time may be ill considered. We may need to look much more closely for other signs of understanding if we are not to underrate and misjudge our pupils. Putnam draws the reader's attention to Michael Polanyi's notion of 'tacit' knowledge. While Putnam talks about the kind of knowing that cannot be 'formalized', Polanyi refers to knowing that cannot be verbalized. It is important in teaching that we seek evidence of children's understanding through actions as well as words. Many children, I feel sure (and shall argue more concretely later), are discouraged and even demoralized by sensing that they know more than they are credited with, or by being convinced that the teacher is right in thinking them 'dumb'. It is likely that, as teachers who are articulate ourselves, we may often be more impressed by what Bruner calls 'articulate idiocy' than by 'tacit understanding'.

If skills are learned in action rather than by analysis, this realization must affect our teaching methods. Where skills are concerned, we need to offer more discipleship, more scope for trial and error, more opportunities for varied experiences, and less exposition. When we discover some new meaning, acquire a skill, diagnose or identify something, or work out a manoeuvre, we usually do it, not by conscious analysis, rationality or calculation but by intuitive leaps that result from having concentrated (or focused) on things we seek as a whole rather than on their elements or the means by which we may achieve our ends. The accomplishment is so 'tacit' that our success may not come at the time we will it hardest, but may perversely come when we are off guard.

The notion of tacit learning means that as teachers we need to sensitize children to problems, encourage them to formulate them and

159

concentrate on solving them, acquiring, in the process, necessary skills. This exciting task is *not* all that a teacher needs to do: but it is a necessary part of her duties. What we must *not* do is to assume that children will necessarily see the meanings in our minds at our bidding. Nor should we think that it is discovery learning if the child is merely asked to play a game (what some people call the Socratic method), that amounts to 'Guess what I am thinking' or 'Find out what I already know.' Possibly this is better pedagogy than unrelieved didactic teaching; but it is no training in learning how to *ask* questions – a point that was raised in chapter 2. 'To acquire new knowledge by prescribed manipulation is to make a survey not a discovery',[12] says Polanyi. He draws many of his examples from the discoveries at the frontier of scientific knowledge. It would be folly to talk of great creativity as if it were identical in process with our humdrum little discoveries of new meanings and skills; but it has been folly, historically speaking, to assume that children make new meanings out of relentless analysis, comprehension questions, or didactic preaching. This point also gives the clue to why Rory Barnes and I discouraged the practice of teaching by an endless series of written assignments (see pp. 40, 45). Even the more successful child may regard them as token tasks rather than as engaging questions. Surveys, of course, have their advantages in acquiring information, but they also have limitations. We have indicated to Maria that it is important to be aware of those limitations.

Polanyi's illustrations of skills that are acquired without being verbalized are helpful to teachers. When we ride a bicycle we do not concentrate separately on our hands, our feet, our eye movements, let alone on the mechanics of motion that explains what keeps us afloat, but on a synthesized action. I recall, in reading around this question, someone quoting Stephen Potter's ploys about how to win without *actually* cheating. If you want to put your golf opponent off his game when he is beating you just draw his attention to some small element in his actions – how he is holding his club, for example. This will probably make him 'take his eye off the ball' – stop him focusing on the ball. Polanyi uses the telling examples of stage fright – 'the anxious riveting of one's attention to the next word – or note or gesture – that one has to find or remember. This destroys one's sense of the context [the gestalt if you like] which alone can smoothly evoke the proper sequence of words, or gestures.'[13] We focus on the goal and are only subsidiarily aware of the means we adopt or the reasons why we succeed, to use Polanyi's terminology again – an observation that strengthens Gough's case against behavioural objectives in chapter 3.

As soon as Maria starts applying this idea to her own teaching she can think of many homely examples. When learning to dance we have to be stopped from watching our feet; when walking a tightrope we look at the destination — woe betide us if we watch our feet; touch-typists are more efficient than typists who look at the keys the whole time; we can learn a poem better by listening to or repeating a whole stanza than by trying to learn it line by line, let alone word by word. And so we could go on finding many examples that we ordinarily take for granted as axiomatic truths.

Maria recognizes that she has tacitly understood all this as a teacher. When a child is focusing on conveying an idea in speech or writing, or on grasping ideas in reading, something has stopped her from inter-fering by correcting a mistake in spelling or punctuation or pronun-ciation. On the other hand, if a child is to read she tries to think of any unknown words in the passage that are central to the meaning, and she explains them in advance or at least during the child's reading. And if the child is stumbling to find the words to express his thoughts, that is the time when she prompts him to explore the language in order better to express his meaning. Acting on this sort of distinction requires the sort of nous found in sensitive teachers and is an example of *their* focal awareness of the child's concerns.

In my experience all young teachers and many experienced ones are troubled about when and how to intervene with corrections of what the child does. Maria's hunches are pretty good on this score, but she is ever doubtful and often in two minds about what is the right thing to do. This raises the question of 'the time and the place' for drill and rote-learning in vocabulary, spelling, punctuation, pronunciation and the like. Though they may be subsidiary concerns when the child is concentrating on exploratory thinking, at another time they can be focused on as integral to, say, word patterns, spelling rules (albeit however idiosyncratic English spelling may be), and comprehension of the written word through sensible punctuation. Paulo Freire and Herbert Kohl give masterly illustrations of how language development can be learned with added meaning by word-building; for example, from the vocabulary students already have. Extending children's range of such skills of expression is central to clarifying and extending their thinking.

When the child reflects on what he has said or written, or on how he wants to express an idea, his focus changes, and he now concentrates on techniques. With added skill he will become concerned later about how his audience might respond to the way he speaks or writes, as he gradually learns to be his own critic. He is still refining his ideas and even extending them, but the grappling now is with fineness of meaning rather than with mastering a new idea or understanding a particular experience. This reflective period is the time when punctuation, spelling, syntax, semantics and vocabulary take on significance and can profit-ably be analysed within a context that would be absent in the study of grammar, say, in an isolated lesson. There is still need for great tact, but there is place for direct intervention.

Let us use a more practical example. We might profitably stop ourselves from jabbing at the billiard ball by practising hitting the ball straight up and down the table until we automatically control the cue smoothly; but we do this because we are concerned to play the game better and not before we have seen the game as a whole or shown any interest in playing it. To take an absurdly extreme example, imagine practising scales on the piano without ever having heard a tune played on it.

Maria is not sure either of why she so stubbornly gave up French at school or why she is now willing to go to Saturday morning Italian class and be drilled in pronunciation, vocabulary and grammar. Perhaps Polanyi is right that we must restore what we are doing in our drill to its total context, for example, by 'saying something that makes use of the word' [14] we have been practising. The tantalizing thing for Maria, for most teachers, and more importantly for pupils is that we cannot fully grasp the beauty of a foreign language until we can think, speak and read in it: we cannot anticipate from elementary skills the possible satisfaction of advanced mathematics; we cannot fully enjoy playing an instrument or singing until we have become proficient at it: but we can get something of a foretaste from small satisfactions, especially if the teacher refuses to dwell unduly on the dissected parts. It is probably no accident that Maria is prepared to endure uninspired teaching in Italian because it is familiar to her whereas she rejected school French. What is more, as a grown person she has greater patience than she had as a child, no doubt because her later education has given her more faith (or is it confidence?) in the pleasures to come.

She is in two minds about whether she should have been pushed harder by her French teacher at school, but she is pretty certain that if she had had a more imaginative teacher she would not have dropped it so eagerly. There is ample evidence, she knows, that a child can correctly use or identify a language concept before he can characterize it in words, and thus it follows that teachers should concentrate on recognition, familiarity and meaning before (and while) breaking off for drilling. Her interest in tacit knowing was first aroused by Bruner's ideas on spiral learning, which became increasingly convincing to her as she gained experience in teaching. Children, she knew, could give the make of a car before they could itemize its features, and there were countless other examples of that kind. Experiments in airforce training showed that men could identify aircraft flashed on a screen at breakneck pace, and they weren't fooled when a shot of Betty Grable was interspersed in the sequence. Again, she thought of her ability to recognize that a plant was sick and even to make a snap and correct diagnosis, if it resembled a sickness she was familiar with. All of this without any explicit, even conscious, analysis.

She is sure that learning experiences should be structured in such a way that a child is introduced to concepts in as many different ways as possible before any attempt is made to verbalize them, let alone analyse them. Thus a child following Bruner's ideas will recognize concepts such as 'life cycle' or 'innate knowledge' by being familiarized with examples from animal and human life presented in pictorial narrative, in silent film, in reading, tapes and discussions. He will keep pets. He will see television and documentaries. Birth and death will become familiar through many media before the child grasps and then can express the concept of 'life cycle'. Similarly, wide reading courses can be seen as an invaluable ingredient in English teaching because children are likely to pick up vocabulary and an intuitive knowledge of punctuation, spelling, syntax and grammar simply by familiarity before any conscious analysis occurs.

In discussing these points with Paul, Maria was surprised at how readily he agreed with her and 'bettered the instruction' by pointing to its corollary that premature analysis can lead children to empty verbalism. He suggested that English classes produced numberless examples of how children could quickly learn to label things without understanding them. He recalled lessons in which he had demonstrated examples of dangling participles which the pupils all could recognize with ease by the end of the lesson, but yet they failed to notice when they used them in their own writing. Similarly they were adept at applying terms like 'false analogy', 'begging the question', 'disagreement of number' or 'mixed tenses' with blind confidence to wrong examples. The moral, said Paul, was that pressing children to learn such terminology should come *after* they had much experience of recognizing the illogicalities. But this, he hastened to add, was different from encouraging experimentalism with vocabulary.

Education as search for meaning

Analysis, as Paul suggests, comes from 'doing' and reflection. Polanyi analyses language use into a hierarchy of abilities, but he points out (and this is a heretical idea to most teachers) that we acquire mastery not by systematically going from the simple to the complex. Rather, in concentrating on expressing our meaning we find the constituent skills for the purpose of conveying it.[15]

> You cannot derive a vocabulary from phonetics; you cannot derive grammar from a vocabulary; a correct use of grammar does not

account for good style; and a good style does not provide the
content of a piece of prose.

That seemingly obvious point is widely disregarded in much teaching. It gives the key to Bill Hannan's observation that generations of
correcting children's non-standard English (such as 'I done it' or 'yous'
or 'he's better'n me' or their non-U accents) have largely failed. Dialects
remain. The reason, no doubt, is that people who can express themselves adequately, indeed fluently and even eloquently, in their own
dialect will choose the quickest, readiest way of getting their meaning
across. To be understood is far more important to the child than to
be 'correct'. Our interventions, then, with non-standard speakers or
writers, should *first* be to assist them to make their meanings clear,
next to make their ideas persuasive by expressing them in a manner and
with a content that takes the nature of the audience into account
(the *Verstehen* again), and finally to give them the option of choosing
U usage or accents. In communicating, learning how to be understood
and a receptiveness to new knowledge are two sides of the one coin. It
is this appetite for new meaning that produces pupils who are question-
askers and that makes audacious teachers who will innovate in the quest
for extended knowledge and better teaching techniques.

Once a child has acquired some power in expression, he can profitably turn to the sort of analysis that would show him the function of
parts of speech, of grammar in general and of syntax, and he can then
see-saw between analysis and integration at will. In schools the order
is reversed when teachers try to build language mastery from grammatical analysis. The practice may work with children who are already
fluent, but all too often in correcting expressions like 'he's better'n
me', children learn 'between you and I' and we wonder why.

Twentieth-century research has discredited the nineteenth-century
belief in transfer of training that was used to justify such practices as
drill, memorization, tough textual or grammatical analysis for their
values as intellectual stiffeners. The swing away from transferability
often overlooks the fact that transfer of training is quite different from
the ability to apply one's existing patterns of meaning to new situations.
To do this depends on having acquired generalized knowledge and
conceptual structures that can be used to incorporate new meanings
and extend old ones. The extremes of neither the new 'progressives'
nor the new 'reactionaries' make this distinction. The first group tends
to eschew structure as being a straitjacket, and the second group
conveys the idea that they want to return to 'old' and 'well-tried'
methods — to 'mindless tasks',[16] to manipulate the child into docility.

In the thirties I went to a 'progressive' school in which the staff made
it quite clear that they thought memorization a third-rate intellectual

skill, and they encouraged it (enforced it if they could) only as a funny sort of punishment! Concentration on the centrality of meaning enables us properly to reinstate some of the unfashionable practices like memorization. It is no mere return to the 'basics' as ends in themselves.

As Maria's mature interest in Italian indicates, rich intellectual experiences will help the student to tolerate some boredom and drudgery. 'Nothing succeeds like success' means, among many things, that the taste of success will predispose the child towards appropriate patience, trust in the teacher's promise of later satisfaction, and a recognition that some failure is inevitable, for there could be no success unless there were failure. We must all fail time and again; but our failure is not endured the better for public display. Ways *have* been found of meeting the promise of later satisfactions not only in language acquisition but in all learning. The oft-failed pupil will have a very low threshold of patience.

We learn not by mindless repetition, but a 'structural change' is 'achieved by a repeated mental effort' that enables us *'to feel our way to success'*, without being able at the time to specify the nature of our groping and eventual skill or discovery,[17] and repetition, even drill, might well be part of this process. Maria is convinced that teachers must break with their almost exclusively analytical and logical teaching, giving far more prominence to the importance of intuition, imagination and feeling in their attempts to develop intellectual skills. This is not to say that she would or should swing into romanticism and leave everything to spontaneity and the feelies.

But she acknowledges that we cannot 'force' children into new understandings simply by the strength of our purpose as teachers. Each child comes into class with a different temperament and a different structure of meaning, and each child therefore is likely to gain different significance from the experiences (or lesson) the group shares. The point is nicely exemplified in Carl Sandburg's poem 'Elephants are different to different people' — a poem which pupils usually enjoy and that leads them to think, too, about the significance of different viewpoints. The educational import of the same phenomenon is persuasively illustrated in the following extract from a talk by a Scots scientist probably early this century.

On a Highland hillside towards the close of an autumn afternoon, stand a Highland gillie, a geologist, an artist, a sociologist, and a theologian. All are gazing with interest around, down the slopes, across the glen to the forests where the deer range, and at times down to the shores of the loch where stand the ruins of a village whose inhabitants some years before were driven out by a grasping landlord in order that the deer might graze, and the grouse and the pheasant flourish. On the same outward things do their eyes rest, but the same modes of consciousness are not stirred in each. The gillie sees the pheasants rise, or the deer move, and he may make some speculations about to-morrow's weather. The geologist reads the history of ages in the rocks of the hills, and in his mind's eye he sees other contours to the land around, another landscape, and other forms of life. The artist is in raptures with the autumn tints, the harmony of the colours of the rocks with the withering herbage and glowing bracken of the surrounding hills; the forests, and even the ruins are to him picturesque features of the landscape. The sociologist thinks of land laws, landlordism, and the value of a stalwart rural population to a nation; while the theologian ponders over justice, human and divine, thinks of the wrong done his country by the ejection, and marvels how it has been transformed into good through the rise of the banished Highlanders in far off Canada. (John Smyth, *The Rural School in Australia*, Melbourne, George Robertson, n.d., but 1914?, p. 53, from an address given by Professor J. Arthur Thomson of the University of Aberdeen)

This sort of observation has at least two sorts of importance for the teacher. If we take another example, the historic television programme of man's first landing on the moon, we might recall that some thought most excitedly about the clods that were being collected, what they were composed of and how they might add to our knowledge of matter; some thought most excitedly about the amount of money expended and how much relief it could have given to those in poverty; some thought most excitedly about the power and glory of the USA, and so we could go on. Those responses were related to the educational and experiential backgrounds of different people, suggesting that education does have more effect than we sometimes pessimistically suspect. At worst, however, it leads us to focus narrowly on an event of daunting importance. Specialization has restricted the possible worlds of understanding that could be made available.

The other point, the one to be stressed here, is that any two children are likely to respond differently to any one lesson that is offered them. Thus one child will be well prepared to leap the gap in his understanding while another remains problem-blind. This, of course, makes mass teaching very difficult and a rigidly prescribed curriculum counter-productive. Polanyi talks about the impracticability of driving headlong towards the solution of a problem.[18]

> Poincaré . . . noted that discovery does not usually occur at the culmination of mental effort — the way you reach the peak of a mountain by putting in your last ounce of strength — but more often comes in a flash after a period of rest and distraction. Our

labours are spent as it were in an unsuccessful scramble among the rocks and in the gullies on the flanks of the hill and then when we would give up for the moment and settle down to tea we would suddenly find ourselves transported to the top.

Whitehead emphasizes the need for rhythm to balance romance and precision. Polanyi uses the same word, 'rhythm', and refers to the phases of preparation, incubation, illumination and verification.[19] And many other creative people, whether scientists, mathematicians or artists observe similar processes. The poet and painter, William Blake, who was unusually aware of his own thought .processes, realized this: 'Improvement makes strait [sic] roads, but the crooked roads without improvement, are roads of Genius.' Those who have evolved a theory of 'personal constructs' make a similar point that in creating meaning we go through a cycle of loosening and tightening our mental constructs.[20] Romance and precision? The Enlightenment produced an extreme school of thought that saw scientific method as being mechanistic. Advances in the natural sciences and technology, it was said, indicated that all human and social problems would eventually be eliminated by scientific rationalism. Gripped by the utilitarian possibilities of scientific advance, reformers dismissed a curriculum based on valuing our cultural heritage as being under the dead hand of conservatism.

The romantic reaction was equally radical. The emphasis on science was seen as an insult to the human spirit and the life of the imagination.[21] Taken to extremes there was a cult of eccentricity and passion whose recent parallel could be seen in the counter-culture − in a deification of uninhibited inspiration and fellowship.

In pointing to these trends we must be careful not to over-generalize about the sources of the antitheses. Some of the most generative correctives to rational positivism have come, and are coming, from scientists, and some of the most vehement criticisms of romantic radicalism come from artists and humanists. I vividly remember hearing Alec Hope (one of Australia's finest poets) a few years ago deploring in a radio talk the retreat from eighteenth-century classicism in the humanities − from the formalistic and disciplined art forms − to romantic spontaneity, reaching its extreme in trip-taking to release individuality. All of this Hope attributed to the desertion of rationality.

The point to be made is that the ideological split that may be polarized as scientific/aesthetic, objective/subjective, mechanistic/ idealist not only divides natural scientists from social scientists, social scientists from artists, but also divides members of each group itself. The purpose of this chapter, however, is to show the effect of the split on children's learning, and to suggest that the antitheses are susceptible

167

of creative, dynamic resolutions (or syntheses, if you like) in curriculum
policy and pedagogy as well as in art, politics, and science.

The integration of language and culture

In pointing to an interaction of Yin and Yang, rather than an 'either/or'
approach that has characterized our attitudes historically, I am led
finally to a consideration of structure. Didactic and authoritarian
methods have ignored the fact that pupils ultimately have to structure
meanings *for themselves*. No one can do it for them. By contrast those
guilty of soft pedagogics have tolerated, indeed fostered, permissiveness
that has inhibited the child's intellectual mastery and maturity. Both
are confused about structure — a deficiency that Piaget, Bruner and
Polanyi, for example, can help us to overcome.

Perhaps the most useful clues available to a teacher are to be found
in Vygotsky, and I shall start to show why and how by way of an
example. Shortly after the Second World War I taught a class of girls
aged about thirteen in a very poor area in south-east London. Most of
them had experienced bombing, and been evacuated. Two-thirds of
them had nervous ticks, or disorders, the most common being bed-
wetting. None, I think, had scored above 80 in the 'eleven-plus' test
of IQ, and their efforts (on the rare occasions when they would make
any) at reading and writing were pitiful. It quickly became evident
that they had a talent for acting, especially for comedy of their own
invention. It took longer to discover how wise and kind they were when
discussing the problems of other girls in the class.

Jean Brown was our greatest worry. She would disappear for weeks
on end. Her two brothers had been in court for stealing and were
already in remand homes. It took no great humility to discover that
my class knew a lot more about how to handle this problem than I
did (there were other areas of experience, too, where they were clearly
my master). *They* advised the staff to send the truant officer to find
Jean and bring her back to school. *They* worked out a programme that
we should all follow when Jean returned. It included such things as
giving her a sense of being among friends but not of our being 'soppy'
when she tried to 'borrow' pens, books and money. A whole network
of unexpressed arguments underlay this elliptical conference — we
knew that she stole but we didn't need to mention this; she had to find
out that that was one of the reasons why we didn't like her; she also
needed to find out that school was a better place if your schoolmates
treated you as a friend. There was no explicit analysis. The next school
that I taught at had very 'bright' children. They could have passed
any number of word tests like picking the odd word in the combination

168

of theft, arson, charity, felony and delinquency; but they would have been pretty blind about what to do about Jean Brown, even though, unlike the London children, they would have known that she was 'delinquent'.

Long before having heard about tacit knowledge, spontaneous concepts or intuited understanding, I discovered that my London girls were ironic and fluent when I talked to them out of school about their own experiences. Their writing improved unrecognizably if they were writing about something they had thought and cared about and if I helped them enough.

For twenty-five years or more I *knew* that they knew far more than school ever elicited from them, but it is only in recent years that I saw how to verbalize it. And for that last point the major footnote must go to Vygotsky. In *Thought and Language* he traces the development of thought and language as originally having separate roots. In the first year of life, babbling, crying, laughing, and the first words uttered are shown not only to be expressions of emotion but are also 'means of social contact', as is the child's response to the speech he hears. Then the child uses grammatical forms, mastering syntax before understanding the logic of it. We may draw a parallel here with Polanyi's tacit knowledge — with his insistence that we know more than we can tell. In Vygotsky's words:[22]

> The child may operate with subordinate clauses, with words like *because, if, when,* and *but,* long before he really grasps causal, conditional, or temporal relations . . . Piaget's studies proved that grammar develops before logic and that the child learns relatively late the mental operations corresponding to the verbal forms he has been using for a long time.

If we can manipulate concepts without being able to verbalize them, teachers like Maria who are dealing with inarticulate children should search for signs of undefined comprehension and mastery as a basis for teaching language. School, Vygotsky says, is the place where children begin to learn to become conscious of their thought processes, and full consciousness depends on verbalization. Writing has a special virtue in this process because it, more than any other form of verbal expression, lends itself to reflective manipulation that makes it a unique medium for the refinement of thought.[23] Seeing language development as a response to the child's society and cultural experiences Vygotsky enhances the status of the school and teachers for he sees the teacher as an integral part of the child's culture.

Vygotsky sees speech as social before becoming individual. Reality is explored in action, enjoyed (or deplored) in speech and other forms of communication, and understood in reflection by means of inner speech, which, he insists, is not a stage to be outgrown, but goes on being generative throughout life. On this point he takes issue with Piaget. In defence, Piaget amplified what he means by 'egocentric speech': it is an inability to shift from one's own limited perspective to other points of view, an inability to place oneself in others' shoes. In language communication this is concerned with vicariously grasping the meanings that are available to others (the *Verstehen* again) in order that discussion may take place. This Piaget chooses to call 'decentring' which he sees as an enlargement of the reality that we internalize. As he puts it:[24]

> For science to shift from a geocentric to a heliocentric perspective required a gigantic feat of decentring. But the same kind of process can be seen in the small child: my description, noted favourably by Vygotsky, of the development of the notion 'brother' shows what an effort is required of a child who has a brother to understand that his brother also has a brother, that this concept refers to a reciprocal relationship and not to an absolute 'property'.

Both men see this 'decentring' as a development of objectivity that is part of the structuring we undertake. Vygotsky's value to Maria and to practising teachers in general is the importance he attaches to adult intervention — to effective teaching. Learning, he suggests, is more than maturation. As teachers we can give it profitable shoves. Activities, conversation, reflections should all be saturated with the experiences that familiarize the child with the concepts we want to teach. We do not hold back waiting for signs of the child's 'readiness'. We strain to enrich the child so that her development is quickened, but instruction must also, if anything, run ahead by anticipating rather than just responding to our recognition of where 'the child is at', otherwise 'instruction hobbles behind development'.[25]

Thus many academic historians both in schools and universities will assert that history cannot be taught until about eleventh year because it requires mature powers of synthesis, interpretation and generalization as well as a time sense. Let us take the last point. Although we know that small children get exasperated if we tell them just to wait an hour (for they have no notion of how long an hour is), they will soon understand and trust us if we regularly come and see them five minutes after we turn off the light. They will, when quite young, take the point that five minutes waiting in a bus queue seems much longer than five minutes playing an enjoyable game, and it is not too difficult for adults to underline the point — thus to help them grasp it. A story of an experience may well illustrate that a night can seem like a month (try Henry Handel Richardson's short story 'And Women Must Weep' with thirteen-year-old girls). One might then try a novel in which all the action occurs, we discover to our amazement, in a day. 'Time flies' or 'time drags' are now becoming so well understood as to be almost clichés. At the same time the youngster is able to begin to understand that time 'accelerates' after the invention of the wheel, between the bicycle and the aeroplane, and between the aeroplane and the man-made satellite.

This illustration leads back to Bruner and the help his notion of spiral learning gave to Maria. The main thing is to keep coming at knowledge that is difficult to understand (such as a time sense) in terms that children can understand progressively in as many different contexts as possible and by a variety of illustrations. This, to think back to chapter 2, is the essence of integrated studies. If we think back for a moment about the 'Equality' topic (see pp. 36-9), we can find that this principle was at work. Through the unit of work, pupils were to look at equality and inequality with as many pairs of eyes as the staff could help to provide with a great variety of illustrations. And so it could have been with the topic that centred on 'Creativity' (see pp. 28-9). The difference between those two units was that in the second one each example was worked through quite separately by staff members who worked in isolation so that no cross links were being made. But 'Equality' and 'Creativity' were rich topics for integrated work whereas 'Movement' (see pp. 28-9) was not. One problem with course planning in schools is that detailed work has usually to be concentrated on a short span of time, like Maria's team's project for year ten, whereas to develop children's time sense in the way that I have just described requires years of effort. There are overriding concepts and intellectual skills that can be acquired only over a long period of time. If a core curriculum was concerned to see that a school deliberately made provision for each child's developing such understandings there could be little quarrel with it. Perhaps (though I am not sure) Skilbeck's cultural map (see p. 119) could be intended to perform just such a function.

Maria is already aware of the subtle, elusive discriminations that have to be made in teaching. Through Bruner she would call my account of how a child might develop a time sense an example of how we intuit meanings before we can verbalize them. Polanyi would call this tacit knowing, and Vygotsky points in the same direction by referring to the 'discrepancy between [the] ability to form concepts and ... to define them'.[26] When Vygotsky writes, 'I have just tied a knot — I have done so consciously, yet I cannot explain how I did it, because my awareness was centred on the knot rather than on my own motions, the *how* of my actions', we could imagine we were reading Polanyi. And for Maria, the significance of this is that it can guide her present intuitions when dealing with pupils about when to push and when to let go. I can figuratively put a blue pencil through many of the questions that teachers, including Maria, ask so pressingly. As Polanyi suggests, if a learner is concentrating on keeping on a bike as a learner, no good can come of diverting his attention to 'why' this and that movement keep him on the seat. Yet Vygotsky shows that ultimately the learner must become aware of both the how and its explanation if he is to 'become fully conscious'. This is certainly true of intellectual skills. The pinnacled human accomplishment Vygotsky calls the 'consciousness of being conscious'.[27] At one stage analysing the how and why can be a stopper, but eventually it must be done in the process of gaining self-knowledge. This comes through meanings that in time can be made explicit. By defining our knowledge and the particulars that comprise it we can become increasingly able to generalize and abstract. Thus language brings order to thought, and Maria gives her pupils every encouragement to discuss their ideas together and with her. By the knowledge she gains of her class she reduces the chanciness of timing correctly her probing questions. The smaller her class and the more time she has with them, the better her judgment can be.

But there is another side to this that also concerns her. It is easier, she thinks, to see how her pupils develop some mastery of abstract thinking than to see how some of them can play a language game that conceals their lack of understanding. What happens, she wonders, when they parade high-sounding jargon that is devoid of meaning? Partly, she thinks, they are just cunning enough to learn the impressive labels and bluff. But Vygotsky might help her here, too, to see that the problem goes a little deeper. It is just as difficult, he notes, to transfer from an abstract idea to a new concrete one as it is to form abstractions themselves. Maria noticed in university seminars that many students seemed to be left with disembodied verbiage, and perhaps it was because they became in time so removed from the process of forming generalizations from experience that they could no longer particularize. This is why, she thinks, learning to teach can provide the necessary corrective, for the teacher must re-create her own mental processes for the pupils, and so much inert or arid knowledge comes to life again by, to use Vygotsky's term, becoming 'saturated with experience again'. The teacher becomes versatile in moving from the abstract to the illustration and back again, each process then enriching the other.

And so we might come back to Yin and Yang — to the interaction of opposites such as the conscious and spontaneous, the general and particular, instruction and discovery, logic and intuition, integration and analysis. In language development there is an interlocking of the social, affective origins with the generative capacity of reflection (inner thought) and the disciplinary exercise of definition and exposition in speech and more markedly in writing. As the great German chemist,

Kekulé, said, 'Let us learn to dream, gentlemen, then perhaps we shall find the truth . . . but let us beware of publishing our dreams before they have been put to the proof by waking understanding.'[28] As Maria sees it, schools are too often destroyers of the dream, but at their best they try to restore the ability to dream to the child who has lost it.

Let us end on that note with the synthesis of Yin and Yang, as that great exponent of it, Mao Tse-Tung, saw it:[29]

> Under the general line of going all out and aiming high to achieve greater, faster, better and more economical results, a wave-like form of progress is the unity of the opposites, deliberation and haste, the unity of the opposites, toil and dreams. If we have only haste and toil, that is one-sided . . . In all our work, we must use both haste and deliberation.

My intention has been to help Maria and teachers like her to verbalize her understanding of the dangers of categorizing teaching as soft or hard pedagogy — as 'progressive' or 'traditional'.

Notes

1 C.P. Fitzgerald, *A Concise History of East Asia*, Penguin, 1974 (first published by Heinemann Educational Australia, 1966), pp. 10–11.

2 For a development of this point see 'Who am I?' and 'Being at risk' in Gwyneth Dow, *Learning to Teach: Teaching to Learn*, London, Routledge & Kegan Paul, 1979.

3 See Ron Toomey, 'Teachers' approaches to curriculum planning: an exploratory study', *Curriculum Inquiry* (Ontario Institute for Studies in Education), 7 (2), 1977, p. 128.

4 For examples of the way in which teaching methods and content are inextricably linked see Dow, op. cit., pp. 119–21.

5 A.N. Whitehead, *The Aims of Education*, New York, Mentor Books, 1949, pp. 50–4.

6 For a recent critique of their contribution see Margaret Donaldson, *Children's Minds*, London, Fontana, 1978.

7 Edward de Bono, *Children Solve Problems*, New York, Harper & Row, 1974.

8 Hilary Putnam, *Meaning and the Moral Sciences*, London, Routledge & Kegan Paul, 1978, p. 76.

9 Ibid., p. 77. See also p. 73, and Lecture VI, passim.

10 Ibid., pp. 72-3.

11 Ibid., p. 75.

12 Michael Polanyi, *Science, Faith and Society*, University of Chicago Press, rev. ed., 1964 (new Introduction — original copyright 1946), p. 4.

13 Polanyi, *Personal Knowledge*, London, Routledge & Kegan Paul, 2nd ed., 1962, p. 56.

14 Polanyi and Harry Prosch, *Meaning*, University of Chicago Press, 1975, p. 40.

15 Marjorie Grene (ed.), *Knowing and Being. Essays by Michael Polanyi*, London, Routledge & Kegan Paul, 1969, pp. 154–5. Since this chapter is essentially a chapter on avoiding dualism in educational practices, it is of some interest that Polanyi uses examples like the language one to argue metaphysically for dualism between, for example, denotative and existential meaning. It is beyond the scope of this chapter to explore Polanyi on this point, but further examples can be found in Polanyi in Grene, op. cit., pp. 128, 140, 147, 151, 153–5, 188, 195; Polanyi and Prosch, op. cit., pp. 39–40. Polanyi, *Personal Knowledge*, p. 58. Marjorie Grene examines this question in 'Tacit knowing: grounds for a revolution in philosophy', *Journal of the British Society for Phenomenology*, 8 (3), October 1977.

16 See, for example, Elliot W. Eisner, 'Humanistic trends and the curriculum field', *Journal of Curriculum Studies*, 10 (3) July–September 1978, p. 198.

17 Polanyi, op. cit., 1962, pp. 61–3.

18 Michael Polanyi, 1964, p. 34.

19 Ibid.

20 D. Bannister and Fay Fransella, *Inquiring Man: the Theory of Personal Constructs*, Penguin Education, 1971, p. 92.

21 Isaiah Berlin, 'General education', *Oxford Review of Education*, 1 (3), 1975, pp. 287–92.

22 L.S. Vygotsky, *Thought and Language*, Massachusetts Institute of Technology Press, 1962, pp. 46–7.

23 This point is stressed in Donaldson, op. cit. See also Jack Goody, *The Domestication of the Savage Mind*, Cambridge University Press, 1977, particularly pp. 150, 159–62.

24 Jean Piaget, *Comments*, Massachusetts Institute of Technology Press, 1962, p. 3.

25 Vygotsky, op. cit., p. 94. For a more detailed exploration of Vygotsky's ideas and a development of his criticisms of Piaget, see Donaldson, op. cit. In particular, on 'readiness', see pp. 100–3.

26 Vygotsky, op. cit., p. 79.

27 Ibid., p. 91.

28 Quoted in G.M. Dow, *Uncommon Common Sense*, Pergamon Press (Australia), 1977, p. 4.

29 Quoted in Stuart Schram, *Mao Tse-Tung Unrehearsed*, Penguin, 1974, p. 106.

Chapter 8

And then?

Gwyneth Dow

In setting up the fictional Maria, we deliberately faced her with teaching problems that gave rise to ideological conflicts. But we did say that she had no doubt that her role was one of 'consciousness-raising'. All contributors would agree on that point — that schools should try to equip pupils to understand their world and to take up the democratic challenge of contributing responsibly to its future by recognizing such power as they can and cannot exercise.

We have no simple answers to the problems ahead of our pupils. Some we can barely perceive, and many, no doubt, have not even occurred to us. In attacking the mechanistic nature of Behaviourism and positivism in the past, Noel Gough, Rod Foster and I are well aware that computerized learning will transform the classroom and possibly make it redundant. If so, however, and if Vygotsky is right as I have suggested at the end of the last chapter, a new social and cultural setting will have to be found, for the act of learning is essentially social as well as private.

Doug White, in seeing the movement for a core curriculum as a desperate attempt to manufacture some sort of cultural unity, is talking about much more than the core curriculum. He is concerned at the way the sources of political power are becoming less and less visible as they become increasingly distant. Midget computers might simplify our daily problems with the household budget but they are also accompanied by the production of satellites that, with their Argus-like eyes, will encourage the control and dissemination of knowledge by combines that make the present trend towards amalgamations in ownership of newspapers, TV, publishing houses and the like miniscule. Our protests in this book are not as Luddites but as humanists.

We are also aware that the trend towards greater inequalities between the world's rich and poor, and the alienation that grows with the size and scale of modern enterprises are likely to increase not

175

diminish. The questions that we address ourselves to in this book are ones that are concerned with restoring the individual and the knowable group whose members can reassert some control over their own lives.

The new phenomenon of youth unemployment is a further reminder that specialization has increasingly debased the labour of many workers and divided thinkers from doers. Both White and Foster develop this point forcefully. Since industrialization, a liberal education has been strained by the increasing divorce between work and leisure. With our first taste of massive structural unemployment, we add to everyman's alienation the further loss of identity that he suffers when he finds the value of hard work that has been dinned into him for centuries now is an outmoded ethic. Perhaps the time has come to reassert the importance of effort in leisure and satisfaction in work. Perhaps a new version of the city state and the social contract would place a premium on the education of everyman. More than that, perhaps everyman can now taste the less bustling satisfactions that come from pursuits well done and understandings battled for for their own sake.

In this book we have avoided the tired arguments about forms of knowledge, realms of meaning and the nature of 'disciplines'. We have also tried to avoid the obscurantist writings on the sociology of knowledge. We are, rather, concerned with the old-fashioned liberal notion of knowledge as power, which is what we mean by 'consciousness-raising'. We are also involved in practical implications of the debate about schooling as 'determined' or 'determining'. We all point to ways in which teachers and schools can make a difference, even in the most work-a-day task that Rory Barnes and I have explored: how the planning and conduct of courses may contribute to social understanding and action, to intellectual growth and to self-knowledge.

The 'back to basics' movement ignores the challenge that schools face. Bill Hannan may be right that schools mostly do a rotten job in their humanities programmes, but it must be remembered that a century ago the basics were minimal literacy and arithmetic. There is no evidence that those standards have fallen, while it is very clear that schools now try to provide the initiation of all pupils into a world of knowledge that is going on multiplying at a blinding pace. A hundred years ago we made practically no attempt to introduce everyman to the then far more circumscribed world of knowledge and ideas. Hannan's discontent lies in the schools' failure to break down more effectively exclusive attitudes to critical knowledge, and this is part of a bigger political question.

We have all, in one way or another, dealt with political paradoxes and with tension as an integral part of learning — a point dealt with more specifically in the chapter 'Being at risk' in my book *Learning to*

Teach: Teaching to Learn. Yin and Yang are in constant tension, but that symbol for harmoniously resolving dualism is dynamic in that the nature of the synthesis is ever changing, is fluid. As the quotation from Mao at the end of the last chapter so beautifully illustrates, there is always in Yin the seed of its opposite, and in Yang the seed of Yin, so that new balances are for ever being formed under the creative pressure of each on the other.

I would suggest that the value of the picturesque symbol, Yin and Yang, lies in its corrective to the preoccupation in western thought with both analysis and logicality as the prized intellectual pursuits which we set above imagination, insight, warmth and certainly (but why?) fantasy. Foster's chapter suggests ways in which Ethology might help to redress the balance by its comparative studies of behaviour which provide evidence of insight and of imagination in problem-solving in contrast to the dominant place of conditioning in Behaviourist learning theory. A new look at psychology might be in sight.

This book also shows school reforms as derived from more than psychology. They must be seen in a democratic context to make proper sense. But many assumptions and practices in schools are at odds with the democratic ideal. Gough has pointed to some ways in which policy-making can be democratized and evaluation made participatory. In our strenuous attempts to revise social and political structures that could revive everyman's sense of belonging and contributing to an effective community, we all see that a proper degree of autonomy must be retained by schools so that they too are effective communities in themselves. If each contributor were to be asked what all chapters had in common, I think that one reply would be a radical belief in democracy that is not marred by the doctrinaire affliction of 'either/or' thinking. Human error cannot be eliminated by fiat. Democracy is risky. But it cannot be created by metaphorically disfranchising ordinary people. They must have experience in trying to make democracy work, and that means that some failures must be tolerated while men gain experience in overcoming them. That is what school-based education is about.

While the tensions between Yin and Yang are revitalizing to both, the ultimate model of *the* circle, and harmony within it, must be seen to be conservative. I prefer to think of a model made up of new circles formed when the boundaries of the old break under intolerable or insistent tension. Each time a new circle forms it spirals until another new one forms.

The view of education that we present is an uneasy one since we concentrate on its problematic nature rather than on such certainties as there may be. Thus, as Gough says, we have to try to do what is best rather than to be paralysed waiting to discover what is 'right'.

As contributors, we might be caricatured as belonging to the 'on the one hand . . . on the other hand' school of thought, or, worse, to the 'there's a time and place for everything' brigade. We do indeed show the importance of discrimination; but we also know the danger that, in seeking the right theory and the right time, the academic can become paralysed by doubt and conflict, because he is asking the wrong question. Nothing so effectively breaks the fruitless search for certainty or the vicious circle as *having* to act, and, as Gough says, *having* to decide what is best.

Of course a teacher's life is made up of innumerable little actions and little decisions that don't seem to her like taking a stance, but that constitute in sum her ideology even though she may delude herself that she is neutral. As Hannan and I argue, decisions that lack insight into alien or contrary positions add up to tacit ethnocentrism, egocentricity or just plain prejudice. It is characteristic of what White calls the 'intellectual culture' that conflicting values and interpretations are understood and respected, are tested against experience rather than resting on authority as a basis of commitment.

A teacher like our Maria welcomed the chance to work with colleagues on a new curriculum for this forced her into self-conscious activity which prompted her to clarify her thinking. Although she was not fully prepared for the conflicts that arose, with time and experience (which we have made the theme of this book) she found them productive rather than debilitating. And that distinction points to another dichotomy that she can rid herself of − the polarization of conflict and harmony.

The contributors to this book hope that Maria has learnt to distinguish between productive or stultifying conflict and to see harmony as the consequent uneasy equilibrium on which our sanity depends. Psychologists have distinguished between being at risk and suffering neurotic anxiety; one being possibly creative, the other self-destructive. Foster's references to our neuroses and even to student suicides are not morbid melodrama − they characterize the individual's response to isolation and despair, the failure to resolve personal conflicts. Liam Hudson in *Contrary Imaginations* defines the neurotic as 'the man who adopts a particular intellectual and personal style, but the one who, having adopted a style, suffers its weaknesses without enjoying its strengths.' Behind this witticism is the vision of a man without authentic meaning. The individual neurotic's failure to face his anxieties may be seen as the microcosm of world neuroses, for our spiralling circle can turn back upon itself. It is not predestined that it must necessarily go forward. And then?

Index

Recent and Forthcoming
Routledge Education Books

Learning to Teach: Teaching to Learn
Gwyneth Dow

★The Common Curriculum
Its Structure and Style in the Comprehensive School
Maurice Holt

★Ideology and Curriculum
Michael W. Apple

★The Politics of the School Curriculum
Denis Lawton

Regenerating the Curriculum
Maurice Holt

School-based Curriculum Development in Britain
Edited by John Eggleston

Teacher Decision-making in the Classroom
Edited by John Eggleston

★Theory and Practice of Curriculum Studies
Denis Lawton, Peter Gordon, Maggie Ing,
Bill Gibby, Richard Pring and Terry Moore

★Women and Schooling
Rosemary Deem

Also available in paperback

Routledge Education Books

Teacher Learning

This book examines just what teachers can and cannot effectively do. It is in part a response to the pessimistic fatalism of much modern sociology that demoralizes, indeed often paralyses, sensitive teachers. It expands the editor's earlier account (in *Learning to Teach: Teaching to Learn*) of educational theories tested and refined by the teacher in action in the classroom and the staffroom. The contributors write of an imaginary, but typical, school that could be in any industrial town in Australasia, Great Britain or America, where a young teacher, 'Maria', finds her beliefs and knowledge severely tested. She and her colleagues are aiming to make the curriculum relevant to the lives of their pupils and to ensure that they experience satisfaction and success in learning. Maria finds herself in conflict about such everyday matters as whether or not to correct her pupils' language usage, or how she should counter the undemocratic and ethnocentric prejudices that bedevil attempts at multiculturalism. When discussing proposals for a new curriculum with her colleagues, she worries about whether they can cross subject boundaries without becoming trapped in a morass, and she is perplexed by specious appeals to science on the one hand and human nature on the other. These are the realities of the school that force her to define her own ideological stance and to examine educational theories in action.

The contributors have tried to distil from their wide experience in educational innovation those ideas and practices that are worth retaining and developing; their examiniation of what they find faulty dwells on positive, rather than destructive, criticism.

The Editor

Gwyneth Dow is Reader in Education at the University of Melbourne. In the early 1950s she taught in London, in one of the first comprehensive schools, and in Melbourne before becoming a university lecturer in 1957. From 1966 to 1977 she was a member of the steering committee of the Curriculum Advisory Board (Victoria), and from 1973 to 1977 she directed the experimental school-based teacher-training course described in *Learning to Teach: Teaching to Learn* (Routledge & Kegan Paul, 1979). Her earlier publications include *Uncommon Common Sense: Signposts to Clear Thinking* (several editions, most recently Pergamon Press, Sydney, 1977) and *Samuel Terry: the Botany Bay Rothschild* (Sydney University Press, 1974).